CHICKASAW REMOVAL

AMANDA L. PAIGE

FULLER L. BUMPERS

DANIEL F. LITTLEFIELD, JR.

CHICKASAW PRESS

© 2010 by Chickasaw Press

ISBN 978-1-935684-00-8

Book and cover design by Carl Brune

Chickasaw Press
P.O. Box 1548
Ada, Oklahoma 74820

chickasawpress.com

CONTENTS

Acknowledgements

THIS BOOK IS THE PRODUCT OF A NUMBER OF YEARS OF EFFORT. It began in 2000 when the three of us, as the research team at the Sequoyah National Research Center, undertook research for a report on the significance of the site of North Little Rock, Arkansas, in Indian removal. Our goal was to convince city leaders that they should be cognizant of removal history as they began to develop businesses and recreation facilities in the city's riverfront area.

Our original study was expanded through a Challenge Cost Share grant from the National Park Service as part of the Park Service's research for the Trail of Tears National Historic Trail project. Although that project focuses primarily on the Cherokees, the Park Service asked us to expand our research to include all tribes who removed through Arkansas. With our expanded report completed in 2003, we decided to write this book about Chickasaw removal.

During the ensuing years, two institutions contributed to the success of our work. We thank the Sequoyah National Research Center at the University of Arkansas at Little Rock, which provided not only the work environment but many of the resources for the research. The staff of the National Archives also made that institution's invaluable resources available to us.

We give our special thanks to Governor Bill Anoatubby who supported the publishing of this book. We would also like to acknowledge Dr. Amanda Cobb-Greetham, Kirk Perry, Robert Perry, Lisa John, and Richard Green of the Chickasaw Nation, who carefully read and critiqued our work.

AMANDA L. PAIGE
FULLER L. BUMPERS
DANIEL F. LITTLEFIELD, JR.

(u)

LIST OF ILLUSTRATIONS

INTRODUCTION

O N JUNE 17, 1820, A YOUNG South Carolinian named Thomas C. Stuart and the Reverend David Humphries arrived in the Chickasaw Nation in Mississippi. Stuart had been licensed to preach by the South Carolina Presbytery, and he and his traveling companion were on a journey to establish a mission among the southern Indians. They had first stopped among the Creeks, but personally revolted by the effects of the black drink upon the Creeks and spiritually repelled by what they considered a heathenish practice, they had moved on to the Chickasaws. They spent their first night at the home of Levi Colbert near Cotton Gin Port, where they learned that a large number of Chickasaws were gathering for a great ball play at the home of George Colbert, Levi's brother, some twenty-five miles away near present-day Tupelo. The two young preachers went on to George Colbert's and made arrangements to attend a council on June 22 at the home of James Colbert near Tockshish, south of present-day Pontotoc. Decades later, Stuart wrote to his friend Humphries, "You remember their young king was conducted to the chair of state that day, for the first time, as king of the Chickasaw Nation. He was an ordinary Indian, and never opened his mouth during the council." The "king" was the young minko Ishtehotopa. That same day, the Chickasaws also granted Stuart permission to establish a mission, and he left to return the next year to begin his work.[1]

(1)

By Stuart's own admission, his and his missionary colleagues' many years of effort among the Chickasaws were relatively fruitless, although they labored faithfully until the Chickasaws removed to the West. Church records seem to bear out his assessment. Years later, curious about the effects of his efforts, he decided to visit his former converts and students in the West.

In the summer of 1856, he arrived in the Chickasaw Nation, where he found the Chickasaw people prospering for the most part. Perhaps more remarkable to him was their new form of government: "They have abolished the office of chiefs and councils for the government of the people, and have organized a regular state government, with a written constitution, after the model of our sovereign states. It was my good fortune to be present at the meeting of their first legislature, and the election and inauguration of their first governor."[2]

Stuart had witnessed a singular set of events: the installation of Ishtehotopa as the last traditional minko of the Chickasaws and the inauguration of Cyrus Harris, one of his former pupils, as the first elected governor of the constitutional Chickasaw Nation!

During the three-and-a-half decades that passed between the two events, the Chickasaw people endured one of the most traumatic periods of their history.

Because they paid the expenses of their removal, they acted independently, to the dismay of government officials. The funds generated by sale of their lands in Mississippi and Alabama made both the nation and individuals targets of fraud by contractors, merchants, and federal officials. Although the Chickasaw national fund was greatly depleted, the Chickasaws were willing to spend what was necessary to remove their entire nation to the West. Many individuals took much property to the West with them, but others suffered deprivation because they were unable to retrieve their funds from the United Sates. Through it all, however, the Chickasaws escaped the factionalism that rent other tribes during removal and were unified in their sense of national identity, which enabled them to separate from the Choctaw Nation and reestablish a national government in the West. Thus Chickasaw removal was significantly different from that of other tribes, and its story, which is presented here, is unique in the histories of Indian removals and stands as a testimony for Chickasaw survival.

NOTES

1. E. T. Winston, *"Father Stuart" and the Monroe Mission* (Meridian, MS: The Press of Tell Farmer, 1927), 63.

2. *Ibid.*, 79.

THE
CHICKASAW NATION
1820–1830

ORCES THAT LED TO INDIAN REMOVAL in the nineteenth century might be said to have started with the arrival of Europeans on the North American continent, but as federal Indian policy, it had begun with Thomas Jefferson after the Louisiana Purchase in 1803. Between then and 1820, the push for removal of the Southeastern tribes, including the Chickasaws, gained momentum. The Chickasaw Nation to which young Thomas C. Stuart had gone in 1820 was grappling with changes that made Chickasaw life difficult and were pushing the people rapidly toward removal. The changes had resulted primarily from the establishment of the American government and subsequent pressures by that government and its peoples. Treaties before 1820 had ceded Chickasaw lands so that by then, Americans were pressing on the nation's borders on several fronts. Although the changes had made significant inroads on traditional Chickasaw life ways, the most rapid changes were yet to come: during the next decade, the Chickasaws would see their government continue to move away from its traditional structure; their country invaded by Americans, some seeking to "civilize" them through Christian religion and American-style education and others to exploit them by usurping their lands and conducting illicit trade; their laws and government extinguished by the states of Mississippi and Alabama; and their existence as a nation placed in jeopardy by the specter of removal.

One of the most significant changes Chickasaw society had undergone by 1820 was governmental. The council that Stuart attended in 1820 reflected the major governmental transition that was taking place within the Chickasaw Nation. The Chickasaw leaders who gathered in council at Tockshish did not only represent the nation at

(3)

large, but also four districts that were of recent vintage. In the early American period, the Chickasaw population had begun to disperse from the concentrated area of their traditional towns, and by 1805 the population had settled in four distinct geographical areas. Ten years later, to make annuity payments more efficient, Chickasaw Agent William Cocke formally organized four districts. The annuity of 1818 was paid to the chiefs of the districts—Samuel Sealy, Coahoma (William McGilivray), Tishomingo, and Apassantubby—who passed the annuity on to the people. Although the districts were numbered, agents commonly referred to each by its chief's name. Tishomingo's district was the northeastern, McGilivray's the northwestern, Sealy's the southwestern, in which the Chickasaw Agency and present-day Pontotoc were located, and Apassantubby's the southeastern in which present-day Tupelo is located.[1] The four chieftainships did not change until Apassantubby died in 1831.

This new structure had revolutionized the centuries-old traditional leadership system. Though the system is somewhat ambiguous today, the Chickasaws had traditionally been led by a minko (called "King" by the Europeans), who was a hereditary peace leader, and the Chief Warrior, often referred to by the Americans as the "Chief" or "principal chief," who achieved rank through warfare or international affairs. By the time the district structure emerged, Chinnubbee was minko and Tishomingo, who opposed the district structure, was at least nominally the chief, although the powers traditionally associated with his position were apparently in the hands of others. When Chinnubbee died in 1819, he was succeeded by his nephew Chehopistee, a twenty-year-old who died after a short time in office.[2] Chehopistee was succeeded by Ishtehotopa, also a nephew of Chinnubbee, and it was Ishtehotopa's induction that Thomas C. Stuart witnessed at the council in 1820. Although Ishtehotopa was destined to be the last hereditary minko of the nation, his position and the Chickasaw loyalties to the traditional leadership later provided a means for the Chickasaws to retain a form of government after the states of Mississippi and Alabama forbade government by chiefs in 1830 and 1832.

The traditional system of minko and chief leadership had become weaker during the preceding decades by the rise to power of the Colbert

(4)

brothers. The Colberts—William, George, and Levi—had distinguished themselves in warfare in behalf of the Chickasaws during the 1790s. William served first as chief. Then, because of George's service in the field as an interpreter, the council elected him their spokesman, and for twelve years he served as their head chief. Late in 1813 he resigned as chief, and he and his brothers joined the fight against the Creeks. Then Levi Colbert became chief and spokesman for the Chickasaw Nation, a position he held until his death in 1834.[3]

Opinions of historians like Arrell Gibson, who long ago described the role of the Colberts during the period leading to removal, have generally gone unchallenged until recent years. Gibson and others have argued that the Colberts were representative of the Chickasaw mixed bloods who rose to power, took advantage of the full bloods to achieve that power, used their position to enrich themselves, dominated the Chickasaw economy and international affairs, and shaped the direction of Chickasaw society. That the Colberts, especially Levi, were self-serving, perhaps even avaricious and open to being bribed, can generally be supported. However, more recent scholarship makes a compelling argument that the full bloods and the mixed bloods were not at odds over the direction of Chickasaw affairs, that the Colberts were acting upon the wishes of a majority of the Chickasaws, and that the actions of the Colberts, in effect, held the Americans at bay in the pre-removal period.[4] Throughout the period of Colbert political domination, the Chickasaws retained the hereditary minko in Chinnubbee, Chehistopee, and Ishtehotopa and the chiefs such as Tishomingo and Emmubbee.

While there is little debate about the political power of the Colbert family, their effectiveness in manipulating the direction of Chickasaw culture has also been brought into question. The most prominent mixed-blood family, they certainly dominated Chickasaw foreign affairs for many years. However, there is little evidence that they were the head of a "clique" of mixed-bloods. Historian James Atkinson argues that there is "no substantial support for Gibson's insinuation that the mixed-bloods as a whole were manipulating and thus altering the general Chickasaw population's cultural, political, and social configurations."[5] There is little doubt, however, that the economic success of the

Colbert and allied families in the first two decades of the nineteenth century contributed significantly to the changing economies of the Chickasaw Nation. However history ultimately deals with the Colbert family, their role was undeniably significant in Chickasaw history during the three decades leading to removal. A good example is their assistance to the missionaries, including the Reverend Thomas C. Stuart, in their early endeavors among the Chickasaws.

Stuart was a harbinger of changes to come. Christianity, to the Americans, was a necessary ingredient of their definition of "civilization." When Stuart returned to the Chickasaw Nation in early 1821, he was intent on bringing "civilization" to the Chickasaws. Only the month before, he had been ordained by the Synod of South Carolina and Georgia as the first missionary to the Chickasaws. Zealous and accompanied by a small party of mission workers, he arrived at the site of the future Monroe Mission, two miles from Tockshish on the last day of January 1821, when they felled the first tree, an event that, to Americans, always symbolized the advent of "civilized" society. He was joined by carpenter Hamilton V. Turner and farmer James Wilson and their families from South Carolina; the Reverend and Mrs. Hugh Wilson of North Carolina; and the Reverend William C. Blair of Ohio.[6]

As the Chickasaw leadership understood it, the primary purpose of the missionary presence in the Nation was American-style education, not religion, for the chiefs found little in Christianity that appealed to them. Thus Stuart and the mission group spent the first two years clearing a farm and building a school, which was ready by the spring of 1822. Stuart first sought out children who lived in the neighborhood, unprepared as he was at the time to take in boarders. With some difficulty he obtained a promise from a local widow to send her two children only after he promised to clothe them and feed them during the day. These children later became known as William H. Barr and Mary Leslie, the first two Chickasaw students to be schooled at the mission, and later, along with their mother, they became members of the church.[7]

In the spring of 1823, the school entered full operation. District Chief Samuel Sealy made an official speech to open the school and enrolled his son, who later became known as T. Carleton Henry. Most

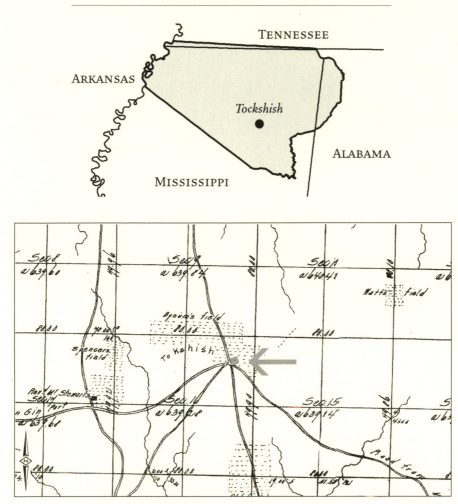

Tockshish. From the Cession Surveys of 1832.

of the fifty students boarded at the school with the mission workers. Also in 1823, the Reverend Hugh Wilson established a school two miles north of Monroe near Tockshish, which outlasted the Monroe school and remained in operation almost until the Chickasaws left for the West.[8] The process was "the Bible and hoe" system. Besides the academic curriculum, there was a daily routine of religious instruction and prayer, and the boys practiced American-style agriculture on the mission farm, where they raised food for the mission's consumption. By 1824, the missionaries had to limit the number of students they admitted. The Chickasaws, they wrote, "begin to see the necessity of a different mode of life from that which they have hitherto pursued." The Chickasaws were turning, they wrote, from game to agriculture.[9]

There was no doubt some truth in what the missionaries said, but American education was most popular among those families that had earlier sought education for their children. In the late eighteenth and early nineteenth century, a few intermarried whites and mixed bloods sent their sons and daughters for private education in Florida, Tennessee, Maryland, and the District of Columbia. As early as 1803, the Chickasaw leaders requested establishment of schools in the Nation, but it was not until a decade later that a short-lived school was established near the agency. Then in 1820, the Cumberland Presbyterians established a school at Levi Colbert's home near Cotton Gin Port. Called Charity Hall, the school opened in his home while a structure was built about three miles south of Cotton Gin Port. The complex consisted of a log classroom, rooms for students, outbuildings, and a mission farm used to teach the boys American agricultural methods. The girls were taught spinning, weaving, and other domestic activities.[10] With these few efforts, education was not widespread among the rank and file Chickasaws.

The Chickasaw leaders, however, saw the need for education. In 1824 the chiefs lent their support to the establishment of schools, appropriating $5,000 to build two additional schools and guaranteeing an annual appropriation of $2,500 to support them. The schools were placed under Stuart's direction. One was called Martyn on Pigeon Roost Creek near present-day Holly Springs and was taught by William C. Blair. Caney Creek School was on the Tennessee River near

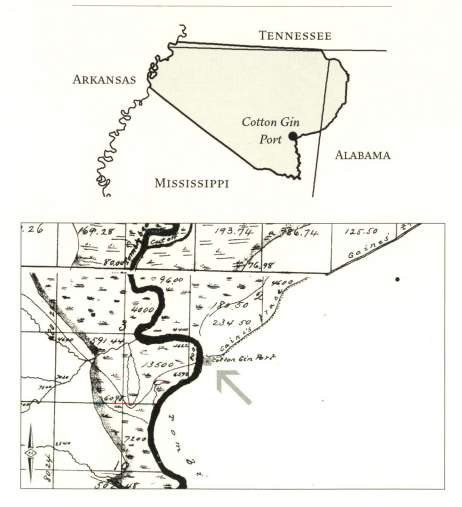

Cotton Gin Port.

IMAGE COURTESY OF THE CHICKASAW NATION
GEOSPATIAL INFORMATION DEPARTMENT.
© CHICKASAW NATION

CESSION AREA OF 1832

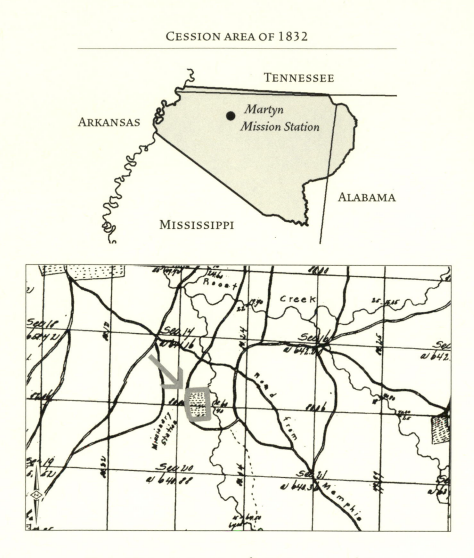

Martyn Mission Station. From the Cession Surveys of 1832.

Tuscumbia, Alabama, and was taught by the Reverend Hugh Wilson, who was replaced at Tockshish by James Holmes of Pennsylvania. The four schools combined enrolled 120 boys and girls, men and women. In 1826, the schools were transferred to the American Board of Commissioners for Foreign Missions. By that time, after having gotten off to a good start, the schools had begun to falter. By 1827, there were preaching stations, as well as schools, at Monroe, Martyn, Tockshish, and Caney Creek. The school at Monroe, however, had suspended for a year, and two of the others were "embarrassed" for lack of teachers.[11]

The alliance with the Board of Commissioners for Foreign Missions gave the schools a lift. By 1831, they enrolled 88 students. The Monroe school had closed in 1830. The school at Tockshish, which had also been suspended, reopened in the fall of 1830. Students who lived far from the school boarded with the mission family or people in the surrounding neighborhood. At Martyn there were buildings and a small farm, supported primarily by the Chickasaw annuity that had been set aside for education. The Chickasaws in that area were primarily mixed bloods who understood English and wanted their children educated in English. In the fall of 1830, the missionaries reported twenty-nine students, both local and boarding, girls outnumbering boys almost two to one. They studied arithmetic, geography, English grammar, and composition. Nearly all spoke English. Teacher James Holmes said, "The girls are taught to work."[12] What Holmes meant by "work," of course, was American-style domestic work. The missionaries touted their successes to their supporters back East as evidence that their "Bible and hoe" method was working, but the number of students was insignificant in comparison to the total number of Chickasaws who followed the systems of knowledge that had been practiced by their people for centuries.

The missionaries also reported what they considered "successes" at Caney Creek. There were thirty-nine students, of whom eight were men between the ages of eighteen and twenty-one. Hugh Wilson, the teacher, put the students into a program that was three or four years old and resembled what was called the "outing" program later in the century at Carlisle Indian Industrial School. The students spent most of the year in nearby areas of Alabama and Tennessee among white families

(11)

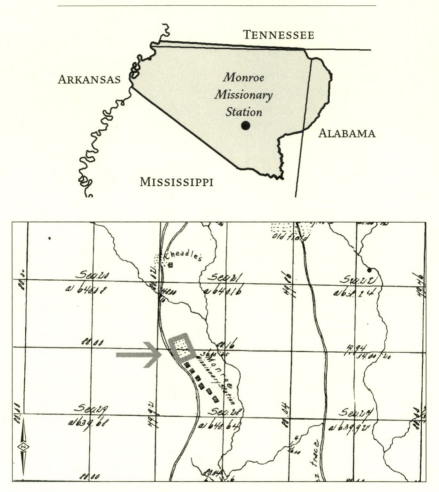

Monroe Missionary Station. From the Cession Surveys of 1832.

The Monroe Mission
Ann Sheffield

IMAGE COURTESY OF THE CHICKASAW NATION ART COLLECTION.
© CHICKASAW NATION

(13)

in order to give them "an acquaintance with the English language" and "the habits of civilized life." All spoke English fluently, it was reported, acted "with a good degree of propriety, and seem[ed] thoroughly domesticated." All could read and most could write. After a year, Wilson was contemplating bringing them back to the Caney Creek station, for he believed his objective had been reached during their stay in white society.[13] Like most zealots in other times and places, Wilson did not realize that the type of education he touted rarely prepared his subjects for life in the American world, nor did it necessarily make them better members of their own society.

What the missionaries might have considered "successes" were in reality short-lived. By the end of 1830, Mississippi had extended its jurisdictions over the Chickasaw lands, and Congress had passed the Indian Removal Act. In the winter of 1832, Alabama extended its laws over Chickasaw lands in that state. The disruption caused by these events in the Chickasaw Nation ensured the demise of the schools by 1834. Martyn and Caney Creek closed in 1832, as did Charity Hall, the Cumberland Presbyterian school at Cotton Gin Port. From the time the missionaries established the schools, Stuart said, they had struggled "under trials and difficulties that always attend a similar enterprise amongst an unenlightened and uncivilized people."[14] Looking back after more than twenty-five years, he judged the educational efforts primarily a failure: "The number who obtained anything like a good English education was comparatively small. Having learned to read and write, many of them left school, supposing they had finished their education. Moreover, the regulations of the school and the requirements of the station imposed such a restraint on their former roving habits that many of them ran off and never returned. This was often a matter of deep regret and a cause of great annoyance to us, but it was one of those discouragements with which missionaries amongst an ignorant and heathen people have always had to contend." The schools did not prove a useful tool in Christianizing the Chickasaws. Stuart wrote, "Comparatively few of our scholars embraced religion and united with our church. In after years a good many joined the Methodist Church."[15]

After the schools had closed, the Chickasaws continued to send some of their children for education outside the Nation. Senator Richard M. Johnson's Choctaw Academy had opened in Scott County, Kentucky, in 1825. When the Chickasaws began sending students there is uncertain, but in 1834 and 1835, they paid for clothing and traveling expenses for John B. Love, Stephen Perry, Maxwell Frazier, William Brown, Levi Perry, John Hall, Logan Albertson, Benjamin R. Albertson, Robert Johnson, Thomas H. Benton, Shtokaway's son, Takintubby's nephew, and others.[16]

The failure of the schools to instill Christianity in its students was due, primarily, to a general lack of interest in the Christian religion among the Chickasaw people. A Christian movement among the Chickasaws had, in fact, got off to a faltering start. The Reverend Hugh Dickson of the Presbytery of South Carolina had organized the Monroe Presbyterian Church in 1823 with only nine charter members, none of whom were Chickasaws.[17] One, however, was a black woman, whom Stuart called "the first fruit of the Chickasaw Mission": "Being a native of the country, she spoke the Chickasaw language fluently; and having the confidence of the Indians, I employed her as my interpreter for several years, in preaching the gospel to them."[18] The first members of Chickasaw households joined in 1824: Abraham, a black slave, belonging to a Chickasaw; Mrs. Tennessee Bynum; and Esther, belonging to Mrs. [William?] Colbert.[19] During the next four years, only 16 members were added, although Monroe sat in the midst of one of the most populous sections of the Chickasaw Nation with an estimated 800 people, of whom approximately 500 were Chickasaws and 300 were slaves and a few white men with Chickasaw families.[20]

In early 1827, however, there occurred what the missionaries termed an "awakening," which started with a revival meeting held by Cyrus Kingsbury, Anson Gleason, and Cyrus Byington, the latter of whom preached in both English and Choctaw. Stuart credited Byington with the revival's success. While a revival was underway at Mayhew in the Choctaw Nation, Byington, imbued with the spirit, went to Monroe and began to preach. The preachers worked hard, however, to prevent "excitement" and calculated to instruct the people in religion by holding inquiry meetings on Saturday nights. Twenty to thirty attended, some coming ten to twelve miles.[21] By mid-summer the revival was widespread, people coming from more than thirty-five miles around "to see what was going on." One communion was attended by about 200 people. The revival, however, netted only twenty-two members: two Chickasaws, three white men, and seventeen slaves.[22]

By 1830, the church had only 119 members in the entire Chickasaw Nation. Only thirty-three were Chickasaws, twenty-five were whites, and the rest were blacks. These latter, Stuart wrote, lived in "considerable number in the neighborhood" of Monroe. "These generally spoke the Indian language; and being on an equality with their owners, and having more intercourse with them than is usual among white people, through their instrumentality a knowledge of the gospel was extended among the Indians. The change, too, in their deportment had a tendency to convince them of the reality and excellence of religion, and to eradicate their prejudices against it."[23] However, by 1830 preaching

(15)

had become sporadic. When James Holmes arrived at Tockshish in the fall of that year, only one sermon had been preached there since spring. He drew large crowds at his sermons, but lack of a large enough building meant that services were held outside, and those attending had to brave cold winds and damp ground through hours of service.[24] In 1831, Holmes was sent to replace Blair at Martyn. He felt confident in leaving, he said, because ninety people took the sacrament at Tockshish and nearly two hundred made up the congregation. He said, "This now has assumed the aspect of a Christian settlement, and the Lord appears to prosper everything undertaken in his glory." On the other hand, at Martyn, only ten took communion, and no more than fifty attended the preaching.[25] While Holmes's estimation of the Tockshish community is glowing, if not overly optimistic, the majority of the Christian community he referred to was white or black, not Chickasaw.

Other denominational missions had been even less effective than Stuart's Presbyterians. From 1799 to 1803, the Presbyterian Joseph Bullen had labored among the Chickasaws but failed to establish a church. No other efforts occurred until Congress passed the so-called Civilization Act of 1819, which made federal funds available for Indian education. The Baptists began working among the Chickasaws and Choctaws in 1819, but it was not until 1828 that they finally established a mission near Tockshish. In 1821, the Methodists included preaching stops in the Chickasaw Nation on their circuit and continued them for several years thereafter. The only mission that approached Stuart's success was Charity Hall, the Cumberland Presbyterian school established in 1820 near Cotton Gin Port. Charity Hall, like the other Presbyterian schools, declined and finally closed in 1832.[26]

Although Stuart's biographers later put a good face on his Presbyterian mission's efforts, the results were far from stellar, in part, because of Chickasaw aversion to Christianity. Despite the changes that had taken place in Chickasaw social and political structures in recent decades, the people retained a strong attachment to old beliefs. Many held a disdain for Christianity, which may have related to their general disdain for the Choctaws. In 1830, one missionary at Tockshish wrote: "The great outcry against the missionaries has been, that they were not teaching school, which, it was said, was their appropriate work, and that, if we kept on this way, we would get the people all crazy and spoiled, like the Choctaws."[27]

In addition to the Chickasaw aversion to mission work, the promising missionary efforts between 1828 and 1830, like those in education, were undermined, in part, by the rapid changes in the Chickasaw Nation that were pushing the Chickasaw people ever closer to removal. In 1820, the year the missionaries came, Mississippi had entered a period of concerted agitation for Chickasaw removal by attempting to extend its laws over the Chickasaw people. By the waning years of the decade, pressures to bring the Chickasaws under state jurisdiction were mounting. In 1825, Secretary of War John C. Calhoun developed a plan for removal and proposed that the Chickasaws could be absorbed by the Choctaws. The following year, the U. S. sent treaty commissioners to the Chickasaws to negotiate their removal, but the Chickasaws refused. Commissioner of Indian Affairs Thomas McKenny visited the Chickasaws the following year, urging them to remove west to relieve the people of the steadily increasing pressures of American society. In 1828 Chickasaw leaders sent an exploring party west to examine the country and search for a suitable site for the Chickasaws to settle, but the party made an unfavorable report.[28] A significant event that precipitated destructive change was the Mississippi legislature's extension of the state's laws over the Chickasaw and Choctaw Nations in early 1829 and placing the Chickasaw Nation under the jurisdiction of county courts. A year later the state placed the Chickasaws and Choctaws and their property under state law and outlawed their tribal governments. The state of Alabama was on the verge of extending its laws over the Chickasaws as well.[29] Part of the anti-Constitutional, states' rights movement to usurp federal authority over Indian affairs, these moves had a two-fold purpose: to gain authority over the rich Indian lands to bolster a developing slave-based cotton economy and to force the Indians from within the boundaries of the state, if possible.

(17)

The Chickasaw leaders looked at the prospect of living under state law with dread. They held out hope even to late 1829 that their faithfulness to the United States government would make the administration save them. If state laws were extended over them, they had no faith that they would be put on an equal footing with the whites. Not understanding the laws, they would become victims of the whites, who would uphold each other. They would be helpless to resist the encroachments of whites upon their property, and in a short time they would have nothing left. They would rather exchange their land for any they could get rather than lose their "native freedom," they said.[30] The Mississippi law "abolished and took away all the rights, privileges, immunities, and franchises held, claimed or enjoyed by those persons called Indians within the chartered limits of that state by virtue of any form of policy, usages or customs existing among them."[31] The Chickasaws sent appeals to the federal government for the United States to stand by the honor of their treaties with the Chickasaws, but officials used the occasion to argue that the only relief for the Chickasaws was to remove to the West.

With suspension of the government by chiefs under threat of fine and imprisonment, the Chickasaws entered one of the most demoralizing periods of their history. White intruders in the Chickasaw country had been a long-standing problem. Though Chickasaw leaders had constantly entreated the federal government to remove the intruders and to uphold the tribe's sovereignty according to the treaties, the United States had steadily refused to do so. In early 1830, sub-agent John L. Allen reported that he had had difficulty preventing whites from violating the federal Intercourse Law regulating trade with the Indians. The Chickasaws called for enforcement of the Treaty of 1816, which required traders to apply for a permit to trade in the Chickasaw Nation. Whites drove their livestock over the state line on to Chickasaw land, made illegal settlements, traded without permits, and stole Chickasaw slaves, horses, and cattle.[32] Intruders became more numerous after Mississippi extended its laws. In applying the Mississippi legislative act, the circuit court of Monroe County claimed jurisdiction over all of the Chickasaw Nation within the state's boundaries and nullified federal law regulating trade and intercourse with the tribal nation. The result was an influx of white squatters, who brought with them large numbers of whiskey peddlers.[33]

According to the missionaries, the Chickasaws entered a period of dissipation. Both federal law and tribal law had forbidden the sale of whiskey within the Chickasaw Nation, and until Mississippi's act, there had been little intoxication. Holmes wrote from Tockshish in the fall of 1830, "But now, multitudes of men and women whenever they get a few dollars, are off with their kegs and pack-horses to the nearest village, and return with their poison, to retail it at 75 cents and upwards per quart." Chickasaws would sell their horses, he said, for a keg of whiskey.[34]

Part of the tribe's demoralized condition was also a result of mounting and intense pressure to achieve the states' ultimate goal: to drive all of the tribes from within their boundaries. After the Louisiana Purchase, Thomas Jefferson and national politicians following his philosophy had considered the Louisiana Purchase as a place where tribes east of the Mississippi could be relocated. The matter did not become an issue of national debate until after President James Monroe formally urged the Congress in 1825 to adopt a removal policy. Action was delayed, however, until the election of Andrew Jackson in 1828. One of his first priorities was removal of the southeastern tribes to the West. His position had its support, which began to erode when it became evident that Georgia and other states were primarily interested in the land rather than the welfare of the tribes. The nation entered a period of intense and bitter debate over the issue of Indian removal. In May of 1830, a bitterly divided Congress passed the Indian Removal Act, which gave the president authority to negotiate the removal of tribes, who would exchange the lands they occupied for lands west of the Mississippi.

(19)

The Indian Removal Act had been the culmination of a decade of drastic change for Chickasaw society and was a portent of even more changes to come. In the wake of the act, the Chickasaw people faced the most demoralizing prospect yet—giving up their ancient homeland and moving to a new and alien place.

NOTES

1. James R. Atkinson, *Splendid Land, Splendid People: The Chickasaw Indians to Removal* (Tuscaloosa: University of Alabama Press, 2004), 208. Apassantubby was succeeded by Isaac Alberson in 1831. An early, rather balanced account of Colbert family motives is Guy B. Braden, "The

Colberts and the Chickasaw Nation," *Tennessee Historical Quarterly*, 17 (March–December, 1958), 222–48, 318–35.

2. Atkinson, *Splendid Land*, 208, 212–13, 311n60.

3. *Ibid.*, 197–98, 201, 207.

4. *Ibid.*, 199–200, 210–11.

5. *Ibid.*, 212.

6. E. T. Winston, *"Father Stuart" and the Monroe Mission* (Meridian, MS: The Press of Tell Farmer, 1927), 69–70.

7. *Ibid.*, 70.

8. *Ibid.*, 70–71.

9. *Missionary Herald*, 18 (1822), 82, and 20 (1824), 131.

10. Atkinson, *Splendid Land*, 217–18; Arrell M. Gibson, *The Chickasaws* (Norman: University of Oklahoma Press, 1971), 110.

11. Winston, *"Father Stuart,"* 71; *Missionary Herald* 24 (1828), 13, 283.

12. *Missionary Herald*, 27 (1831), 9, 44, 45, 251, 351–52.

13. *Ibid.*, 351–52.

14. Winston, *"Father Stuart,"* 70.

15. *Ibid.*, 71, 72.

16. Atkinson, *Splendid Land*, 220.

17. Winston, *"Father Stuart,"* 71–72; John Wilson, "Old Monroe Presbyterian Church and Cemetery, 1821–1823" (Algoma, MS: n.d.), 5. Wilson's typescript contains the session minutes for the church through 1842. Copy used here is from the Pontotoc Public Library, Pontotoc, MS.

18. Winston, *"Father Stuart,"* 72.

19. Wilson, "Old Monroe Presbyterian Church," 5.

20. *Missionary Herald* 24 (1828), 13, 56.

21. Winston, *"Father Stuart,"* 73.

22. Winston, *"Father Stuart,"* 17; Wilson, "Old Monroe Presbyterian Church," 6; *Missionary Herald* 24 (1828), 13, 56, 119, 283–84.

23. Wilson, "Old Monroe Presbyterian Church," 5; Winston, *"Father Stuart,"* 72.

24. *Missionary Herald* 27 (1831), 44–45.

25. *Ibid.*, 45; Winston, *"Father Stuart,"* 72–73.

26. Gibson, *The Chickasaws*, 107–10.

27. *Missionary Herald*, 26 (1830), 33, cited in Gibson, *The Chickasaws*, 114.

28. Gibson, *The Chickasaws*, 170.

29. Muriel H. Wright, "Notes on Events Leading to the Chickasaw Treaties of Franklin and Pontotoc, 1830 and 1832," *Chronicles of Oklahoma* 34

(Winter 1956–1957): 465–68.

30. John L. Allen to War Department, February 7, 1830, National Archives Microfilm Publications, Letters Received by the Office of Indian Affairs, Microcopy M234, Roll 136 (this source hereafter cited as M234, followed by the roll number).

31. Grant Foreman, *Indian Removal* (Norman: University of Oklahoma Press, 1972), 21, citing, 23rd Congress, 1st session, *U. S. Senate Document 512*, III: 361.

32. Allen to War Department, February 7, 1830, M234-R163.

33. Gibson, *The Chickasaws*, 170–71, 174.

34. *Missionary Herald* 27 (1831), 45.

Articles of a Treaty made and entered into between Genl. John Coffee being duly authorised thereto by the President of the United States, and the whole Chickasaw Nation, in general Council assembled at the Council House, on Pontotock Creek on the Twentieth day of October 1832.

The Chickasaw Nation find themselves oppressed in their present situation; by being made subject to the laws of the States in which they reside. Being ignorant of the language and laws of the white man, they cannot understand or obey them. Rather than submit to this great evil, they prefer to seek a home in the West, where they may live and be governed by their own laws. And believing that they can procure for themselves a home, in a country suited to their wants and condition; provided they had the means to contract and pay, for the same. They have determined to sell their Country and hunt a new home —

The President has heard the complaints of the Chickasaws and like them believes they cannot be happy, and prosper as a nation, in their present situation and condition, and being desirous to relieve them from the great calamity that seems to await them if they remain as they are — He has sent his Commissioner Genl. John Coffee, who has met the whole Chickasaw nation in Council, and after mature deliberation, they have entered into the following articles, which shall be binding on both parties, when the same shall be ratified by the President of the United States by and with the advice and consent of the Senate —

Article 1st For the consideration hereinafter expressed, the Chickasaw nation do hereby cede, to the United States, all the land which they own on the East side of the Mississippi River, including all the country which they at present own and occupy.

Article 2nd The United States agree to have the whole Country thus ceded, surveyed, as soon as it can be conveniently done, in the same manner that the public lands of the United States are surveyed in the States of Mississippi and Alabama, and as soon thereafter as may be practicable, to have the same prepared for sale. The President of the United States will then offer, the land for sale at Public Auction, in the same manner, and on the same terms and conditions as the other public lands, and such of the land as may not sell at the Public Sales shall be offered at private sale in the same manner that other private sales are made of the United States lands —

Article 3d As a full Compensation to the Chickasaw Nation for the Country thus ceded, the United States, agree to pay over to the Chickasaw Nation, all the money arising from the sale of the land which may be received from time to time, after deducting therefrom, the whole cost and expenses, of surveying and selling the land, including every expense attending the same —

Article 4th The President being determined that the Chickasaw people shall not deprive themselves of a comfortable home, in the Country where they now are, untill they shall have provided a Country in the West to remove to and settle on, with fair prospects of future comfort and happiness — It is therefore agreed to by the Chickasaw Nation that they will endeavor as soon as it may be in their power, after the ratification of

the

NEGOTIATING REMOVAL

LONG DEBATE IN WASHINGTON and in the American press over the question of Indian removal culminated in the Indian Removal Act, which became law on May 28, 1830. The act provided for western lands in exchange for those of the Indians living in any state and for the Indians' removal west of the Mississippi River. The states of Mississippi and Alabama had recently undermined the Chickasaw government by passing laws that made the Chickasaws subject to state laws, did away with tribal laws, and called for fines and imprisonment for leaders who presumed to carry out their duties. President Andrew Jackson turned a deaf ear to Chickasaw appeals for the federal government to intervene in their behalf according to treaty agreements.[1] Federal officials immediately began to use the Removal Act to pressure the tribes to remove. Although the prospect was staggering, the Chickasaws faced the reality of it and quickly began negotiation. They had one major fact in their favor. Unlike the other tribes, they had not engaged in factional strife. The issue of removal had not rent them as it had the others. They faced the future as a unified people and, because of that, were able to forestall removal years, to negotiate better terms of removal, in some ways, than the other tribes were be able to do, and lay the groundwork for recovery of their nation in the West. Though they were unified, the price of the long negotiations of the Treaty of Franklin, the Treaty of Pontotoc, and the Supplemental Treaty of 1834 was costly. During the seven years the process took, Chickasaw society underwent more damaging changes as their country was overrun by whites and the people's morale reached, perhaps, an all-time low.

(23)

◀ *Preamble, Treaty of Pontotoc*
COURTESY THE NATIONAL ARCHIVES

The economic changes that had taken place among the Chickasaws during the previous two decades made the economic possibilities of the Chickasaw domain tantalizing and, therefore, desirous to Americans. In the early days of 1830, the War Department asked sub-agent John Allen for a report on the condition of the Chickasaws. It is wise to remember that such reports were generated to support removal policy, and the agents in the field told the central government officials what they wanted to hear. There was one central theme in such reports: The Chickasaws were on their way to becoming "civilized," but they needed time to complete the process and therefore should move safely beyond the whites until it was completed. Although Allen's report should be read in that light, much of its content can be verified by other evidence.

Of first significance to Allen—and to avaricious Americans—was the land. The best land was located along the major streams, but much of the remainder was fit only for summer range, except the smaller steam bottoms, which contained cane brakes that provided range throughout the winter for horses and cattle. The Chickasaws maintained large herds of horses that had earned a reputation for their toughness and stamina long before removal. Allen said of the Chickasaw and their horses: "They have a plenty of horses of a superior quality as at least well adapted to the use of Indians, they use them on their farms with much less food than is generally given those animals that are raised and used by the whites, and when traveling through their country, they travel from thirty to fifty miles per day never feed them but let them subsist on what grass or cane they can procure for themselves when hobeled [*sic*] out at night."[2]

The Chickasaws, Allen reported, were embracing the domestic and economic practices of the Americans. They had given up the hunt as a major source of sustenance. The buffaloes and bears had disappeared, and only a few deer were left. The rifle was now used for "recreation, and entertainment." The Chickasaws had turned to agriculture, raising cotton, corn, wheat, oats, peas, and potatoes, and to raising livestock, with herds of horses, cattle, and goats, and flocks of poultry of "every description." A thirst for gain had gripped the Chickasaws, Allen said, the profit motive resulting in exports of cotton, beef, and pork. Allen expected their cotton export to reach 1,000 bales in 1830. After their profits purchased what they needed, the Chickasaws indulged in what Allen called the "Luxuries of life: (to wit) slaves, shugar [sic] coffee, as well as dry goods of various descriptions, which are calculated to render them comfortable and ornament their persons." During the past preceding eight years, Allen asserted, the men had taken more responsibility for working the fields and took on cultivating chores while the women attended to household affairs, weaving and making their own clothes, milking, making butter and cheese, and rivaling white women in their fashions. Allen also asserted that "many" Chickasaws professed Christianity.[3]

Without question, Chickasaw society was undergoing change, but it had not conformed as closely to the model of the American yeoman farmer as Allen's report would lead his readers to think. How accurate his report was may be judged by his assertion that many Chickasaws had embraced Christianity. His statement was apparently based on one camp meeting he had attended in late 1829, when he saw Chickasaws taking the sacrament for the first time. He no doubt over-generalized other elements of Chickasaw life as well. Nevertheless, his report served its purpose. It told United States officials what they wanted to hear: The Chickasaws were well on their way to embracing a lifestyle similar to that of Americans. However, they had not reached a point where they could compete with the whites pressing on their borders and invading their lands. Only removal, government officials argued, could save them, and they turned a deaf ear to Chickasaw appeals that the government enforce the Chickasaw treaties.

Without recourse at either the state or federal level and pressured by government officials, the Chickasaws entered into negotiations in the late summer of 1830. United States Secretary of War John H. Eaton and John Coffee, Andrew Jackson's confidant and husband of Rachel Jackson's niece, met with the Chickasaw leaders at Franklin, Tennessee, where they were joined by Jackson himself. The Chickasaws were represented by Levi, George, and James Colbert, William McGilivray, James Brown, Isaac Alberson, and others. John McLish was secretary and Benjamin Love interpreter. What the government proposed was grievous to the Chickasaws. The president asked them, they said, to take land in fee simple west of the Mississippi "in exchange for the country we now possess in fee simple" (or to use his own words, "as long as the grass grows and water runs"). They said, "We the Chickasaws have occupied the country not only where we now live from time immorial [sic], but a large portion of the rich and fertile lands of Tennessee and Alabama where is now covered with large farms, flourishing citys [sic] and villages, we have from time to time sold piece after piece of our Country to our white brothers to serve their views and interests; until we have but a small home left that is barely sufficient to subsist upon while living and to bury our bones when we are dead." Their ownership rested in that immemorial occupancy. "It is acknowledged," they said, "that we were the first to build fires upon the land we now occupy." Now they were told that they must go to the West if they hoped to preserve themselves. While they felt inclined to concede to the wishes of the president, they would not agree to go to the West until they found a land "equal to the one we now occupy," they said.[4] Such was the talk with which the Chickasaw delegates, with George and Levi Colbert at the head, opened the negotiations at Franklin.

Understanding that land was the driving force behind removal, the Chickasaw negotiators sought, upon agreement to remove, to guarantee each Chickasaw a reservation of 160 acres or the equivalent in cash, as well as compensation for property left at removal. Failing there, they sought an annuity of twenty dollars for each Chickasaw for ten years. Coffee and Eaton argued that the Chickasaw demands were too costly. They came to agreement, however, in the Treaty of Franklin, August 31, 1830, which granted warriors, widows with families, and whites with Chickasaw families a half section of land and single individuals a quarter section in fee simple. The Chickasaws then were to decide whether to remain on their land or to remove. If the latter, they could sell their reservations; if the former, they would become citizens of the state. The treaty contained other provisions: the U. S. would pay the Chickasaws an annuity of $15,000 for twenty years; five leaders, including Levi Colbert, were each granted reservations of four sections of land; other leaders were granted smaller reservations; and the U. S. would pay for removal and provide subsistence to the Chickasaws for a year following their removal. Meanwhile, the Chickasaws would send a delegation to the West to find suitable lands to take in exchange for those in Mississippi and Alabama. However, if the Chickasaws failed to find a "suitable" country, the treaty would be null and void.[5]

On October 15, 1830, an exploring party of Chickasaws from the eastern part of the nation left for the West, led by Levi Colbert. They were joined at Memphis by Chickasaw agent Benjamin F. Reynolds.[6] Besides Colbert, the Chickasaws in the party were Eiochetubbee, In-mahhoolatubbe, Thomas Sealy, Ishtahiyahatubbee, Ahtokomah, Pitman Colbert, Newberry, James Brown, Ohhucubbee, Ishkettake, Okelabhacubbee, Shumachabe, Kin-hi-che, Henry Love, and Elaplink-bahtubbee. The latter had lived among the Pawnees in the West for a long time and spoke their language. From Memphis they plunged into the Mississippi Swamp in eastern Arkansas, and on the third day out, Kin-hi-che fell ill and had to return home.[7]

Jackson and the War Department wanted the Chickasaws to settle with the Choctaws in the West. Thus, once in Indian Territory, they planned to join an exploring party of Choctaws accompanied by George S. Gaines near the mouth of the Canadian River and explore that river's south side to a point as far up as they wanted to go, travel south to the Red River, and go down that stream to the Blue. The army outfit-ted the Chickasaws and Choctaws at Fort Gibson. They retrieved rifles, powder, flints, and lead from storage at Fort Smith, and at Fort Gibson picked up iron, a pack saddle, rope, and rations of flour, beef, pork, salt, and soap. They were afraid of attacks by the Pawnees and requested that some troops accompany them. Matthew Arbuckle, commander at the post, reluctantly sent a small unit to join them enroute.[8]

The Chickasaws and Choctaws met at the mouth of the south fork of the Canadian and from there launched their exploring expedition. They looked at the lands on the South Canadian and then followed the North Fork with the intent of going as far as the Cross Timbers. Two of the marks of a good land were fertile bottoms along streams and suf-ficient cane brakes to provide winter forage for livestock. These quickly played out as they ascended the south fork of the Canadian, and the uplands along the stream looked unpromising to them. The Red River watershed was more promising. The False Washita, Blue, Boggy, and Kiamichi had wide bottoms and cane, and the uplands had timber and

(27)

generally rich prairies. Reynolds and Gaines thought it might be possible to relocate the Chickasaws along the Canadian watershed, using the ridge between the South Canadian and the Red River watershed as a dividing line between them and the Choctaws.[9]

Reynolds and Gaines' hopes for a union of the two peoples as a single nation were set back. The Chickasaws were generally unimpressed by the western lands. The Choctaws seemed willing to take the Chickasaws in as members of the Choctaw Nation, but Levi Colbert caused the Choctaw delegation to withdraw when he asked them to sell a part of their land to the Chickasaws. Having no instructions to discuss a sale, the Choctaws would not continue discussions. Reynolds and Gaines, however, always putting forward the American argument for removal, wrote, "Combined the two nations could make one of the strongest, wealthiest and most respectable communities of aborigines on the continent of America with the means in their own hands of soon becoming civilized, educated, independent American citizens."[10]

Dissatisfied with the Choctaw lands, Colbert and four of his captains, including Shumache, left the party to visit the Caddoes south of the Red River in search of suitable lands in Mexican territory. Although Reynolds approved Colbert's sojourn into Texas, he was highly critical of him. Colbert had gone west, Reynolds claimed, with a bias against the Indian Territory. He had been a part of an exploring party in 1828 and 1829 that had reached a point only a few miles west of the mouth of the Canadian, where they discovered a moccasin track, turned around immediately, and had gone back to Fort Smith without seeing any of the good lands of the area. Colbert had been reluctant to go out with exploring parties under Reynolds' direction and seemed unimpressed with even the good lands along the Red River. Colbert, Reynolds said, would "not like to live under [Greenwood] Leflore and I know his thirst for power is such as to form an obstickle [*sic*] in his mind adverse to a union" with the Choctaws. Reynolds began to doubt the sincerity of Colbert's statements at Franklin supporting a union, for he was heard to observe on the way west, Reynolds said, "that he knew there was no country in the west for his people and that he was traveling to humor the president." Reynolds said, "He acts childish. It took him a time to realize that he was not going out on a frolic like he did the other time,

(28)

and when it occurred to him that this was serious he threw obstackles [*sic*] in the way for a considerable time. He sent word to the President that he went south of the Red River to find a suitable land for his nation." While Colbert was exploring Caddo country, the remainder of the two parties traveled with Gaines and Reynolds back to Memphis by way of Washington in southwestern Arkansas and Little Rock, arriving at Memphis in mid-February. Reynolds fitted them out on February 20 for their return home from there.[11]

A council of the Chickasaw leaders convened in May 1831 to hear the report of the exploring party; they made it clear that a major driving force in Chickasaw affairs was the Chickasaws' desire to maintain their national identity. On May 28, they reported to Andrew Jackson. The country the party had explored, they said, had enough good land for only the Choctaws, who refused to "sell one foot." Their wish and hope, they said was "to preserve our independence & our Nation and our names to the latest generation." Thus, they explained, five of them had crossed the Red River near the place where the eastern Choctaw boundary struck it and explored the country west of the Louisiana line between the Red and Sabine rivers. They liked the Mexican country. "If this country can be purchased for us," they wrote, "our Nation will remove and be satisfied, we see no other country which we think would suit us so well." They did not want Jackson to think that they wished to escape the control of the United States. But Jackson had promised to move them beyond the control of laws such as those of Mississippi, which bore heavily upon them. "We know that you do not speak with a forked toung [*sic*]," they said, and appealed to Jackson to renew his pledge to find them a new land they could be happy in.[12] Because they had not found a suitable land, the Chickasaws, in effect, had nullified the Treaty of Franklin.

Americans acted as if Chickasaw removal was imminent and poised themselves to take over. Shortly after the Treaty of Franklin, they had begun to flood into the Chickasaw country, and friction arose between the two peoples. Before leaving for the West, Reynolds had posted signs throughout the Chickasaw Nation and placed notices in Mississippi, Alabama, and Tennessee newspapers, warning whites against settling on Chickasaw land. Some intruders had already made perma-

(29)

nent improvements. For years, others living in Tennessee had planted
corn and cotton crops across the line in Chickasaw country. They had
been routed the year before, but were expected to return. Whites had
also driven large herds of cattle onto Chickasaw land each winter, and
frequent strife had arisen between them and the Chickasaws over ownership. Whites had hunted on Chickasaw land and killed Chickasaw
cattle. By October 1830, the number of whites had so increased that
Reynolds advocated calling out a military force. Sub-agent Allen, on
the other hand, suggested sending a number of undercover or "confidential," men to find and arrest the intruders.[13]

Peddlers represented another form of intrusion. In October 1830,
Alexander and Wilson McCowan, armed with a letter from John
Coffee, took a wagonload of dry goods from Franklin, Tennessee, to
the Chickasaw Agency in order to obtain a permit to sell goods to the
Chickasaws under the Treaty of 1816. When the McCowans arrived at
the agency, both Reynolds and Allen were gone. Mrs. Reynolds urged
them to remain at the agency and wait. John McLish, secretary for the
Chickasaw Nation, told them that they could retrieve their goods and
trade with whites and blacks but not Chickasaws. More than a dozen
Chickasaw men took up surveillance of the McCowans, accused them
of trading with Chickasaws, confiscated their wagon, and stored the
goods in the agency. When Allen returned on November 11, he found
fifteen to twenty Chickasaws standing guard around the McCowans'
wagon, charging them with violating the Treaty of 1816, and the
leaders demanded half of the goods be given to the Chickasaw Nation
according to the Treaty. Instead, Allen held the goods and awaited
orders from the War Department. McCowan claimed that he had sold
dry goods only to whites and blacks in the nation, except Isham McLish,
a "half breed," who had bought a pair of yarn socks. Eliza Carter, also
half Chickasaw, had obtained some silk thread by having Allen's wife
and agent Reynolds's wife purchase it for her. Others testified that
McCowan had sold goods to "negroes." But the peddlers conveniently
did not think that McLish was a Chickasaw and considered the sale to
Miss Carter a sale to white women. McCowan stirred up the whites in
his behalf. Several young men, who according to Allen, had no visible
means of support except gambling, urged the McCowans to retake the

(30)

goods and sue Allen for "misdemeanor in office."[14]

With difficulty Allen maintained order. The "lawless" whites stayed around the agency for days, offering to help McCowan break into the agency and take the goods by force. "One of the mob, a Mr. Humphreys engaged in a combat with me," Allen said, "and at lenth [*sic*] he becoming weary of the contest retired in disgust." Allen contemplated asking for troops and urged U. S. officials to write the Chickasaw leaders in McCowan's behalf. General Coffee came to McCowan's defense, arguing that he did not intend to violate the treaty and suggested that the secretary of war station troops along the Tennessee-to-Natchez road. In January 1831, Allen released the government's half of the goods to McCowan and advised Pistalatubbee, who had confiscated the goods, to release the other half, which he did.[15]

The Chickasaws' insistence on enforcing treaty law placed them in direct confrontation with the laws of Mississippi. The leaders wrote to Jackson in the spring of 1831, "Father, we are told that the laws of these states are written in more than a hundred big books we cannot read, we cannot understand them and altho we love our white brethren, we cannot see in the extention [*sic*] of state laws over us any thing but injustice and suppression.... Your red children is [*sic*] now oppressed by new laws & customs executed by white officers whose words we do not understand."[16]

Legal disputes became common between Chickasaws and whites. In late 1830, missionary James Holmes reported one case in which a Chickasaw was hauled into court in a neighboring county, charged in the white court, and prosecuted by whites. He won his case, but his defense cost him $200. The missionaries thought some civil proceedings against the Chickasaws were "novel," suggesting that they were aimed at inducing the Chickasaws to remove.[17] Holmes called the application of Mississippi laws "grievous oppression." Crimes involving outsiders increased as time passed. In early fall 1831, for example, Reynolds arrested a slave for killing a white man, and he pursued a gang of whites who stole blacks and other property from the Chickasaws.[18] In another case a Chickasaw was the object of a fraudulent suit by a white. Civil authorities confiscated the Chickasaw's property, forcing him to sue for its return. He won, but he was gone several weeks from home and

(31)

CESSION AREA OF 1832

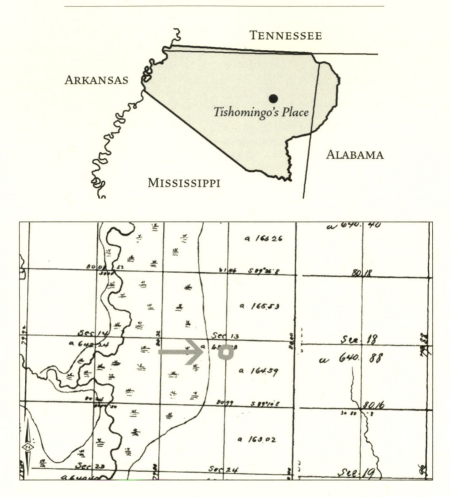

Tishomingo's Place. From the Cession Surveys of 1832.

"sustained great loss," besides having to pay his expenses while away from home and to hire a lawyer, all of which cost him about $1,000. Holmes also charged that in civil cases arising in the Chickasaw Nation, the Chickasaws were "uniformly the defendants, who had to bear their own expenses of hiring lawyers and attending court."[19]

One victim of the court system was none other than the aged and venerable Tishomingo, the surviving head chief from the earlier days of hereditary government. Pistalatubbee, who had seized McCowan's goods, and Tishomingo had repeatedly complained to Allen about intruders settling on Chickasaw land, driving livestock on to the Chickasaw domain, and peddling goods. The old chief, fulfilling his role as a traditional head chief as he would have in earlier days of the Chickasaw Nation, seized and sold the goods of John Walker and Marshall Goodman. The two men were intruders who were in the Chickasaw Nation illegally; thus Tishomingo kept half of the goods and gave the other half to Allen, who sold some to Chickasaws on credit and charged the items against the next annuity payment. Walker and Goodman brought charges in the Monroe County district court against Tishomingo and Allen for criminal trespass. In September 1832, the two defendants were jailed at Athens and went to trial that November. Tishomingo and Allen based their defense in treaty stipulations forbidding illegal trade in the Indian nations. The jury found them guilty and fined them $593.09. The judge ruled that Tishomingo had no authority to act and that there could not have been a treaty violation because Tishomingo had seized the goods before any were sold. Tishomingo appealed. Allen asked the War Department to help Tishomingo: "The nation would regret to see their much beloved chief harrassed [sic] on the amount of that transaction, which was done in strict conformity to our official duty." *Mingo & Allen v. Goodman* was heard in Jackson, Mississippi, in early 1837, when the High Court of Errors and Appeals affirmed the decision of the lower court.[20] By the time this final judgment was rendered, the Chickasaws had negotiated for a permanent home in the West, and preparations were under way for their removal.

By the end of 1831, the year Tishomingo was charged, an anxiety gripped the Chickasaw people. James Holmes wrote from Martyn, "The expectation of a removal beyond the river seems to have concentrated

(33)

every thought to that one point. Even those who are determined to re-main on reservations, as in the case with this neighborhood, are far from enjoying tranquility of mind." They feared that they could not live peacefully among the whites, but the alternative, "being buried in a western wilderness," was a disturbing thought to them. Even the small number of Chickasaws who had joined the church deserted it, few attending the preaching, some backsliding. Their apathy, Holmes charged, directly related to "national affairs." Some stalwarts began a temperance society, and the leaders tried to suppress intemperance among the people.[21] However, there was little they could do officially under Mississippi laws to stop the whiskey trade, especially in the wake of Tishomingo's arrest.

Although the Treaty of Franklin was null and void, uncertainty about removal was kept alive by negotiations between the Chickasaws and Choctaws during the winter of 1831 and the spring of 1832. Coffee and Eaton pushed Reynolds to continue pressing the Chickasaws to find suitable homelands in the West. At a council at the agency, he urged the Chickasaws to begin negotiating with the Choctaws for a portion of their newly acquired land. In December 1831, Eaton and Coffee met with the Chickasaws and Choctaws without results. Then early the next year, at Jackson's directions, Coffee, Eaton, and Thomas Hinds negotiated again with the two nations. Despite the government's belief that the two could merge as a single entity under the Choctaw govern-ment, both nations opposed the idea and insisted on their separate-ness. In addition, the Chickasaws did not like the land proposed for them, claiming it was mainly prairies with little timber and good land. Although Reynolds believed that the tide of opinion among the Chick-asaw leaders was turning toward removal,[22] negotiations between the tribes were commonly discussed among the Chickasaw people, who be-lieved they could not reach agreement with the Choctaws. Some took heart in that fact, hoping that they might be able to remain where they were. Their hopes were bolstered by the U. S. Supreme Court decision in the Cherokee cases that established the right, though not enforced, of the Cherokees to their separate nationhood and freedom from state control.[23] The so-called "common" Chickasaws began to believe that they could avoid removal.

(34)

Having failed with the Treaty of Franklin and negotiations with the Choctaws, Andrew Jackson ordered new treaty negotiations with the Chickasaws. Once more, he appointed Eaton and Coffee, but gave them no instructions. Circumstances prevented Eaton from attending, and Coffee was left to his own devices.[24] Historian Arrell Gibson indicates that in 1832, John Coffee had his way with the Chickasaws and "drove a treaty down their throats," primarily because Levi Colbert was ill and absent.[25] Colbert, though ill, was, in fact, on the treaty grounds and read early drafts of the treaty.[26] But the treaty was not a contest between Coffee and Colbert, and the event was not as one-sided as Gibson's language suggests. Coffee may have had his way, but the Chickasaws put up strong resistance to a number of his proposals.

With John Terrell, an Alabaman, as a go-between, the discussions went back and forth for days. On the one side were Coffee and what Colbert called the "half-breeds" or "half people," who wanted to salvage the Treaty of Franklin. On the other were Colbert and the Chickasaw leaders. Also there were interest groups, including whites and Chickasaw mixed bloods, who tried to influence both sides. First, as Coffee's emissary, Terrell sought to induce Colbert to sell the Chickasaw lands. Colbert refused, saying that any proposition should come from Coffee. A few days later in general council, Coffee handed Colbert an outline for an agreement. The Chickasaw leaders had two major objections. First, Coffee proposed that the lands reserved to individuals before removal would be sold by the government, but the Chickasaws wanted control of sales. Second, Coffee proposed that the proceeds from sales be invested by the United States. "We wanted this money in our own power," said Colbert, "to pay the debts of my Nation, which must be done before we go," to search for and purchase new lands in the West, and to pay for the people's subsistence while they reestablished themselves in the West. Colbert also said, "There was in this treaty no guard against speculation. The selection of reservations, and the valuation of improvements, I believe belonged to our National Council, and not to the President, because exclusively, this is my Nation's interest and business, the national funds pay for it, and the valid interests of my Nation very much depend on it." The Chickasaw leaders also objected to establishment of two land offices, extra clerks

(35)

Cession Area of 1832. From the Cession Surveys of 1832.

(36)

and officials, and treaty reservations of land to certain persons. The only reservation that the Chickasaws in council had agreed to was Colbert's Island on the Tennessee.[27]

Coffee used various tactics to try to move the Chickasaws to accept his plan. On the last point, he began to threaten. He called the treaty commissioners to his tent and told them that the president would not like it if there were no reservations given to the Chickasaw negotiators and seemed baffled that they denied themselves reservations. Colbert said, "I told him that the great body of my Nation was against reservations and my mind was with them. He asked me what was my mind about the Franklin Treaty, if it was proper to receive any part of it. I asked him if that treaty lived. He said the government had failed to fulfill its part, it was bad, but as the Chickasaws were always ready and willing to fulfill all their contracts, it might be proper to receive some part of it. I told him it was useless to talk about the dead." On the question of investing Chickasaw funds, Coffee shrugged off the Chickasaws' argument that they needed the funds. He and the "half breeds" harangued Colbert and the other leaders to no avail. After several days, the Chickasaws were beginning to get uneasy. The treaty conference occurred at the time the annuity for 1832 was supposed to be paid. Coffee had the payment withheld to try to press the Chickasaws, whose camps were running out of food, but getting nowhere, he angrily threatened to write a treaty that he thought was right. If the Chickasaws refused to sign it, he would go home. "So we parted as we met," said Colbert, "except a little more heat."[28]

A day or two later, Coffee returned to the treaty grounds with what became the Treaty of Pontotoc. As in earlier drafts, one article gave to "Indians, half breeds, and some white men not of Chickasaw families, 39,860 acres of choice land in fee simple." Among these people were Chickasaw treaty commissioners in league with Coffee, according to Colbert. Another article gave more than 5,200 more to "half breeds and white men with Indian familys [*sic*]. The very persons against who the chiefs had been so long contending." The Chickasaws objected to the draft treaty. Coffee then wanted the full bloods and "half breeds" to meet in council without Levi and Pitman Colbert present. Wrote Colbert, "The parties meet, the half breeds after these talks, asked the chiefs, one by one if they would allow reservations, one by one the old chiefs answered No, and turn'd to the warriors and asked them if they would defend them in this Question, the warriors replied they would. So they parted as they met."[29]

Then Coffee apparently tried to bribe Levi Colbert, or at the least, compromise him by including a reservation of 9,920 acres for him. Terrell tried to convince Colbert of "the immense value of 9,920 acres of well selected land, which might be got [*sic*] in the very bosom of stream navigation." Colbert said that he told Terrell, "When Genl. Coffee attempts to buy my honesty, he must have a pile of money as high as my head, then I will keep my honesty still, and the money must come from the United States Treasury and not from my Nations pocket to put [in] mine, and then my honesty shall stay with me still."[30]

(37)

The reservations question stymied the treaty negotiations for three weeks. Colbert and the old leaders had discussed the question of land sales and investment of funds with Henry Cook, attorney William Cooper, John Terrell, and sub-agent John Allen, all white men, who, Colbert said, were trusted by the Chickasaws. Colbert believed that the Chickasaws had gone a long way toward making a treaty when the reservations question intervened. The question drove a wedge between the old leaders and the "half people," who supported Coffee. Coffee threatened to treat with just the "half breeds." Colbert responded that they had no power. Coffee, angry, ordered Terrell and the other whites from the treaty camp.[31]

To Colbert this was a turning point. The Chickasaws found themselves at a disadvantage. "He was a man of experience and education," Colbert said of Coffee, "we were made from the hand of nature. He had his secretaries and other enlightened friends around him, we were deprived of the few friends on which we could rely." Colbert and the older leaders felt betrayed by the "half breeds." The nation had borne the expense of educating them, needing their help in councils. The nation had paid their debts to protect them from state laws. "They are the first of our nation," Colbert said, "to turn against what the steady old chiefs believe, the most solid good for this nation. They seem to calculate for their own pockets forgetful of their country." Colbert repeatedly asked Coffee to listen to the old leaders. At one point he said, "I told him if he would let them half breeds and two or three white men who were troubling his ears alone, in four days we could finish a good treaty." And another time he told Coffee, "I wished he would shut his ears to this half people and let us make a treaty all satisfied old friends." What Colbert apparently did not know was that Terrell and Cook, land speculators in whom he had confidence, also had the confidence of not only Coffee but of Andrew Jackson and were working both sides of the treaty negotiations until they were expelled. In addition, Terrell was a special agent for Andrew Jackson and had for years worked among the Choctaws urging removal.[32]

John Coffee drafted another treaty and imperiously demanded that the Chickasaw leaders sign it. The Chickasaws were uneasy about its provisions. Deprived of the white men whom they considered their friends, they distrusted the language of some provisions, fearing they gave the "half breeds" the right to remain on the land or give long leases even after removal. Colbert was now so ill that he was confined to his camp. The Chickasaw leaders brought the treaty to him, and they deliberated for two days but could not understand it and refused to sign. Food was running low, and some of the leaders had left. Coffee called those remaining together, dismissed their objections, and berated the leaders as ignorant, duplicitous, and mean, charging them with "trifling with his official character as well as his private feelings." If they did not sign, he threatened, he would leave and the government would refuse to treat with them again, leaving them to the state laws. He left, pretending to go, but came back and started berating the leaders again. During all of this, Colbert was absent, ill, in his camp. Some of the leaders signed.[33]

Then Coffee turned to trickery. The day after the first leaders signed, Coffee brought another paper for them to sign. He told the Chickasaws that Colbert and others had read the document and approved it so that there was no need to read or interpret it to them. On the belief that Colbert had read it and approved, they signed it. The following day, Coffee and his allies brought a supplement, which he read and said that it cured all of the ills of the first document. All of this time, Levi Colbert was absent, ill, and he later claimed that he had read neither document. On the night before Coffee left, Colbert sent word by his son (probably James) and Pitman Colbert, asking for copies of the papers that had been signed. Coffee "very harshly" denied his request. Colbert said, "I should very much like to know, what was in that dumb paper because the paper gives me much uneasiness as does the supplement, for I never saw either."[34]

(39)

Whether Coffee drove the treaty down their throats or not, the treaty that was signed on October 20, 1832, reflected Chickasaw thinking regarding disposal of their land, thinking that had remained consistent at least since 1805: the Chickasaws did not want to give up their land wholesale but to dispose of it on the open market in order to realize the market value for their property.[35] Other evidence indicates that Chickasaw resistance to Coffee's original intent to simply reaffirm the Treaty of Franklin had much to do with the shaping of the treaty provi-

Pontotoc Creek Treaty
Ann Sheffield

sions.[36] Colbert's rejection of Coffee's offer of a reservation certainly helps explain why grants of land to leaders were conspicuously absent from the Treaty of Pontotoc in 1832.

In the Treaty of Pontotoc, the Chickasaws ceded all of their lands east of the Mississippi with stipulations, however, ostensibly aimed at safeguarding individual Chickasaw wealth and property until removal. The treaty called for a survey of the land as quickly as it was convenient and provided allotments according to the needs of each household. Each family numbering five or fewer received two sections of land, each with six to nine received three, and each with ten or more received four. Those owning ten or more slaves were given an additional sec-

Jno Coffee [Seal]

Ish-te-ho-to-pa (King) his X mark [seal]

Tish-o-min go — X [seal]

Levi Colbert X [seal]

George Colbert. X [seal]

William McGilvery X [seal]

Samuel Sely X [seal]

To pul Kah X [seal]

Isaac Albertson X [seal]

Em ub by — X [seal]

Pis-Tah-lah-tubbe X [seal]

Ish-tim-o lut-ka X [seal]

James Brown X [seal]

Im-mah-hoo-lo tubbe X [seal]

Ish-ta-ka-chah X [seal]

Lah-fin-tubbe X [seal]

Shop-pow-me X [seal]

Nin-uck-ah-umba — X [seal]

Im-mah-hoo-lo tubbe X [seal]

Illup-lah-umba — X [seal]

Pitman Colbert [seal]

Im-mush ka-ish hah X [seal]

James Wolfe [seal]

Bah-ha-kah-tubbe X [seal]

E Bah-kah tubbe — X [seal]

Capt. Thompson X [seal]

New-berry — X [seal]

(41)

Treaty of Pontotoc: Chickasaw leaders' signatures

COURTESY THE NATIONAL ARCHIVES

Memphis to Cotton Gin Port Road.
From the Cession Surveys of 1832.

(42) tion; those owning fewer than ten received an additional half section. Single men having reached twenty-one years of age received one section. These homesteads guaranteed the Chickasaws secure homes until they removed, at which time they would sell the allotments. The money received from the sale of surplus land would become a national fund held in trust by the federal government. This fund would be used to pay for expenses of land surveys, land sales, removal, and subsistence of the people for one year following removal. Individual Chickasaws were guaranteed compensation for the improvements on their homesteads that they abandoned when they removed. To guard against speculation, the Chickasaws inserted other provisions. The land was to be sold in public sales; only land that did not sell in that manner could be disposed of in private sales. The treaty forbade sales in parcels smaller than one-quarter section unless the Chickasaws approved, and

West Tennessee to Tuscumbia Road.
From the Cession Surveys of 1832.

it forbade combinations of buyers.[37] Unfortunately, the Chickasaws later found when land sales began that these attempts to prevent land speculation were futile.

The supplement, dated October 22, which Levi Colbert questioned, did, after all, address some of the chiefs' concerns. Provisions regarding the land were paramount. The supplement prohibited leasing allotments "to any person, either white, red, or black, or mixed blood of either." All land was to be sold at a minimum price of three dollars per acre until the nation decided to reduce the price. Still fearful of land buyer combinations, the Chickasaws asked the president to devise a plan for overseeing private sales. The supplement also corrected some provisions of the earlier treaty regarding reservations. Instead of using age twenty-one for single men, they reduced it to seventeen, "as the Indians mature earlier than white men, and generally marry younger."

Also, orphan girls of seventeen whose families did not provide for them and widows in similar condition were given reservations. Finally, the Chickasaws cleared up some of their debts and made provisions for certain whites. Colbert Moore, who had always lived in the Chickasaw Nation, and his family were given a reservation like the Chickasaws. Robert Gordon received a section of land to satisfy a note he held on James Colbert. The Chickasaws gave a section of land for the land office and asked for establishment of two mail routes, one from Tuscumbia, Alabama, to Rankin, Mississippi, and one from Cotton Gin Port to Memphis. Finally, John Donley, who had carried the mail by horseback from the time he was a boy, was offered a section of land to use until removal if he were given a contract to oversee the mail service.[38] Whether these were the "whitemen" that Colbert alleged to have influenced Coffee is uncertain. Other whites present and witnesses to the treaty were George Wrightman of Mississippi, D. S. Parris of Tennessee, S. Daggett of Mississippi, William A. Chism, G. W. Long, W. D. King, and John M. McKennie.

Objections to the treaty soon followed. Levi Colbert's name appears on the treaty and supplement, although he claimed not to have signed either. A letter surfaced, critical of Coffee, which Colbert and the chiefs had sent to Andrew Jackson. According to Coffee, the source of dissatisfaction was not Colbert but about fifty white men and mixed bloods who wanted reservations under the treaty but had been refused. Primary among them were John D. Terrell and John L. Allen, the Chickasaw sub-agent who was married to William Colbert's daughter, Margaret. Coffee had ejected Terrell and other non-citizens from the treaty council ground because of their interference, he claimed. Terrell was a planter from Marion County, Alabama, who was in league with Henry Cook, a merchant and land speculator at Tuscumbia, who had been at the treaty and whom Colbert had considered a friend to the Chickasaws. Terrell not only had long been Cook's point man, but had also been sent by Andrew Jackson years earlier to promote pro-removal sentiment among the Choctaws and Chickasaws. It was probably he who spread the rumor that Levi Colbert did not like the treaty, for he took Colbert's and the chiefs' letter to Washington on December 20, 1832. He informed Cook that Colbert was "completely dissatisfied," and he apparently tried to increase tensions between Colbert and General Coffee.[39]

Terrell and Coffee were once more playing both sides. Coffee tried to make it appear to the government that he had tried to protect the Chickasaws from reservations for whites, while Levi Colbert insisted that it was Coffee who was set on including them. Terrell and Henry Cook, who had gained the Chickasaws' confidence, were without question land speculators. Terrell, claiming to have business in Richmond and Washington, carried Colbert's letter to Jackson, claiming he had been sworn to secrecy and had shown the letter to no one, even though he had divulged its contents before he left Alabama.

His letter clearly shows that Colbert understood the political reality of the Chickasaws' situation. On the one hand, he knew how close Jackson and Coffee were, and he balanced his criticism of Coffee with appeals for justice. "The Chickasaws feel a native born attachment for their Country," Colbert said, "and it seems to me true, that nature presents nothing in the west, which can make the Chickasaws more happy there—than here, their Native and beloved land." Yet they had been willing to sell their land, "to put down that bitter question of State Sovereignty, to keep peace in the white family to preserve the Union of the United States whose friendship and protection we want, and ourselves, to get away from the troubles which our white brothers fixed upon us."[40] Of course, such appeals to Jackson fell on deaf ears.

(45)

Terrell, who claimed to be in Washington on business, had in reality accompanied a Chickasaw group that he and Allen had rallied to go to Washington to oppose the treaty. In fact, even before the treaty was negotiated, Terrell had planned a meeting for early November at the Monroe County Courthouse to draft a protest to the treaty. He wanted Cook to attend because he knew, he said, that Cook had "the confidence of Levi." There was nothing to be lost, he told his partner, but much to be gained. "I gave Coffee rope. Now let us draw it up." The Washington delegation that came out of the meeting originally included Levi Colbert, Pitman Colbert, Tishomingo, Ishtemolutka (Greenwood), John L. Allen, and John A. Bryan.[41] With them were J. H. Perry, Benjamin Love, and G. W. Long. However, Levi Colbert and Tishomingo did not make the trip. Before leaving the Chickasaw Nation, the group refused to share their intentions with either Agent Benjamin Reynolds or John Coffee, with whom they were clearly at odds. In fact, few people in the Chickasaw Nation knew their intentions. To the missionaries, it appeared to be a rift between what they called "half-bloods" and "Reds" over the question of titles to allotments, whether the titles were to be issued in fee simple or remain nationally owned. Reynolds believed the delegation was part of an anti-treaty intrigue led by Allen. He ordered his sub-agent back to the Chickasaw Nation, but Allen boarded the stage at Tuscumbia with the rest of the delegation for the overland trip to Washington. The purpose of their trip was clear: they sought to have the treaty amended.[42] The missionaries were correct in concluding that the issue was land, but reservations motivated the white members of the delegation more than title. The main interest of Terrell and Cook, the driving force behind the delegation, was Chickasaw land and resources and how to get at them.

The delegation remained in Washington from late 1832 to March 1833, urging a revision of the treaty. A major concern of the Chickasaws in the delegation was disposition of Chickasaw funds derived from the treaty. Coffee tried to blunt their effect by alleging the message from Colbert delivered by Terrell was full of falsehoods about his behavior at the treaty ground and was meant to "injure" him. He questioned the authority of the delegation and tried to defend himself before individual senators.[43] On January 19, 1833, Coffee and Eaton met with the Chickasaw delegation—George Colbert (who apparently replaced Levi), Ishtemolutka, Pitman Colbert, and John L. Allen—who asked that the funds be taken out of federal control and turned over to the Chickasaws, which Levi Colbert and the chiefs had advocated during the treaty "negotiations." Because of their allegations against him, Coffee withdrew from the conference. Although he questioned the authority of the delegation, it had been approved by Ishtehotopa and the chiefs. The language of their directions, however, delegated the authority to make a new treaty to seven people "united" in their decision.

Eaton followed Coffee's lead and argued that the money would waste away if left in Chickasaw hands, and he finally dismissed the delegation on a technicality because only four Chickasaws were there, and they did not include Levi Colbert or Tishomingo, who had not made the trip. The delegation then attempted to get a hearing in the Senate, which was considering ratification of the Treaty of Pontotoc. But Eaton urged the secretary of war to retain control of Chickasaw funds and stressed that further discussion with the Chickasaws should cease. Jackson and his administration did not want the millions in Chickasaw money to slip from their control. There seemed to be a suspicion on Jackson's part, as well, that Levi Colbert would use the money to purchase Mexican land and thereby escape American control completely. Thus he urged the Senate to act quickly on ratification.[44] Although the treaty was proclaimed on March 1, 1833, the issues raised by the delegation had some validity, as negotiations the following year would show.

Chickasaw society continued to suffer because, according to the missionaries, anxiety resulted from American agitation for removal and the application of Mississippi, and, after the winter of 1832, Alabama laws to the Chickasaws. Monroe County, Mississippi, claimed jurisdiction over the lands of the Chickasaw Nation that lay within Mississippi's boundaries. At the November 1832 circuit court, a judge ruled that the Intercourse Law of 1803 had been made null and void by the extension of Mississippi laws over the Chickasaws. Intruders were emboldened by the ruling, and Agent Reynolds reported that whiskey traders, peddlers, and other intruders overran the country. He had been able to control them to some extent before the ruling, but after the state had defied Congress by declaring its act void, the intruders were uncontrollable.[45]

The missionaries, as well, laid the major blame on the state's assertion of its power. From Martyn in December 1832, Holmes reported the increasing number of whites brought whiskey "and other means of corruption." Anxiety and worldliness prevailed, he said. The situation was made worse by the cholera, which killed a number of Chickasaws. The Reverend Thomas Stuart had reported in mid-January 1833 that within the previous three months, more than three hundred gallons of whiskey had been brought into the neighborhood by white traders. One set up shop within a half mile of his church. "Thinking" Chickasaws complained, he said, but the traders boasted of protection by Mississippi laws. Temperance societies were at work and may have had an impact, for there was less drinking in the nation than in previous

(47)

years. But, the missionaries reported, "the overthrow of the Chickasaw government by the extension of the state laws over the nation, forbidding any Indian to make or enforce laws as a chief, has much embarrassed the sober and intelligent Indians in their efforts to accomplish these objects." Holmes said of the class of whites who were coming into the nation: let the Chickasaws have contact with such people for a few years and they would have no need for a new home, influence of the whites was so pernicious.[46]

The society suffered as well because of uncertainty about the treaty. Even before the Treaty of Pontotoc was ratified, the influx of white population had little opposition from local or federal authorities. Planters from Alabama moved in or sent their slaves into the Chickasaw country to begin cultivating farms. The general impression was that Chickasaw land would soon go on the market, and rumors spread that one company had formed and sent agents through the southern states, finding subscribers to a capital of $4 million to create a monopoly on the lands. One observer commented that if the intruders were not stopped, what had happened in the Creek country would happen in the Chickasaw.[47] When intruders ignored the advertisements setting deadlines for them to remove, Agent Reynolds asked local lawmen to remove the illegal intruders, but the lawmen denied having authority. Orders from the War Department and threats of ordering out troops failed to get results, as did the posting of public notices and threats of civil action. By the beginning of 1834, not a single intruder had been removed. Instead, they continued to arrive, especially along the Chickasaw-Choctaw line and the Chickasaw-Tennessee border. In early 1834 the Chickasaw leaders gave tacit approval for those of "good character" to remain and listed those they wanted to have removed. Without authority to act, however, their statements were simply words. Names of intruders appeared in newspaper advertisements, but to no avail. By April, fear of hostilities rose, and the leaders called for federal troops. The local marshal, however, warned that a thousand troops could not remove the Americans, and he predicted dire consequences if they tried. There were many who opposed the federal government and would likely urge the intruders to resist with arms. Many were personal friends with each other and with the president, and to remove them would mean near ruin for them,

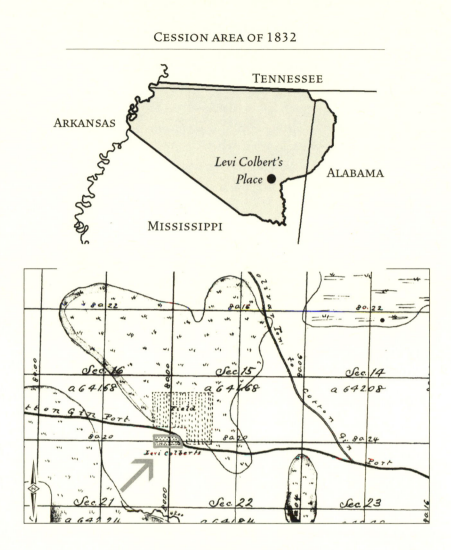

CESSION AREA OF 1832

TENNESSEE

ARKANSAS

Levi Colbert's Place ●

ALABAMA

MISSISSIPPI

Levi Colbert's Place.

they claimed. Loss of Tishomingo's case had opened the door to merchants and whiskey peddlers. Shopkeepers and peddlers with their wagons plied the Chickasaws with goods, resulting in riotous action, disorder, violence, and even murder.[48]

Still more anxiety among the Chickasaws resulted from the failure of Chickasaw delegations to find a suitable home in the West. Another had gone west in 1833. At Indian Affairs Commissioner Elbert Herring's urging, Reynolds visited the old chiefs in their homes, urging them to look for a new home in the West. Ishtehotopa called a meeting at Levi Colbert's home on June 7. For six days Reynolds lectured the Chickasaw leaders about what the immediate effects of the Treaty of Pontotoc would be: survey of Chickasaw lands and an influx of whites, which they were already experiencing. They understood the urgency, the Chickasaws responded, but the cholera epidemic that was then raging along the western waterways made them hesitate. Some Chickasaws who had been trading in Memphis had contracted the disease and died. Thus the Chickasaws said they would wait until the sickly season was over. Reynolds agreed that October, November, and December were the best months for traveling. The Chickasaws asked Reynolds to delay paying the summer annuity until after the corn crop was in. Reynolds suspected that they wanted ready cash to be available near the time of their departure to the West. He had learned, he said, "that Chief Levi Colbert has been flattered into the belief that by taking with him Twenty Thousand dollars, it would enable him to buy a country for his people from the Caddo Indians, who live south of the Red River."[49]

The delegation, duly appointed by the chiefs, set out for the West on October 16, their expenses borne by the Chickasaw Nation. At Tuscumbia, a part of the delegation outfitted with blankets and overcoats, cotton and flannel shirts and drawers, pants, vests, shoes, stockings, flannel, cassinette, knives, powder, lead, and tents. Others outfitted at Memphis, where the two parties joined. The twenty-one chiefs and captains were led by Reynolds, William Hunter of Tennessee, and Milton Guy of Alabama. At Memphis, Reynolds, Hunter, Guy, the Chickasaws, their hired servant, and a "boy" (probably a slave) had their horses shod and saddles repaired. They laid in supplies of medicine, bacon,

CESSION AREA OF 1832

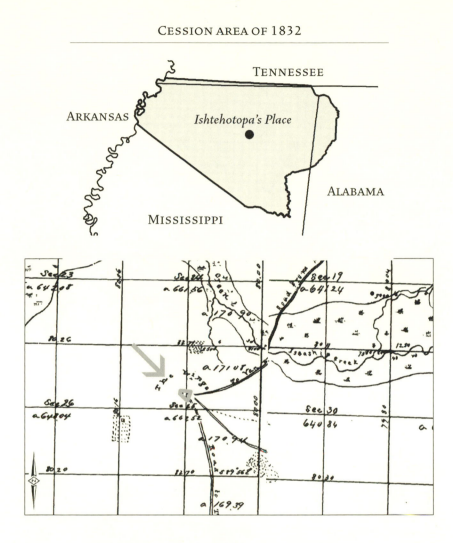

Ishtehotopa's Place. From the Cession Surveys of 1832.

56052

flour, bread, sugar, coffee, and tobacco, and the party with their forty-three horses crossed the Mississippi.[50] They plunged into the Mississippi swamps on the Arkansas side, reached Little Rock on November 9, and crossed the Arkansas River for the last leg of their journey to Fort Towson in the Choctaw country. At Little Rock, Reynolds fell ill. Hunter and Guy had the horses shod and bought clothing and provisions for the next leg of their journey. After several days, some of the party found grazing land for their horses about ten miles west of Little Rock while they waited for Reynolds to recover. Meanwhile, the old chiefs stayed with Reynolds.[51]

While he was recovering, Reynolds assessed his delegation, made up of old chiefs and "some of the most intelligent of the nation." He sensed a lack of unity among them, although they seemed to be "in good cheer and fine spirits." The old chiefs wanted him to stress to the War Department that a vast majority of the Chickasaw people were dissatisfied with the Treaty of Pontotoc. If a delegation could go to Washington after their return from the West and amend the treaty to give the Chickasaws control of their money, they said, the people would be quieted and would be united in removing.[52]

When the Chickasaw delegation met the Choctaws on December 31, the latter flatly refused to consider the sale of any of their land. However, Reynolds and William Armstrong, the western superintendent for Indian affairs, reported that the Choctaws might likely be willing to assign a district to the Chickasaws, who would have equal rights and privileges under Choctaw law. Although Reynolds believed he had worked out such an agreement between the two groups, when they met again, Levi Colbert pushed for a purchase. The Choctaws refused. Instead, they put Reynolds' idea forward, inviting the Chickasaws to become part of their nation.[53]

The Chickasaw delegates considered alternatives. A part of them decided to take up the Choctaws on their offer by going to the western district and selecting home sites. They had concluded, they told Reynolds, that it was time for heads of family or clans to provide a home for their people instead of waiting on the nation to act. Calling them some of the "respectable and wealthy" of the Chickasaws, Reynolds applauded the delegates' actions. Others, Levi Colbert among them, were still interested in finding land in Mexican Territory among the Caddoes. Although they had concerns about their security outside American territory, most of this group decided that they would recommend that the Chickasaws purchase Caddo land.[54] Thus split over what course to take, the delegation returned to Mississippi.

Delay in finding an adequate country to remove to was directly related to some of the provisions of the Treaty of Pontotoc. Growing American desire to be rid of the Chickasaws made U. S. officials more amenable to their wishes. A council at Ishtehotopa's house on March 7, 1834, appointed Levi Colbert, Isaac Alberson, Henry Love, Martin Colbert, and Benjamin Love as a delegation to Washington to amend the Pontotoc treaty. Levi Colbert fell ill at the Chickasaw Agency near Tuscumbia and became too ill to continue, so he gave his brother George Colbert free authority to act for him. Apparently sensing that he was near death, he wrote Andrew Jackson: "I am admonished by the days that I have seen—that I should not look for two [sic] many more, & I now take you by the hand perhaps for the last time under full confidence that you will listen to the words of our delegation & grant us such relief as will again unite us as we were when you first became acquainted with the Chickasaw people." Colbert signed his letter "your Dutiful Red Son."[55]

The delegation, headed by George Colbert, left for Washington in March 1834 and in May negotiated amendments to the Treaty of Pontotoc regarding reservations and land sales. Under the new agreement, families with ten or more people would receive allotments of four sections of land, those with at least five but fewer than ten would receive three, and those with fewer than five would receive two. Slaveholders with fewer than ten slaves would receive an additional half section, and those with ten or more would receive an additional section. Orphans were granted a half section. Money generated through sales of surplus land would go into a general tribal fund to be invested in stocks and against which the government would charge the expenses of land survey and sales and removal. Titles to individual reservations were to be given in fee simple, and when the land was sold, the money would go to the individual. The supplemental treaty established the Chickasaw Commission, whose task was to oversee the sale of each reservation

Due to his considerable economic and political power within the Chickasaw Nation, George Colbert was one of the primary negotiators of removal treaties between the Chickasaws and the United States government.

and determine the competency of the holders to manage their own affairs and thus receive their payments.[56] Each land sale would require the signature of at least two of the commissioners, who were Ishtehotopa, Levi Colbert, George Colbert, Martin Colbert, Isaac Alberson, Henry Love, and Benjamin Love.

The Treaty of Pontotoc had been remarkable among Chickasaw cession treaties because it had not provided large gifts to the negotiators. The supplemental treaty of 1834 corrected that aberration to some extent by granting reservations to individuals, but the gifts are modest compared to some, such as those Levi Colbert had received in the past.

In this case, Colbert received four sections of land. It is likely he never knew about the gift, for he died within days after the agreement was worked out. Minko Ishtehotopa and Benjamin Reynolds each received two sections, and the following received one each: Margaret Colbert Allen (wife of John L. Allen), George Colbert, Martin Colbert, Isaac Alberson, Henry Love, Benjamin Love, Mintahoyea (a widow of Levi Colbert), Emmubbee, Ishtemolutka, Ahtohoway, Pishtahlatubbee, and Samuel Sealy. Attorneys William Cooper and John Davis were awarded a joint reservation of one section for their service as legal advisors to the Chickasaws. In addition, George Colbert received acreage between his old home and ferry on the Tennessee River as well as Colbert's Island.[57] It is interesting that these grants went to some of the people who had gone to Washington in 1833 to try to amend the Treaty of Pontotoc. Cooper and Davis had been the legal team who defended Tishomingo.

As the Chickasaw Nation moved ever closer to removal, it became imperative that the Chickasaws find a new home. After the failure of the delegation in the fall of 1833, Reynolds had sought to have the Choctaws, accompanied by a few Chickasaws, explore their land to the west. A good report might encourage the Chickasaws to agree to settle on Choctaw terms. By early 1835 some Chickasaws had decided to move on their own, some settling with the Choctaws and others in what later became the Republic of Texas.[58]

How long the major population of Chickasaws could remain occupants of their lands in Mississippi depended on location of new land that suited them. Thus, accordingly, Reynolds sent another exploring party west on October 17, 1835. Headed by William L. Henderson with James McLaughlin as interpreter, they traveled to the Choctaw Agency West where Superintendent William Armstrong assisted them in looking over the land. They explored the land along the Blue, Boggy, and Washita Rivers, but they could not agree to the Choctaw demands that their district should fall under the laws of the Choctaw Nation. Armstrong grew fearful that the chasm between the two peoples could not be bridged. However, he believed that there was no way to effect Chickasaw removal except to make the Chickasaws a permanent part of the Choctaw Nation.[59] Thus this excursion, like those before it, failed to result in a homeland for the Chickasaws.

Meanwhile, the Chickasaw people continued to suffer in a state of social disruption. By the time the 1835 exploring party went west, the missionaries had given up in despair. Never successful, their church and school efforts had become weaker over the years. The preaching station and school had closed at Monroe in 1830 and at Martyn and Caney Creek in 1833, when the latter was moved to Tipton County, Tennessee, where it lasted two years longer. The station and school at Tockshish lasted until 1835, when Chickasaw mission work shut down altogether. Stuart remained at Tockshish, preaching to Chickasaws and whites whenever he found an opportunity. In 1836, mission authorities blamed their failure on the condition of the Chickasaws: "Under the influence of strong temptations, they give themselves up to idleness, gambling, and intoxication; and are, of course, disinclined to listen to instruction." Whereas membership had been over 100 in 1835—although most of those were not Chickasaws—there was now "fatal apostasy," they said.[60] The deteriorating condition of the Chickasaws resulted in part from further disruption following the Treaty of 1834. Local authorities had given up on removing intruders and vowed to so only on direct orders from Andrew Jackson. Chickasaw lands were surveyed in the summer and fall of 1835, and Chickasaws had to select individual homestead allotments. Reynolds found that they had sold their 1834 crops to whites in order to subsist, and few had made crops in 1835.[61]

(56)

One should take reports of intoxication among the Chickasaws with a note of caution. Reports of widespread drinking came primarily from the missionaries associated with Monroe Mission. It was common practice for missionaries to other Indian tribes to blame whiskey for their failure or lack of progress with their "Bible and hoe" agenda. The Monroe Church was never strong among the Chickasaws as a result of widespread opposition to Christianity because they did not like it as it was practiced by the Choctaws. As the missionaries steadily lost ground in the early 1830s, they may have overemphasized the role of whiskey in their failure. The fact was that many Chickasaws were not wasteful and amassed and held large amounts of wealth in slaves and other personal property, particularly livestock, which some had begun to pass on to their posterity. Much Chickasaw property belonged to the women, who tended not to drink.

Implementation of the provisions of the Treaty of 1834, which had established heads of household for the purpose of allotment, threatened to dispossess many of the women of Chickasaw society. Government officials generally held that when a Chickasaw had two or more wives at the time of ratification of the treaty, the wives and their respective children were enrolled as one household with the husband at the head. The minko and the old chiefs and others protested that that was not the interpretation of *head of household* that the Chickasaw treaty makers had in mind. Their intent was to secure the rights of every Chickasaw family, without exception. The question to the leaders was what constituted a Chickasaw family and who should determine what a family was in terms of Chickasaw "customs and manners of life." Did the language of the treaty say that plural wives and children should be entered as one family, the chiefs wanted to know?[62]

To the Chickasaw leaders, the several wives and their children did not constitute a single Chickasaw family. Matrimonial bonds between men and women were "slight," they said, "contracted without formality," and "dissolved at the pleasure of either party." The line of descent, they said, was "always traced through the maternal line, the succession of the Kings ever having been determined that way." The father was not under any obligation to support his children, whose care and nurturing were exclusively the mother's duty. Upon her death, the father assumed no responsibility for the children; their care became the responsibility of the mother's female relatives. When the father died, whether he had only one wife or more, the children did not inherit his property; instead, it went to his oldest collateral relatives, who often stripped the wife and children of all his property. "It is an ancient and universal law among the Chickasaws," the Chickasaw leaders said, "that the wife has a separate estate in all her property, whether derived to her from her relations or acquired by her, with full liberty to dispose of it in any manner she may please."[63]

The Mississippi courts recognized Chickasaw women's rights of property in the well publicized Betsy Allen case. When Mrs. Allen died, her estate of personal property was extensive: horses, cattle, fowl; household furniture including beds, clocks, tables, chairs, writing

(57)

desk; household items such as mattresses, pillows, blankets, coverlets, sheets, and table cloths; kitchenware such as bowls, plates, teapot, china, dishes, cups and saucers, sugar bowl, knives, forks, spoons, grater, and shears; books; utensils, including a hand mill, flat iron, pots, and kettle; loom; tools such as plows, shovel, scythe, auger, and axes; and slaves.[64]

The rule that a man and all his wives and children constituted one family had dire economic implications for many Chickasaws, the leaders argued. Under the American system, if a man died, his wife and children inherited his property. But what if there were more than one wife? Some men had several. Some of the richer Chickasaws had "plantations and stock-farms" at a distance from their residences, which at times were located in poor but healthy sections of the country. Their wives were generally kept at separate homes, usually distant from one another. Rarely, and only if they were sisters, did the wives live in the same house. The children claimed no relationship to their father's children by other wives but were, as the chiefs said, "to each other as strangers." In these various homes, a Chickasaw man often had more than ten children. A good example touted by the chiefs was the late Levi Colbert, who had several wives and "left upwards of twenty children." The treaty provided for four sections for a household of ten or more. What might be adequate for ten would not be adequate for thirty or forty, they argued.[65]

The matter was made more complex by the application of Mississippi laws to the Chickasaws since 1830. The fourth article of the legislative act validated all marriages recognized by the Chickasaws. However, the law made no provisions for Chickasaw marriages made after January 19, 1830. A number of young Chickasaw men who had become educated by the Americans claimed that their acquisition of an education had qualified them to have more than one wife. What were the implications of the system of allocating reservations for those marriages?[66]

In addition to redefining the Chickasaw household, preparations for transferring the common land to individually held plots rapidly transformed the Chickasaw landscape. Survey of the Chickasaw lands had begun in early 1834. By the end of that year, the survey had been completed, and Chickasaw reservations were being laid out. With the land laid out in townships and sections and land offices established near Pontotoc and the Chickasaw Agency, the process attracted more Americans. From early 1830, Monroe County, Mississippi, had claimed civil and criminal jurisdiction over all of the Chickasaw Nation within Mississippi's boundaries. Counties were laid out in the Chickasaw lands in 1835, and towns like Pontotoc began to emerge. An observer described Pontotoc in 1836 as follows: "At present it resembles a Methodist Camp ground. Its buildings are a collection of rude ill constructed huts, with the exception of a few neat little framed dwellings. These are tenanted by a collection of people from every State, and from many foreign countries. In this collection is centered perhaps more shrewdness and intelligence than can be found in any other congregation of the same size."[67] The first house was built in 1835, and within a year there were nearly 2,000 people and 40 stores. Much of the population was made up of what one observer called "speculators and adventurers," who were there for the land sales. They supported the "entirely ephemeral" prosperity by supporting the "extensive mercantile establishments and expensive taverns."[68]

Despite the Chickasaws' hope to prevent speculation, it began in earnest as soon as the Treaty of 1834 was signed. Capitalists who backed the speculation used merchants as their middlemen. One local company was Gordon & Bell of Cotton Gin Port. Gordon was an attorney who had received land in the treaty, and Bell, the son of a former missionary, had been surveyor of the Chickasaw lands and had long pushed for removal. Gordon & Bell acquired more than 600 sections. These merchants and others, such as Daniel Saffarans and William Carroll, Andrew Jackson's close friend and the government's land agent, loaned money or gave credit to Chickasaws in return for an agreement to sell their allotments to the creditors. The merchants helped the Chickasaws select their allotments, making certain that they selected good land, which the merchants ultimately sold to capitalist speculators. The merchants and their agents, often half bloods, scoured the country to arrange agreements with other Chickasaws to sell their allotments, although sales had not started. Most of the population was ignorant of the value of land and of the laws governing sales. Fortunately, the Chickasaws received what they had asked for the land because speculators were convinced that the land would become more valuable as cotton land. Large companies, such as the American Land Company, the Chickasaw Company, and the New York and Mississippi Land Company, had formed to buy up vast tracts of the country, much of it resold to them by local speculators.[69]

Among the Chickasaws hired by the land companies was later the first governor of the Chickasaws to serve under the constitutional government in the West, Cyrus Harris. Harris, born in 1817 south of Pontotoc, was descended from William Colbert through his daughter Molly Colbert Oxberry, whose daughter Elizabeth had first married James Harris and then Malcolm McGee. Cyrus Harris had entered Monroe Mission School under the Reverend Thomas Stuart and later gone with the Reverend Hugh Wilson to Caney Creek School. After he left school in 1830, he and his mother and uncle, Martin Colbert, resided at Horn Lake where he remained until 1835. He returned to Pontotoc where he worked as a clerk and agent for the land and banking firm of Gordon & Bell during the sales of Chickasaw lands.[70]

The survey and sale of Chickasaw land created perhaps the greatest disruption that Chickasaw society had yet seen. A presidential proclamation opened the land sales on the first Monday in January 1836. In addition to having been subjected to state and local laws for several years, the Chickasaws now had a steady flow of money into their hands as their land was sold. A vast majority of the sales were consummated long before Chickasaw removal to the West. For example, in 1836 more than 1.3 million acres sold for almost $2.2 million, and in 1837 almost 193,000 acres sold for nearly $320,000. In 1838 more than 280,000 acres sold for over $195,000, and in 1839 about 640,000 acres sold for more than $246,000.[71]

The drop in sales after 1837 was significant. Joint stock companies made up of eastern investors obtained nearly 35% of Chickasaw allotments. Companies like Saffarans and Lewis, and Gordon & Bell bought up huge tracts. Individual speculators like Daniel Saffarans, a merchant and land dealer from Gallatin, Tennessee, and Felix Lewis of Columbus, Georgia, bought thousands of acres. Saffarans, who was speculating in Choctaw scrip in 1835, obtained almost 82,000 acres and Lewis almost 25,000. David Hubbard, an Alabama congressman

(60)

from Florence and Courtland, Alabama, was head of the Chickasaw Company, the second largest land company dealing in Chickasaw land, obtaining nearly 30,000 acres. Speculators held as much as 80% of the Chickasaw cession at one point during the flush times of speculation. However, as the 1830s wore on, the banking industry became weaker. Until mid-1836, land offices took paper money in land sales. Speculators borrowed money to purchase land and used the land as collateral to borrow more money. As the cotton economy began to slow down after 1836, creditors found it more difficult to collect. Paper money prevailed, and was being discounted in every transaction. Land speculation in the early to mid-thirties, especially in Creek, Choctaw, and Chickasaw land, contributed to the weakening banking business that resulted in the Panic of 1837. And the flush times that had built white towns like Pontotoc and Holly Springs began to fail.[72]

While generally one might consider the acquisition of money a good thing, in this case it was not necessarily so. Some Chickasaws spent lavishly, some remained idle, and some were intemperate. Slone Love, one of the Chickasaw commissioners in the West, was about thirty-five years old in 1842, when he said "that he could remember the time ... when the Chickasaws were almost as wild as the wild Indians west of the Cross Timbers." After a time they became "industrious and ingenious in manufacturing a number of articles particularly articles of cotton cloth." With the money that came from sales of land, they gave up "both industry, and art."[73] Benjamin Love, one of the original commissioners, later said that when the sale of land was announced, the change in habits of the people was "sudden" and their wants became "urgent, in this new state of affairs." Businesses in Pontotoc and elsewhere were supported by Chickasaws who had sold their reservations. "Hundreds of these are now in the streets," said one writer, "many drunk and most of them wasting their money as fast as they can. It is amazing to see their displays of finery: The dress are all of the most fanciful kinds—of every variety of cut and colour. Some of them are ridiculously gaudy, while others are rich and tasty—giving the wearer a martial and splendid appearance."[74]

For three years, land sales and preparations for removal consumed the population. Many Chickasaws never saw their money but lived on credit, supplied by the merchants, who waited for the Chickasaws that the Chickasaw commissioners deemed "incompetent" to be paid or waited for Chickasaws to transfer their allotments. Wealthy Chickasaws like Love also supplied credit, he claimed, with which the people bought horses, provisions, and clothing. Litigation became common as Americans began suits to dispossess Chickasaws from their homes, ignoring the guarantee that they could remain on their lands until they removed.[75] Others tried to eject Chickasaws from home places they had occupied for years. A good example was the merchant-speculator Robert Gordon, a Scotsman who started out as a trader at Cotton Gin Port about 1825 or 1826. Through his partnership firm of Gordon, Wrightman Co., he held a note of indebtedness by James Colbert. Gordon presented a claim for settlement during the negotiation of the Treaty of Pontotoc. The Chickasaws in council decided to assume the debts of Colbert and granted a section of land in the treaty to Gordon as payment. Gordon, whom a historian in recent years has called "thoroughly unscrupulous," began a campaign in 1835 to unseat Roberson James from his allotment on a prime piece of real estate that Gordon had chosen for his land grant under the treaty.[76]

By the middle of 1836, the Chickasaw leadership recognized the precariousness of their people's situation. They tried to alleviate conditions by pleading that the "incompetents" be given a third of the money due them, saying that "most of the money has been placed in the hands of the women, who are distinguished for their economy and judicious application of money for the use of their families." The leaders were afraid that creditors would "use coercive measures and distress the Indians."[77] In September a council of leaders sent a memorial to Jackson, complaining about the state of affairs. Whites had intruded upon their lands since the treaty of Jackson until now they found "their people without home, surrounded by men whose language they can neither speak nor understand, subject to laws of which they were wholly ignorant, degraded, debased, and ruined by strong drink and vicious habits, and pursuits."[78] They were ready to negotiate with their "old allies and neighbors, the Choctaws" but wanted control over their national affairs and to maintain their national character.[79]

Thus in November, another Chickasaw exploring party went west.

Consisting of John McLish, James Perry, Pitman Colbert, James Brown, and Isaac Alberson, the group had instructions to procure that "suitable" land for the Chickasaw Nation west of the Mississippi, if not from the Choctaws then wherever else they found a fit land. Ishtehotopa and the headmen stressed the need for a speedy removal, given the declining condition of the people. Their limit was one million dollars to be billed against the proceeds from Chickasaw land sales. The delegation took with them Henry R. Carter, a white man, as their conductor.[80]

In the West, Western Superintendent William Armstrong made arrangements for the delegation to meet with the Choctaws. He used the December payment of the Choctaw annuity as a means of getting the scattered Choctaws together. He first got the chief and captains on the Arkansas to agree to send a delegation to meet with their counterparts from the two districts on the Red River and negotiate with the Chickasaws. Then at Fort Towson, he made similar arrangements with the leaders of the Red River districts.[81]

With authority on both sides to negotiate an agreement, the Chickasaws met the Choctaw negotiators at Doaksville on January 11, 1837, and began talks. Colbert, McLish, Brown, and Perry opened with a statement of their purpose: to procure from the Choctaws, whom they called "our old friends and neighbors," a district for their "destitute and homeless people," whom they called upon the Choctaws to save "from the destruction which now seems to await them!" The district they sought was to be governed by Chickasaw laws and regulations. In response, the Choctaws—represented by Peter P. Pitchlynn, George W. Harkins, Israel Folsom, Robert M. Jones, John McKinney, Eyachahopia, and George Pusley—called the Chickasaws "brothers" with whom they were "united together by every tie of friendship that binds one people to another," but they flatly refused to provide them a new land by purchase.[82]

As a counter offer, the Chickasaws made concessions. They proposed "the privilege of forming a District within the limits of their country, to be called the Chickasaw district of the Choctaw Nation." The Chickasaws would be placed on equal footing with the Choctaws except that they would not participate in the Choctaw annuity and reserved the right to control their own funds and to elect such district officers as they saw fit. In response, the Choctaws regretted setting aside part of their country for any purpose. "The subject is one which calls to memory past events which almost makes our hearts bleed," they said. But because the Chickasaws' situation was one that demanded sympathy, "especially that of the Red Man," they agreed provisionally to the Chickasaw proposal. This was a strange situation for them, claiming to be unused to transacting business except by trade or bargain, and it called for frankness: "What are you willing to give our people for the privilege which you ask?"[83]

With the question of price on the table, the two sides haggled over place. The Chickasaws would have to know what section of the country the Choctaws were willing to assign them before they could make an offer. The Choctaws described the boundaries of a district in the western part of the Choctaw Nation. That would not do, the Chickasaws countered. What they wanted was a place where their people could practice a "system of improvement," where they could "abandon the precarious mode of subsisting by hunting, so prejudicial to civilization" and could pursue agriculture and "become generally enlightened." Those goals would not be possible in the district the Choctaws had described. From their own knowledge and from what others had told them, the country would not suit them. The soil was sterile, it was covered with prairies, and it had little timber. Could not the Choctaws offer something better, perhaps more north and east?[84]

(64)

The Choctaws now appeared insulted by the Chickasaw response. They had offered a "favorite" section of their country and the privilege of settling elsewhere among the Choctaws. They had nothing left to negotiate about. They meant no disrespect, the Chickasaws replied. They had an obligation to get the best agreement they could for their people. They had been "misinformed" about the country and were now willing to accept it. Apparently properly contrite, they appealed to the Choctaws: "We must earnestly ask you in the name of your old friend & allies to negotiate further with us on this subject, that our homeless and destitute people may have a spot where they can rest & continue to be your friends &neighbors." The Choctaws, now apologetic themselves, could gracefully reenter the negotiations. The Chickasaw explanation had been "reasonable." Sympathy for the Chickasaws' plight had made the Choctaws amenable to entertaining their request for a district, and they regretted "that an impression on our part was formed that our brothers, the Chickasaw Commissioners, were trifling with our liberal offer. We therefore hope our correspondence in future will be carried on in a frank & candid manner usual among Red men."[85]

This classic give and take in Indian diplomacy put the second proposition back on the table along with the question of how much the Chickasaws were willing to give. They had instructions to offer up to $1 million, but they offered $500,000 to be paid however the Choctaws desired. How much did they expect to receive from the sale of their lands in Mississippi, the Choctaws wanted to know? No more than eight or nine hundred thousand, the Chickasaws replied, $500,000 of which they had offered the Choctaws. With what remained they had to pay for their own removal and subsistence in the west. They could not be precise, given the state of land sales. The Chickasaws later offered an additional $35,000. On January 16, 1837, the Choctaws accepted the offer and agreed to meet the next day to make a formal agreement.[86]

On January 17, the Chickasaws and Choctaws drafted an agreement. It set aside a Chickasaw district, placed on an equal footing with the Choctaw districts. The Chickasaw district would have equal representation in the Choctaw Council, and the Chickasaws would be subject to Choctaw laws. However, the Chickasaws retained control over their financial matters. They were to pay the Choctaws $530,000. Carter took the agreement to Washington, where it was quickly approved by the government.[87]

(65)

The Chickasaws had proved themselves able negotiators. This was the last of a number of visits to the West during the preceding decade to find a suitable home. After the failed Treaty of Franklin and the negotiation of the Treaty of Pontotoc and its Supplemental Treaty, the Chickasaws had experienced the social and economic disruption that came with the survey and sale of their lands. The agreement at Doaksville may not have been what they would have liked, but it provided a solution to their dilemma in Mississippi. The negotiators returned to Mississippi with an agreement, which removed the last major obstacle to the nation's removal. But they had also laid the groundwork for the eventual reestablishment of the Chickasaw Nation as a political entity separate from the Choctaws. The boundaries of the new district,

Chickasaw District in Indian Territory.

IMAGE COURTESY OF THE CHICKASAW NATION
GEOSPATIAL INFORMATION DEPARTMENT.
© CHICKASAW NATION

(66)

poorly defined by the agreement, would be a future point of contention between them and the Choctaws, and they would also disagree
on whether the $530,000 was a purchase price or simply rent for the
privilege of living on Choctaw land. It is unlikely that in early 1837 they
could foresee these developments. Their concern with removal was too
immediate.

NOTES

1. Arrell M. Gibson, *The Chickasaws* (Norman: University of Oklahoma
   Press, 1971), 170–71.

2. John L. Allen, Report of the Chickasaws, February 7, 1830, National
   Archives Microfilm Publications, Letters Received by the Office of
   Indian Affairs, Microcopy M234, Roll 136. Citations from this Microfilm
   Publication are hereafter cited as M234, followed by the roll number.

3. *Ibid.*

4. Chickasaw Chiefs to John H. Eaton and John Coffee, August 25, 1830, M234-R136.

5. Gibson, *The Chickasaws*, 171–73; Muriel H. Wright, "Notes on Events Leading to the Chickasaw Treaties of Franklin and Pontotoc, 1830 and 1832," *Chronicles of Oklahoma* 34 (Winter 1956–1957): 468–74.

6. Benjamin Reynolds to Eaton, October 16 and 20, 1830, M234-R136.

7. Reynolds to Eaton, June 19, 1831 and Statement Showing the Number of Chickasaws Composing the Exploring Party in 1830–1831, M234-R136, frames 217 and 404.

8. M. Arbuckle to Eaton, December 2 and 11, 1830, M234-R136.

9. Reynolds and George Gaines to Eaton, January 19, 1831, M234-R136.

10. *Ibid.*; Gaines to Coffee, February 1, 1831, M234-R136.

11. Gaines and Reynolds to Secretary of War, February 9, 1831, and Reynolds to Eaton, March 27, 1831, M234-R136, frames 188ff.

12. Reynolds to Thomas L. McKenney, April 1, 1830, Reynolds to Eaton, May 5, 1831, McKenney to Reynolds, June 7 and 9, 1830, Ishtehotopa, et al. to Andrew Jackson, May 28, 1831, enclosed in Reynolds to Eaton, June 10, 1831, M234-R136; Gibson, *The Chickasaws*, 174.

13. Allen to Eaton, October 23, 1830, M234-R136.

14. Alexander McCowan to Eaton, November 14, 1830, Allen to Eaton, November 12, 1830; and Coffee to Secretary, November 18, 1830, M234-R136.

15. Allen to Eaton, November 13 and November 14, 1830, and January 21, 1831, M234-R136, frames 142ff.

16. Chickasaw Chiefs to Jackson, May 28, 1831, M234-R136, frame 208.

17. *Missionary Herald* 27 (1831): 45.

18. Reynolds to Lewis Cass, October 6, 1831, M234-R136, frame 229.

19. *Missionary Herald* 28 (1832): 117.

20. Allen to Elbert Herring, September 13, 1833, and Allen to Eaton, January 21, 1831, M234-R136, frames 361 and 142; Cecil Lamar Summers, "The Trial of Chief Tishomingo, the Last Great War Chief of the Chickasaw Indians," *The Journal of Monroe County History* 3 (1977): 28–38.

21. *Missionary Herald* 28 (1832): 117–18.

22. Levi Colbert to Jackson, February 23, 1832 and Eaton to Herring, December 20, 1832, M234-R136, frames 256 and 264; James R. Atkinson, *Splendid Land, Splendid People: The Chickasaw Indians to Removal* (Tuscaloosa: University of Alabama Press, 2004), 227–28; Gibson, *The Chickasaws*, 175.

23. *Missionary Herald* 28 (1832): 260, 334.

24. Eaton to Herring, December 30, 1832, M234-R136, frame 264.

25. Gibson, *The Chickasaws*, 175.

26. See Atkinson, *Splendid Land*, 228 for a rebuttal of Gibson on this point.

27. Colbert and Chiefs to President, November 22, 1832, M234-R136, frame 275ff.

28. *Ibid.*

29. *Ibid.*

30. *Ibid.*

31. *Ibid.*

32. *Ibid.*; Mary Elizabeth Young, *Redskins, Ruffleshirts and Rednecks: Indian Allotments in Alabama and Mississippi, 1830–1860* (Norman: University of Oklahoma Press, 1961), 42.

33. Colbert and Chiefs to President, November 22, 1832, M234-R136, frame 275ff.

34. *Ibid.*

35. See quotation, Gibson, *The Chickasaws*, 176.

36. Atkinson, *Splendid Land*, 228.

37. "Articles of Treaty, October 20, 1832," *Public Statutes at Large of the United States of America*, ed. Richard Peters (Boston: Charles C. Little and James Brown, 1846), 7: 381–87.

38. *Ibid.*, 388–90.

39. Atkinson, *Splendid Land*, 229; Young, *Redskins*, 42–43, 131. According to Young, Terrell's partner Cook later bought 22,819.51 acres of patented Chickasaw land.

40. Colbert and Chiefs to President, November 22, 1832, M234-R136, Frames 275ff.

41. Young, *Redskins*, 42; Hotopa, et al Power of Attorney, undated, M234-R136, frame 385.

42. Young, *Redskins*, 43; Atkinson, *Splendid Land*, 229–30. Historian Young, like others, wants to make the controversy conform to the old idea that mixed bloods like Colbert took advantage of the full bloods, but the "facts" do not clearly fit the theory and leave her somewhat confused. See, e.g., her page 43.

43. Coffee to Secretary of War, February 15, 1833, M234-R136, frame 368.

44. Eaton to Cass, January 18 and 21, 1833, M234-R136, frames 375 and 377; Monte Ross Lewis, "Chickasaw Removal: Betrayal of the Beloved Warriors, 1794–1844." Ph.D. Dissertation (North Texas State University, 1982), 101–05.

45. Reynolds to Cass, December 9, 1832, M234-R136, frame 335.

46. *Missionary Herald* 29 (1833): 23, 29, 132–33.

47. Thomas M. Barker to Cass, January 14, 1834, and I. Lane to C. C. Clay, December 29, 1833, M234-R136, frames 480 and 488.

48. Reynolds to Herring, March 31, 1834; William Gwinn to Cass, April 8, 1834, January 4 and 14, 1834; Allen to Herring, October 3, 1833; S. W. Dickson to Cass, November 19, 1833, M234-R136, frames 363, 373, 470, 474, 475, and 505; Lewis, "Chickasaw Removal," 107–09.

49. Reynolds to Herring, June 19, 1833, M234-R136, Frame 411.

50. Lewis, "Chickasaw Removal," 112; 29th Congress, 1st Session, *House Document 8*, 50–51.

51. Reynolds to Herring, October 14 and 31 and November 14, 1833, M234-R136, frames 443, 457, and 464; Lewis, "Chickasaw Removal," 112–13.

52. Reynolds to Herring, November 14, 1833, M234-R136, frame 464.

53. Lewis, "Chickasaw Removal," 113–14.

54. Lewis, "Chickasaw Removal," 114; Gibson, *The Chickasaws*, 177.

55. Colbert to Jackson, March 31, 1834, M234-R136, frame 499.

56. Gibson, *The Chickasaws*, 177–78; Atkinson, *Splendid Land*, 230.

57. Atkinson, *Splendid Land*, 230–31.

58. Lewis, "Chickasaw Removal," 115–17.

59. *Ibid.*, 117–28; William Armstrong to Herring, November 18, 1835, M234-R136, frame 571.

60. *Missionary Herald* 32 (1836): 22.

61. George Adams to Cass, August 5, 1835, M234-R136, Frame 562; Lewis, "Chickasaw Removal," 121.

62. Ishtehotopa, et al. to Jackson, December 24, 1835, M234-R136, Frame 608.

63. *Ibid.*

64. See, A memorandum of the appraised property of the Estate of the Deceased Mrs. Allen, Tockapulla, September 27, 1837, Pontotoc County Records, Estates (Book of Wills), Book 1, p. 23ff; Book 2, pp. 55, 104. See also Deed Book 3, pp. 420–22. For the legal question of women's right to property, see *Fisher v. Allen* (1831), *http://www.chickasawhistory.com/Fisher–htm*, retrieved July 26, 2004 and Kerry M. Armstrong, "Was It James or John Allen?" *http://www.chickasawhistory.com/allen.htm*, retrieved June 23, 2004.

65. Ishtehotopa, et al. to Jackson, December 24, 1835, M234-R136, frame 608.

66. *Ibid.*

67. Letters of John Bell, March 31 and December 17, 1835, M234-R136, frames 515, 532, and 535; quotation is cited in Atkinson, *Splendid Land*, 232.

68. Atkinson, *Splendid Land*, 233.

69. Young, Redskins, 116–22; James Colbert to President, June 5, 1835, M234-R136, frame 614.

70. Richey Henderson, *Pontotoc County Men of Note*, (Pontotoc: Progress Print, 1940), 27.

71. Proclamation [July 1835], M234-R136, frames 684–685; James W. Silver, "Land Speculation Profits in the Chickasaw Session," *Journal of Southern History* 10 (February 1944): 85. See also, "Mississippi Chickasaw Land Sales—1836," *http://www.chickasawhistory.com/land_p_1.htm*, retrieved January 10, 2004.

72. Silver, "Land Speculation Profits," 84–92; Young, *Redskins*, 66, 118, 131, 132, 166–68.

73. Atkinson, *Splendid Land*, 233; Ethan Allen Hitchcock, *A Traveler in Indian Territory*, ed. Grant Foreman (Cedar Rapids, Iowa: Torch Press, 1930), 174–75.

74. Atkinson, *Splendid Land*, 233.

75. Benjamin Love to J. R. Poinsett, May 15, 1840, 28th Congress, 2nd Session, *Senate Report 160*, 15–16. For litigation, see, e.g., Pitman Colbert to Cass, February 27, 1836 (C354), M234-R137; Robert Gordon to Herring, September 19, 1835, M234-R136, frame 637. See also frames following 714.

76. Jerry Anderson Harlow, "Cotton Gin Port," in Monroe County Book Committee, *A History of Monroe County, Mississippi* (Dallas: Curtis Media Corp., 1988), 53; *The Public Statutes at Large*, 7: 389.

77. Reynolds to Herring, May 27, 1836, M234-R137, frame 60.

78. Gaston Litton, ed., "The Negotiations Leading to the Chickasaw–Choctaw Agreement, January 17, 1837," *Chronicles of Oklahoma* 17 (December 1939): 418.

79. *Ibid.*

80. *Ibid.*, 419.

81. *Ibid.*, 420.

82. *Ibid.*, 420–21.

83. *Ibid.*

84. *Ibid.*, 422–23.

85. *Ibid.*, 424.

86. *Ibid.*, 424–26.

87. *Ibid.*, 426–27.

ON FEBRUARY 17, 1837, CHICKASAW leaders endorsed the Doaksville agreement and expressed their willingness to remove. They sought to ensure a "speedy removal to their new home, and thereby prevent the many evils which they now suffer." Claiming "a considerable portion" of the Chickasaws would be ready to remove by the first of May, they agreed to a plan developed by William Armstrong, Superintendent of Indian Affairs in the Western district. Because Creek removal had made provisions scarce along removal routes in the West, they asked the government to buy provisions in Kentucky or Tennessee and ship them to points on the Mississippi where the boats could pick up Chickasaws on their way west. They did not want private removal contractors, like the Creeks had had, whose primary concern was profit and not the welfare of the people but wanted, instead, a government agent to superintend their removal. Finally, given the bad roads west of the Mississippi, they wanted chartered steamboats to transport as many of their people as possible to the mouth of the Canadian River in the Choctaw country and wanted transportation to be provided from there to their new district in the Choctaw lands.[1]

Unfortunately, the government officials read this plan differently from the way they did. Assuming that the entire Chickasaw Nation would move in May, the U. S. government made the first of a number of mistakes costly for the Chickasaws and laid the groundwork for the ultimate loss of a large portion of the Chickasaw national fund: the War Department began procuring rations immediately and shipping them to the Indian Territory, where many of the goods spoiled because of inadequate storage, while local officials waited for Chickasaws who failed to remove.

(71)

Armstrong's plan, though based on the realities of conditions in the West, was far too simple for those realities and was doomed from the start. The Chickasaws hoped to avoid the problems the Creeks had with contractors—problems which they had witnessed firsthand. Some of the early overland Creek parties, driven hard by contractors to protect their profits, had marched through Chickasaw country. In 1834, for example, a party of 630 Creeks had traveled from Fort Mitchell, Alabama, by way of Tuscaloosa and Columbus, Mississippi, and then through the Chickasaw Nation on the Cotton Gin Port to Memphis road. Poorly clothed, the Creeks had suffered greatly from cold and forced marching by the private contractors.[2] During that and subsequent removals, a large number of Creeks "deserted" in Chickasaw country and were sent west later when the Chickasaws removed. In the West, located as he was at the Choctaw Agency West, Armstrong was well informed on the prices of commodities and the availability of goods. The Chickasaw exploring party had experienced bad roads firsthand, and those Chickasaws engaged in business understood the practical advantage of buying provisions farther north: Southern banks were failing at a rapid rate as the banking crisis known as an economic recession began to grip the nation in early 1837. Thus firsthand experience caused the Chickasaws to be wary of overland travel. But the scheme to coordinate the transportation of provisions and Chickasaw passengers was one that only a bureaucratic mind could have hatched. Conditions of travel on western waterways, particularly the Arkansas, made remote the chance of executing the plan without difficulty.

In addition, the response of Commissioner of Indian Affairs Carey A. Harris to the Chickasaw leaders' plan was in some ways downright naïve. On orders from the president, he took immediate steps to set the plan in motion. He promised to send agents to the Chickasaws soon to make arrangements and urged them to "at once commence their preparations for departure and perfect them" to prevent delay in leaving.[3] Tennessean and friend of Andrew Jackson that he was, Harris was overanxious to be rid of the Chickasaws, but he should have known that a quick departure was unlikely. Choctaw removal had taken years, Seminole removal had been halted by the ongoing conflict in Florida, Creek removal had been going on for years, and the Cherokees had

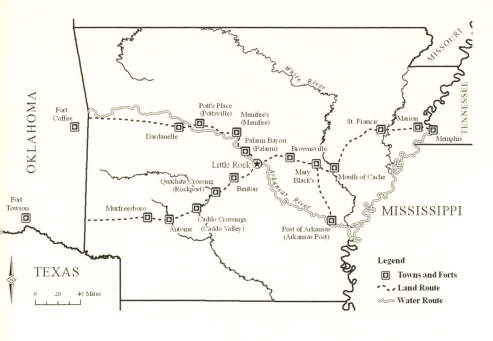

Removal Routes
© CHICKASAW NATION

resisted removal since the treaty of 1835. He was asking too much of the Chickasaws. Yet he set the plan in motion with extraordinary speed. Even before he replied to the Chickasaws, he had made Cincinnati the headquarters for procuring Chickasaw removal rations and had already made contracts with suppliers. He took literally the date of May 1 as the date of removal. However, as subsequent events showed, his understanding of what the Chickasaws meant by "speedy removal" and of "a considerable portion of their people" was not theirs.

Procurement of rations was the task of Lieutenant J. D. Searight, who arrived in Cincinnati on March 19 and immediately advertised for bids to supply rations at three stations: Memphis, Little Rock, and Fort Coffee, located on the Arkansas River west of Fort Smith not far from the Choctaw Agency, which also had a landing. The standard ration for Chickasaw removal was the same as rations provided to soldiers in the American army: twelve ounces of salt pork and one pound of wheat flour or a pint and a half of corn or corn meal per person each day. Salt was distributed at the rate of four quarts per hundred rations. By the middle of April, Searight had made contracts with Ohio businessmen

for supplying Memphis and Little Rock. The Memphis contract went
to William Thoms, whose bid, though late, Searight considered a "private" contract, one of many such agreements with favored suppliers.
The contract for the Little Rock depot went to Christopher Niswanger
and David Deshler of Columbus, Ohio. Searight had rejected four bids
for the Fort Coffee depot because they were too high,[4] but they were the
result of uncertain water levels in the Arkansas River above Little Rock
that were anticipated during the next six weeks. The delivery date was
May 30, which preceded the usual spring rise. If the water was high
enough, the rations could be taken by steamboat, but if low, it would be
impossible to get 100 tons of supplies up the river by keel boat.[5]

Another concern was the size of the contract. It called for one million rations at Fort Coffee in contrast to 100,000 at Memphis and
200,000 at Little Rock. Theoretically, the latter two would be only
temporary stops or depots for small overland parties, primarily those
driving livestock to the West. Fort Coffee would be the subsistence depot for the Chickasaws while they were establishing themselves in their
new lands. To lessen the potential loss for a single contractor, to guarantee that such a huge quantity of rations could be amassed, and to ensure that some, if not all, rations reached Fort Coffee in time, Searight
asked the Commissioner to allow delivery of part of the provisions by
May 30 and the remainder in June. Also, because it might be difficult

to amass one million rations of "first quality" pork, Searight asked permission to substitute bacon or lower quality "prime" pork. Searight
also wanted four or five smaller contracts instead of one contract for a
million rations. It would be difficult for one person to amass supplies
of that quantity, especially corn, and, because of a growing national
banking crisis, it was becoming difficult to obtain the money. Contractors could buy provisions for cash only, and banks could not loan the
$50,000 to $100,000 in cash that a single contract would require.[6]

At the time Searight began to procure the Chickasaw rations, the
banking system was on the verge of a nationwide panic. In the wake
of Andrew Jackson's successful "war" against Nicholas Biddle and the
United States Bank, a banking frenzy occurred in the states. While only
329 state banks existed in 1829, the number grew to 788 by 1837. Corre-
spondingly, bank note circulation increased in the same period by over

$100 million, and the total of loans went from $137 million to $525 million. The frenzy was particularly strong in the West and South and was fed in large measure by speculation in slaves, internal improvements, and land. Speculation in land was fed by two government policies. The United States pumped its money into the banks without establishing any form of oversight. In addition, the government opened great tracts of land to sale, much of which was land vacated when the tribes moved, or prepared to move, to the West, including the Chickasaws. A speculator could buy public land for $1.25 an acre, use the land as collateral for loans, and use the money borrowed to buy more land. The government further increased the speculation by accepting payment by paper money issued by the state banks. The result was that banks issued far more paper money than they had gold or silver specie to back. In response to criticism, even from his own backers, Jackson issued his famous "Specie Circular" in July of 1836. After August 15, all land had to be paid for in silver or gold, except by those who purchased no more than 320 acres; they could use paper money until the following December. The exception was aimed at assisting the small farmer to buy land, while at the same time curtailing speculation. Land sales dropped immediately, the banks faced huge amounts in loans that they could not collect and began to fail, and by early 1837, coincident with the procurement of Chickasaw rations, the great Panic of 1837 set in. Suppliers were anxious to deal with the United States because the government paid in dollar coins.

(75)

By April 15, supplies for the Memphis depot were on their way from Cincinnati, although lines of authority and communication had not been established to deal with receiving them. Captain Joseph A. Phillips, disbursing agent for Indian removal east of the Mississippi, was not in Memphis at the time, so there was no federal agent to receive and inspect the goods. David Vanderslice, an assistant agent for Chickasaw removal, arrived on the same day as the first shipment and had the rations stored with commission merchant Marcus B. Winchester until Phillips arrived. However, with no inspector present, Thoms was still liable for the cargo, which meant that his agent had to remain at Memphis until an official released him. To add to the confusion, contractors for rations and transportation were uncertain who was to pay them, Phillips at Memphis and Captain R. D. C. Collins, who was Phillips' counterpart west of the Mississippi at Little Rock, or Searight in Cincinnati.[7]

The confusion resulted primarily from the appointment of Captain R. D. C. Collins to replace Captain Jacob Brown at Little Rock as disbursing agent for Indian removal west of the Mississippi, which occurred in the midst of the ration procurement. In 1831 the Army sent him to Arkansas where he was in charge of surveying routes and superintending construction of military roads. He was well liked by the local citizens, who considered him a kind man "with a suavity of his manners."[8] The *Gazette* at Little Rock said of his appointment, "No selection, we are sure, could have given more general satisfaction to the citizens of this State."[9] As history proved, however, some of those who praised him and were prone to take advantage of his control over Chickasaw funds found him an easy tool because of his addiction to alcohol.

Besides uncertain lines of authority, other uncertainties plagued the operations at Memphis. Phillips did not arrive until May 12, at which time he inspected the rations, released the contractor, and returned immediately to Louisville, where his wife was gravely ill. Meanwhile, no operating funds were available at Memphis or in the Chickasaw Nation because of the growing failure of the banking system. Phillips had taken with him to Memphis a draft for $10,000 on the Agricultural Bank of Natchez, payable at its branch at Pontotoc, Mississippi. Because all of the business of removal was done in silver coins, Phillips had to find cash. The Natchez bank, however, had suspended payment of specie. In fact, no banks in Mississippi or Tennessee were solvent, except one at Memphis, the only bank in the region still redeeming its own paper. "But whether she will be able to withstand the general prostration of business and confidence in bank paper and the consequent demand for specie, is a question of some doubt," wrote Vanderslice. Nevertheless, Phillips ordered him to go to Pontotoc to protest the draft and try to get it cashed. After several days' delay, the bank agreed to pay the funds.[10]

Supplying the Little Rock depot was done quickly and without difficulties. By the end of April, cargo under a transportation contract with James H. McClure & Company of Cincinnati arrived there and was inspected by Captain R. D. C. Collins, who issued payment for the 200,000 rations for $32,000 and had them stored in government warehouses.[11]

Despite early problems, supplying the Memphis and Little Rock depots was rather simple compared to the monumental task of sending one million rations up the Arkansas River to Fort Coffee. Commissioner Harris appointed army Lieutenant Gouverneur Morris to oversee the process. W. A. M. Brooke, appointed to assist him, arrived at Cincinnati ahead of Morris in late April to find that Searight had not yet purchased the Fort Coffee provisions. Commissioner Harris was displeased with Searight's contract with McClure & Company to transport the goods because it was high at 2.5 cents per pound. Searight had difficulties obtaining even that low of an offer because of boat owners' concern about the water levels above Little Rock. One boat owner had offered to take freight to Little Rock for a penny per pound and on to Fort Coffee for an additional cent if the water was high enough. No owner would agree to unconditional contracts but insisted that their captains have the option to offload cargoes and turn around if water levels fell.[12] Thus uncertainties abounded about logistics from the start.

The bid of Clark and Buckner of Louisville indicates the owners' fear of losses, not only from the condition of the Arkansas River but from the scarcity of money. They offered to take 1,200 tons to Fort Coffee in three excursions—one third before May 30, one third before June 15, and one third before June 30, at $2.90 per hundred—provided there was water in the Arkansas. If they were stopped by low water, they wanted $150 a day per boat until the water rose or the contractor unloaded the goods. If they were stopped, they agreed to try to obtain light-draft boats, "lighters" they called them, to lighten the loads so that the steamboats could proceed, towing the "lighters" as far as they could go. In addition, the owners wanted an advance of $1,000 or $1,500 per boat to be paid at Little Rock and the remainder to be paid at Louisville or Cincinnati after the boats returned. It was not until Morris arrived in Cincinnati that he realized that supplying the Fort Coffee depot would be much more expensive than the Commissioner had originally projected. Thus he asked Harris for $30,000 to $40,000 more than his original budget.[13]

(77)

By late May, by which time Chickasaw removal was to have begun, nearly all of the rations for Fort Coffee had been bought and shipment had begun. The first shipment of 862.5 tons left Cincinnati on May 22, consisting of 3,438 barrels of pork, 750 barrels of flour, 29 barrels of salt, and 3,700 sacks of corn, containing about 6,300 bushels. Morris hired John M. Caldwell to accompany the shipment while he and Brooke purchased the rest of the corn. Caldwell was supposed to build storehouses if he found storage space unavailable at Fort Coffee. The second shipment left on May 27. Morris and Brooke followed the shipment to Arkansas, leaving Searight to purchase the remaining provisions. By that date, the government had bought 2,134 barrels of mess pork at $18 per barrel; 1,616 barrels of prime pork at $16; 707 barrels of super-fine flour at $5.50; 43 barrels of fine flour at $5; 1,250 bushels of salt at 45 cents per bushel; and 8,173 bushels of corn at 56 cents, for a total of $73,644.83. Searight chose to substitute corn for the remaining breadstuffs, some 12,000 bushels of corn that would cost an additional $8,000. If Searight had to buy flour instead, the price would double.[14] All of this expense, of course, was charged against the Chickasaw fund, and officials seemed oblivious to, or unconcerned about, the growing cost.

The officials and the facilities at Fort Coffee were not prepared to receive such large shipments of cargo. It was not until Morris left Cincinnati for Fort Coffee that preparations had even begun for receiving the provisions. Captain R. D. C. Collins ordered Lieutenant Jefferson Van Horne, assistant disbursing agent for Creek removal at Fort Gibson, to build sheds to store the million rations at Fort Coffee. Van Horne immediately encountered problems. The enclosure at Fort Coffee could not accommodate ten sheds built twenty by forty feet. If they were built outside, the goods would have to be hauled up a hill behind the post, a long distance from the river, and would be unsafe unless the sides were walled, which would be costly. Van Horne could not use troops to do the work but was required to hire laborers; who were scarce. The Panic of 1837, which was growing deeper, created other problems. Van Horne was on the verge of finally making a contract with local workers when word came that all Southwestern banks had ceased payment of specie. The workers refused to work, for Van Horne's only alternative was paper money from the Planters Bank of Tennessee and the Union Bank of Louisiana. Stymied, Van Horne obtained permission from the commander at Fort Coffee to use one of the Fort's structures that could hold 1,000 barrels on the condition that Van Horne later build a shed of equal size to store the post's hay. He decided to ask the steamboat captains to unload the remaining cargo at the government warehouses at the Choctaw Agency landing, at the abandoned commissary store and block house at Fort Smith, which Van Horne would have to repair, and, if necessary, at the government warehouse at Pheasant Bluff on the Canadian, thirty miles above Fort Coffee. These were government buildings that could be occupied without cost and were as convenient to the Chickasaw country as Fort Coffee. Without funds, Van Horne personally pledged to pay a group of soldiers who would be "voluntarily employed" in helping to store the provisions.[15]

Van Horne had barely put this emergency plan together when two steamboats carrying the first shipment arrived. On the lead boat, the *Princeton*, was John Caldwell, who had funds and authority to build storehouses. However, he refused to take charge, convinced that Van Horne's plan was the most workable. Though reluctant, Van Horne continued in charge, not wanting the rations to spoil, and immediately stored the load of corn and part of the flour in the one available building and set about securing the remaining provisions.[16]

When Lieutenant Morris arrived ten days later, Van Horne had stored two cargoes at Fort Smith, where buildings had been prepared, but the remainder of the 883.5 tons that had arrived was still in the open air. Van Horne had been unable to induce most steamboat captains to unload at the Choctaw Agency landing or at Pheasant Bluff. Without Arkansas River pilots, they were afraid of grounding and wanted $500 plus a guarantee of an allowance for each day they were delayed. He finally induced James McClure to unload the *Indian*'s cargo of corn at the Agency landing, and he unloaded the *Mississippian* at Fort Coffee, where Van Horne had begun to erect storage sheds, although he was still having difficulty finding laborers. Those he did find demanded exorbitant wages.[17]

Meanwhile, the rations began to spoil. Many of the barrels were defective and had leaked their brine; thus a large quantity of the pork had been stored without brine. In addition, the last shipment had been exposed to high temperatures for a time at the mouth of the White River, where it had been delayed. Preserving the pork would require re-brining. Van Horne decided to use part of the salt rations to re-brine the pork after the storage sheds were finished.[18] The pork was undoubtedly rank if the brine had leaked out and the barrels had sat in the summer sun. The large stores of corn were also destined to spoil. Morris and Brooke had brought more corn with them in the *Echo's* keelboat. The *Indian* had offloaded about 1,000 sacks at the Agency landing, where it got wet in two days of rain. Van Horne feared that some of the flour would also spoil because of exposure. He ordered 40,000 feet of pine plank to be used in building temporary shelters for the corn. "Responsible men," he said, had offered to take part of the corn off his hands and promised to replace it from local sources when the Chickasaws arrived, but Van Horne was powerless to act on the idea without official approval. Meanwhile, construction of the storage sheds at Fort Coffee continued.[19]

By the end of the third week in June, Van Horne had nearly completed four buildings at Fort Coffee. However, the cargoes of the *Express* and the keelboat of the *Echo* were in bad condition because of delay and exposure on the trip. Afraid that these would be lost, Van Horne took the advice of Superintendent Armstrong and Captain John Stuart, commander at Fort Coffee, and contracted with John Drennen, a Van Buren, Arkansas, merchant, to take the two cargoes, consisting of 1,365 sacks of corn and 60 barrels of flour and later to replace them upon a 60-day notice.[20] This transaction was the first of a number of such agreements with Arkansas merchants that ultimately cost the Chickasaws thousands of dollars. While Van Horne was undoubtedly sincere in his desire to save the Chickasaws from loss, the success of his plan relied on the good faith of the merchants, but merchants like Drennen were not always trustworthy.

Preparations for arrival of the Chickasaws were nearly complete. Caleb Langtree, appointed to oversee the Chickasaw stores, reported on July 4 that all provisions had arrived except about 300 sacks of corn, which he expected immediately. All provisions, he falsely claimed, were well stored and in excellent condition.[21] On that day, the first

Chickasaw removal party reached Memphis on its way to Fort Coffee—not the whole nation as War Department officials had anticipated, but less than a tenth of that number. Gathering even that many had been difficult. Thus overstocking Chickasaw rations and failing to prepare adequate storage for them had not been the only major miscalculations made by War Department officials.

The War Department had made even greater miscalculations in its removal plan. Officials were late appointing removal agents and getting them into the Chickasaw Nation. Secretary of War Benjamin F. Butler appointed A. M. M. Upshaw of Pulaski, Tennessee, as Superintendent of Chickasaw removal and David Vanderslice of Georgetown, Kentucky, John M. Millard of Maryland, and W. A. M. Brooke of Washington, D. C., as assistant agents. Upshaw did not arrive at Pontotoc until early May and held his first general meeting with the Chickasaws on May 13, well past the date officials had originally thought the Chickasaws would be ready to remove.[22] By that time, nearly all of the Chickasaw provisions had arrived in the West, and many of the stores were rotting in the open air.

Upon his arrival in the Chickasaw Nation, Upshaw witnessed scenes like those that had been all too familiar to the Chickasaws since their land had gone on sale in 1836. Local white merchants and whiskey peddlers were preying on them, working to delay removal until they could extract every dollar of Chickasaw wealth they possibly could. Upshaw applauded a decision of the Chickasaw Commission to withhold funds due those Chickasaws they deemed "incompetent" to do business and pay them after they arrived in the West. The high incidence of drunkenness he observed caused him to bemoan the fact that funds had not also been withheld from the "competent" Chickasaws as well. But the Chickasaws' reluctance to leave could not be laid entirely on the whites. Upshaw was simply too optimistic in expecting the Chickasaws willingly to make a quick exit from their homeland. Upon his arrival, local residents had told him that very few would remove before fall, but after he had been in the nation a week, he thought he could get 1,000 to start in June.[23] Upshaw found, in time, that the local residents were right.

When Upshaw met with the principal leaders of the nation on May

13, he urged "a speedy removal." In patronizing fashion, as spokesman for their "Great Father," he informed them that rations were in place, ready for their arrival. "There are a great number of your people," he said, "who are spending all their money & making no crops, they get drunk & lose their money & white men make them Drunks to cheat them of their property & their wives & children are suffering for something to eat." Those with crops in the field should sell them, he said, and use the money when they arrived in the West to buy what they needed from the Choctaws. And Upshaw made a promise that would remain a point of contention for the Chickasaws long after removal: the "incompetent" Chickasaws would receive their money soon after they arrived in the West to buy livestock and other necessities. He urged one chief from each district to rally the people for removal and to avoid the mistake of the Choctaws: "Some of us went with the Choctaws, they went late & suffered greatly, they did not have time to build Houses to keep the cold & rain off." As for settlement of debts, he argued that the creditors of the "incompetent" Chickasaws could prove their accounts in Mississippi and have some suitable person collect them in the West. In response to Upshaw's talk, the four district chiefs agreed to hold district councils on May 28 to organize the people for removal and set June 7 as the date to rendezvous to begin their trek.[24]

(82)

Meanwhile, Upshaw worked to prepare for departure. William R. Guy and Francis G. Roche, both Tennesseans whom he described as "the best of clerks and gentlemen," were enrolling agents. He also appointed John Mizell as principal interpreter, a white man who received the endorsement of the chiefs and whom Upshaw characterized as a man of "sterling integrity" and one called "the best interpreter in the nation." During the next few weeks, Upshaw also used Levi Camp, J. James, and Cyrus Harris as interpreters. He remained confident that he could get 1,000 to 1,500 on their way west by the middle of June, although he had come away from his meeting with the chiefs concluding, "Indians are slow in their movements & will take time."[25] And time was against him. Although Guy had been appointed enrolling agent in early May, he remained at Pontotoc for nearly three weeks before entering the field, riding from camp to camp and house to house to enroll people for removal.[26]

Upshaw's optimism flagged somewhat after the four district meetings. He believed that no more than 600 or 700 would go in June. He met strong resistance in McGilivray's district, where a majority of the chiefs had signed the petition to the president to remove in the spring but were now "very contrary" to removing. He laid much of the blame on John McLish, whom he characterized as an ambitious "half-breed" whose plans to "make a fortune" from removal had been thwarted by Upshaw's appointment as superintendent. The grog shops, too, he complained, had a large hand in attempting to delay removal temporarily in order to wring as much wealth from the Chickasaws as possible, and he again urged the policy of withholding of cash payments to the "competent" Chickasaws as well as to the "incompetent." In opposition to these forces, Upshaw had a strong ally in Emmubbee, whom he described as "counciller to the king," a man of "great influence of fine mind and good judgment" who worked in behalf of removal. Upshaw claimed that Emmubbee had asked him to write the president that the great Father had "four sons" in the Chickasaw Nation, apparently referring to the district chiefs, three "good" and one "bad," although Upshaw listed only three: Isaac Alberson, Ishtehotopa (the king or minko), Eoichetubby (i.e., Eiochetubby, apparently chief of Sealy's District), and McGilivray, respectively. Despite the opposition, Upshaw retained the belief that he could get all of the Chickasaws out of the country by November 1.[27]

It may have been Emmubbee's support for removal that caused his murder by a white man named Jones shortly thereafter. The newspapers reported the dramatic event: "When Jones presented his rifle at him, he leaped from his horse, spread his breast, and said 'Shoot! Emubby is not afraid to die.' The wretch did shoot and the Indian fell."[28] Although the news reports said that Emmubbee was killed without provocation, Upshaw was strangely quiet concerning the event. One historian suggests that the killing resulted from difficulties caused by "designing merchants who sought to keep the Indians in their debt as long as they had any money or property."[29]

As Upshaw worked into June, it became clear that the merchants were responsible for the declining numbers of Chickasaws who were preparing to remove. Vice President Richard M. Johnson, who had

(*83*)

traveled through the region in April, had been convinced that the traders would do whatever possible to slow down removal as much as they could by getting the Indians into their debt. Now, Upshaw was having "considerable difficulty" with people the Indians owed. Benjamin Reynolds, the agent, William Carroll, in charge of the land sales, Upshaw, and the chiefs addressed the Chickasaws and recommended postponement of debt collection until after removal. Upshaw reemphasized his belief that stopping payment of funds to all Chickasaws would help greatly in getting them on their way. He had pitched camps at three locations and by June 13 no more than 300 had come in. Nevertheless, he planned to leave about June 25 with however many had come in by then because he believed that sending a few to the West would "be of great service towards getting them off in the fall."[30] These figures represent the miserable failure of his original plan.

He was apparently able to gather as many as he did only because the merchants relented. Under the acts of 1829 and 1830, extending Mississippi's laws over the Chickasaw lands, Chickasaws who were competent to contract debts could sue and be sued. By the time of removal, some had accumulated debts of sizeable amounts, and cases had proceeded through the courts. "Incompetents" had also accumulated debts based on the assumption that they would eventually receive their funds. To merchants and others, removal meant that the Chickasaws might escape payment. Thus when the first removal party was gathering at the juncture of the Tippah and Tallahatchie Rivers, creditors and officers of the law descended on the camp. The Chickasaws became agitated and refused to be listed for removal by enrolling agents. Upshaw sent for James Davis, general counsel for the nation, who called the Chickasaws into assembly and then, later, the creditors and Mississippi officials. He promised both sides that the "incompetents" would be paid upon their arrival in the West and was finally able to allay fears sufficiently to allow removal to go forward.[31]

Commissioner C. A. Harris had given Upshaw specific instructions regarding the organization of removal parties. They should consist of no more than 1,000 persons, and Upshaw was to take care not to divide families. He was to divide each detachment into companies of about fifty, again without dividing families. The head of a family in

(84)

each company, known as a captain, was to be in charge of the company during the trip to ensure that his people received rations, had transportation, and were not left behind as stragglers. Because the Chickasaws were paying for the removal, Harris directed Upshaw to "consult" their views and wishes and to gratify "all their reasonable desires" but to use a "judicious economy." A good example was baggage. War Department regulations allowed each person on the removal trail to take only thirty pounds of personal effects. However, Upshaw had permission to relax the rules somewhat and allow the Chickasaws to take forty pounds each of "property valuable and essential" to them in their new homes. From their gathering point, he was to take the parties overland to Memphis to board steamboats, which would take them down the Mississippi to the Arkansas and up the Arkansas to the mouth of the Canadian.[32]

The designated route resulted in anxiety for Upshaw. Usually, the high water on the Arkansas began to recede, and navigation was interrupted, by the middle of June.[33] By the time the first group started west, the window of opportunity was closing on the Arkansas.

The size of the party was not nearly what Upshaw had first envisioned. They numbered between 400 and 500, and he expected some 50 or 60 more to join him before he reached Memphis. Still, it was a larger number than most people in the Chickasaw Nation had thought he would get together. Opposition to removal plagued him even on the road. On the day the party was due to arrive at Memphis, someone organized a great ball play at Horn Lake, Upshaw believed, to prevent Indians of that region from coming in the day before for removal.[34]

The Chickasaw leaders' request in early in 1837 for a speedy removal set in motion a series of events based on miscalculations by federal officials. They had acted hastily, procuring and sending a million rations to Memphis, Little Rock, and Indian Territory, believing that the Chickasaw people would all remove late that spring. By the time the first small party left for the West in July, many of the goods, improperly stored, were wasting away. Although this first removal reflected a major miscalculation regarding Chickasaw affairs, their removal had begun. This party, made up primarily of people from Sealy's district, would make Upshaw and other officers begin to realize that it was the Chickasaws, and not they, who were in charge of their movements.

(85)

NOTES

1. 27th Congress, 3rd Session, *House Report 271*, 60–61, hereafter cited as *House Report 271*.

2. Grant Foreman, *Indian Removal: Emigration of the Five Civilized Tribes of Indians*, New ed. (Norman: University of Oklahoma Press, 1972), 126–28.

3. *House Report 271*, 61–62.

4. J. D. Searight to C. A. Harris, March 19, April 10, April 13, and April 22 (Chickasaw Emigration S255, S264, S265, and S277), National Archives Microfilm Publication M234, Roll 143, hereafter cited as M234, followed by the roll number.

5. Searight to Harris, April 10, 1837 (Chickasaw Emigration S264), M234-R143.

6. *Ibid.*; Searight to Harris, April 15, 1837 (Chickasaw Emigration S270), M234-R143.

7. David Vanderslice to Harris, April 18 and April 30, 1837, and Searight to Harris, May 10, 1837 (Chickasaw Emigration V23, V27 and S305), M234-R143.

8. *Arkansas Advocate*, July 12, 1841.

9. *Arkansas Gazette*, March 7, 1837.

10. Vanderslice to Harris, May 12, 1837; Upshaw to Harris, May 21, 1837; and Phillips to Harris, May 23 and 28, 1837 (Chickasaw Emigration V3, U7, P127 and P129), M234-R143.

11. Vanderslice to Harris, April 30, 1837, and Searight to Harris, May 10, 1837 (Chickasaw Emigration V26 and S305); Subsistence Receipt No. 149 and Transportation Receipt (1837) No. 2 (Chickasaw Emigration C186), M234-R143.

12. Gouverneur Morris to Harris, April 19, 1837, W.A.M. Brooke to Harris, April 26, 1837, and Searight to Harris, May 12, 1837 (Chickasaw Emigration M106, B214, and S312), M234-R143.

13. Searight to Harris, May 12, 1837, and Morris to Harris, May 12, 1837 (Chickasaw Emigration S312 and M114), M234-R143.

14. J. Van Horne to Harris, June 3, 1837, with enclosures, Morris to Harris, May 22 and 27, 1837, Searight to Harris, May 27, 1837 (Chickasaw Emigration V35, M119, M121, and S339), M234-R143. For receipts in procuring Chickasaw supplies, see Receipts, April 15–June 30, 27th Cong., 3rd Session, *House Document 65*, pp. 3–4, hereafter cited as *House Document 65*.

15. Van Horne to Harris, June 3, 1837, with enclosures (Chickasaw Emigration V35), M234-R143. Van Horne, a graduate of West Point,

served as commissary for migrating Indians from 1832 to 1839. He later
served in the Florida War and the Mexican War.

16. *Ibid.*

17. Morris to Harris, June 16, 1837, and Van Horne to Harris, June 18, 1837,
with enclosures (Chickasaw Emigration M137 and V36), M234-R143.
See Receipts July 4–July 30, 1837, *House Document 65*, pp. 4–7, for details
of the work of storing the Chickasaw goods and building storage
structures.

18. Van Horne to Harris, June 18, 1837, with enclosures (Chickasaw
Emigration V36), M234-R143. See Receipts for W. Mullen, F. Parrish, F.
Richard, J. Williams, J. Witham, J. Sharer, J. Jeumans, James Gaines, and
A. Perry, September 30, 1837, *House Document 65*, p. 26.

19. Van Horne to Harris, June 18, 1837, with enclosures (Chickasaw
Emigration V36), M234-R143.

20. Van Horne to Harris, June 21, 1837 (Chickasaw Emigration V38),
M234-R143.

21. Caleb Langtree to Harris, April 30, May 13, and July 4, 1837 (Chickasaw
Emigration L180, L190, and L239), M234-R143.

22. Upshaw to Harris, March 27, 1837, Vanderslice to Harris, March 17, 1837,
J. M. Millard to Harris, April 18, 1837, and Brooke to Harris, April 19,
1837 (Chickasaw Emigration U2, V17, M107, and B210), M234-R143;
Harris to Vanderslice, April 4, 1837, and Harris to Upshaw, June 15, 1837,
Chickasaw Vol. 1, pp. 141–42, 143–46, National Archives Record Group
75, Records of the Commissary General of Subsistence, Entry 253,
Chickasaw Removal Records.

23. Talk to the Chickasaws and Upshaw to Harris, May 15, 1837 (Chickasaw
Emigration U5), M234-R143.

24. *Ibid.*

25. *Ibid.*; Upshaw to Harris, May 21 and June 2, 1837 (Chickasaw Emigration
U7 and U10), M234-R143. See also receipts for Harris, Camp, James,
Mizell, and Guy, *House Document 65*, pp. 9, 10.

26. Upshaw to William Medill, May 1, 1848 (Chickasaw Emigration U35),
M234-R144.

27. Upshaw to Harris, June 2, 1837 (Chickasaw Emigration U10), M234-R143.

28. Foreman, *Indian Removal*, 205, citing *Jacksonville* [Alabama] *Republican*,
August 24, 1837.

29. Foreman, *Indian Removal*, 204–05. Although Upshaw and others often
refer to such merchants and whiskey peddlers, they offer few details.
The relationship of indebtedness to resistance to removal needs to
be researched in fraud and claims records, as well as in the records of
Pontotoc, Lee, and other counties in Mississippi.

30. Felix Lewis to Jacob Thompson, May 4, 1840, 28th Congress, 2nd Session, *Senate Document 160*, p. 23, hereafter cited as *Senate Document 160*; Vanderslice to Harris, April 18, 1837, and Upshaw to Harris, June 13 and 20, 1837 (Chickasaw Emigration V27, U11, and U12), M234-R143.

31. James Davis to David Hubbard, December 31, 1839, *Senate Document 160*, p. 20.

32. Harris to Upshaw, June 15, 1837, Chickasaw Vol. 1, pp. 143–46.

33. *Ibid.*

34. Upshaw to Harris, July 4, 1837 (Chickasaw Emigration U14), M234-R143.

REMOVAL
FROM SEALY'S DISTRICT

SEALY'S DISTRICT, FROM WHICH the first group of Chickasaws departed, was located in the southwestern part of the Chickasaw Nation. Samuel Sealy, chief of the district for about twenty years, had apparently died after the Treaty of Pontotoc. In 1837, the chief of the district was known as Eiochetubby, who may have been a Sealy.[1] Samuel Sealy's place at the mouth of the Tippah on the Tallahatchie was where A. M. M. Upshaw had chosen to gather the party for departure. Under conductor John M. Millard's direction, this party followed the Cotton Gin Port road to Memphis with their personal belongings, slaves, and livestock. On July 4, some 432 people crossed the Mississippi and went into camp. Dr. C. G. Keenan served as directing physician, and Alexander Mizell and John Mizell served as interpreters. Horses, wagons, and 23,604 pounds of provisions and baggage followed the people across the river. Some Chickasaws had joined the party on the road, for Millard's roll at the outset contained 402, consisting of 95 households.[2] The *Memphis Gazette* said, "They presented a handsome appearance, being nearly all mounted, and, with few exceptions, well dressed in their national costume. It has been remarked by many of our citizens, who have witnessed the passage of emigrating Indians, that on no previous occasion was there as good order or more dispatch. . . . "[3] Once across the Mississippi, this party demonstrated the Chickasaws' willingness to deviate from the government's plan, a tendency that the commissioner of Indian affairs and his agents had not anticipated. This removal provided the first exhibition of independence that marked subsequent Chickasaw removals.

Although Chickasaw leaders had expressed a preference to remove by water, this group had determined to travel by land. Even the chiefs

CESSION AREA OF 1832

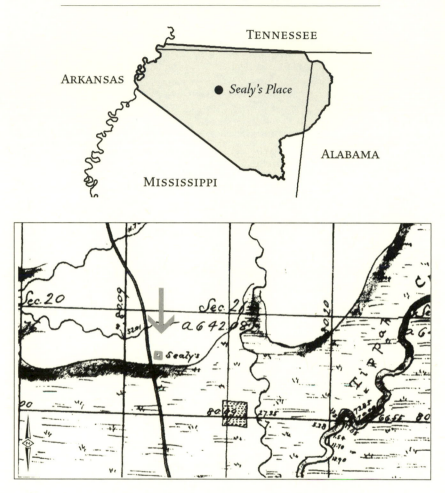

Sealy's Place. From the Cession Surveys of 1832.

IMAGE COURTESY OF THE CHICKASAW NATION
GEOSPATIAL INFORMATION DEPARTMENT.

© CHICKASAW NATION

who had earlier recommended they travel by water now refused to do so. Thus, with the original plans abandoned, the alternative was traveling the most formidable road in Arkansas west across the Mississippi Swamp some forty miles to William Strong's place just beyond the St. Francis River and from there southwest to the White River crossing at a village called Mouth of Cache, now Clarendon, Arkansas, and then to the North bank of the Arkansas River at Little Rock. From there, government agents expected them to follow the Military Road toward Fort Coffee, Indian Territory. Conductor John M. Millard was assisted by William R. Guy. Captain Joseph A. Phillips, disbursing agent for Indian removal east of the Mississippi, decided to travel with them as far as Little Rock because Upshaw had no disbursing authority by which to buy supplies. In addition, communications between Upshaw and other officials had been poor. Fearing that the disbursing agent at Little Rock might be absent, Phillips sent David Vanderslice, Upshaw's assistant and protégé of Richard M. Johnson, ahead to prepare for the Chickasaws' arrival. What lay beyond Little Rock was uncertain, for Upshaw, at that point, did not know whether agents would be at Fort Coffee to receive the Chickasaws upon their arrival.[4]

The road ahead of the Chickasaws was the main overland route from Memphis to Little Rock, authorized in early 1824, as a military road providing a direct overland route to the western frontier of Arkansas. By 1827 much of the road to the sixty-fourth mile west of Memphis had been completed when construction was halted by the impassable bottom lands of the Cache River and Bayou de View. The route was changed to go from the sixty-fourth mile marker southwest to the White River ferry at Mouth of Cache. William Strong had built this segment of the road in 1828. That year, as well, the road from Mouth of Cache to the headwaters of the Bayou of the Two Prairies between present-day Furlow and Jacksonville, Arkansas, was completed in fairly short order because the terrain through which it passed was high grassland known as the Grand Prairie.[5]

Meanwhile, construction had gone forward on the western end of the Memphis-to-Little Rock road. Prior to construction of the Military Road, few roads existed in the area surrounding Little Rock. In addition to the Southwest Trail from St. Louis, a road from Cadron (near

(91)

present-day Conway, Arkansas) went directly east to Crossroads, where it intersected the Southwest Trail, went on to Oakland Grove (later renamed Austin, now called Old Austin), skirted the headwaters of the Bayou Meto and the Bayou of the Two Prairies, and went southeast through the Grand Prairie to Arkansas Post. After the Military Road from Mouth of Cache to Little Rock was completed, the road from Arkansas Post was rerouted to connect with that road at Mrs. Mary Black's public house near present-day Tollville. In 1827, fifteen miles of road from Little Rock to the Bayou of the Two Prairies had been built. In addition, by the end of 1827, the Military Road from Crittenden's Ferry at Little Rock to Fort Smith had been completed.[6] When removal of the tribes from the Southeast began, a system of roads connected Memphis and Indian Territory. Although their condition was often bad, the roads had been used by the Choctaws and the Muscogees before the Chickasaws began their trek.

Departure of the first Chickasaws from the Mississippi opposite Memphis was delayed for nearly two days. They remained in camp on July 5, 1837, and waited for another group that was allegedly on its way to join them. On the following day, apparently because of some mismanagement by the Memphis ferry operator, they did not receive forage and subsistence rations until late in the day and so again did not get off. To prevent the teams from having to pull heavy loads through the swamp, Upshaw sent subsistence for the first leg of the trip by boat from Memphis, down the Mississippi, and up the St. Francis. Dr. Keenan also sent two or three Chickasaws who were ill on the supply boat to spare them the hard trip. On July 7, after a delay caused by the loss of some Chickasaw horses, the party finally struck camp at ten in the morning.[7] What Upshaw and Keenan had hoped to spare the ill Chickasaws was forty miles of the worst road conditions they would encounter as they trudged west from Memphis through the Mississippi Swamp, crossing on ferries at Blackfish Lake and the St. Francis River. From the St. Francis, the road crossed Crowley's Ridge by way of Village Creek to William Strong's public house north of present-day Forrest City.

The first day's trek was not difficult because topography was in their favor. U. S. civil engineer William Howard wrote in 1834, "A curious fact respecting the banks of the Mississippi, which has long been known, is, that these banks, where subject to being overflown, are generally the highest at the immediate edge of the stream, and the surface of the ground is found to become lower as we proceed into the swamps behind." From Memphis, this higher ground extended northward for a number of miles. The road followed this high ground to the village of Marion, where it turned to the west.[8] The Chickasaws made thirteen miles before they were forced to stop by heavy rain. On July 8, after five miles' trek, they came to the end of a newly constructed segment of the road and plunged into the swamp, which Millard called "almost impassable."[9]

Engineer Howard described in detail what they faced in what was known as the Mississippi Swamp. "The surface of this swamp presents at ordinary times," he wrote, "an alternating appearance of lakes, bayous, cypress ponds, and marshy ground. The lakes and bayous lie mostly in a direction nearly perpendicular to that of the proposed road, the former free from any growth of timber, except of cypress growing in the water close to the banks. The bayous proper are free from timber; but they frequently lie in broad and deep valleys, wooded, but less thickly than the higher ground, and containing comparatively little undergrowth. The valleys are, in many cases, inundated to the depth of fifteen or twenty feet, or even more. The ponds are mostly filled with very large cypress trees growing in the water, where the depth does not exceed three or four feet, except in time of overflow. The marshy ground is filled with trees of immense size, principally gum and sycamore in the lower places, and white oak and hickory in those that are a little higher and dryer, having occasional brakes of cane, very thickly set, and frequently rising to the height of twenty or thirty feet, and of proportionate diameter."[10]

The party reached Blackfish Lake about half way between the Mississippi and the St. Francis, minus two wagons, which had bogged down in mud and were left on the road two miles east of the lake. The next day was spent at the lake, which Millard described as about 150 yards wide: "The water is clear and its surface smooth, although there is a tolerably strong current, which empties into the St. Francis." The Chickasaws spent July 9 crossing the lake, bringing up the wagons, horses, and people who had been left on the road the day before, and resting the horses, fatigued during the twelve-mile march of the previous day.[11]

On July 10 they took up the march again, passing the heads of Shell Lake and Bevin's Lake, traveling "over boggy roads and through mud and water," frequently up to the axletrees of the wagons. "The distance we came today," wrote Millard, "is about eight miles and by every person acquainted with the roads considered a good drive." The party crossed the St. Francis on William Strong's ferry, and on July 11 they camped three miles west of the St. Francis, apparently near William Strong's residence, thankful, Millard said, that "good fortune has taken us through the great Mississippi swamp." They were, at the time, near or within the confines of present-day Village Creek State Park, where segments of the road they traveled are still dramatically visible. There they were joined by the few convalescing sick, who had been sent up the St. Francis aboard the supply boat. William Strong's place for several years had provided a welcome respite for travelers who had trekked through the Mississippi Swamp. He had been a contractor for the Memphis to Little Rock road and ran a store and a post office known as St. Francis.[12] Strong had made a good bit of money from earlier removal parties of Choctaws and Muscogees. His place had earned the reputation of being one of the public houses that had been erected at intervals on the Military Road for the accommodation of travelers. The Sealy district party remained in camp at Strong's on July 12, repairing wagons, "adjusting the baggage, examining the rolls and attending to other indispensable business."[13]

The next leg of their journey took them toward the White River crossing. They went west, across the L'Anguille River, which was bridged, to the sixty-fourth mile west of Memphis, where they turned southwest, to Mouth of Cache and the ferry across the White River. When they took to the road on July 13, Millard said, a few of the party "lingered behind at a grocery," probably William Strong's, and got drunk. During the next four days, the Chickasaws made their way over a bad road, made boggy by continued heavy rain, spending their nights at places Millard named Camp L'Anguille, Cypress Camp, Camp Upshaw, and Camp Keeling. At the latter on July 16, they were joined by 39 Chickasaws who had followed them, bringing the number of the party to about 500.[14] This party was apparently conducted by Alexander Mizell, who had been up and down the line of march from their outset from the Mississippi opposite Memphis. He had traveled with the main party beyond Marion, but on the day they reached Blackfish Lake, he had returned to Marion and the next day to the Mississippi, apparently to pick up the new party. Two days later, he was back at Marion and reached William Strong's on the St. Francis a day after the main party had departed. On July 16, he, along with the small party, joined the main party on the road to the White River.[15] On July 17, the combined parties traveled the fourteen miles from Camp Keeling to Mouth of Cache,[16] which was little more than a plantation and a cluster of a few cabins.

One major obstacle remained between the party and the Grand Prairie: the White River bottoms. They spent July 18 and part of the next day crossing the river on a ferryboat that was in a bad condition. Later on the nineteenth, they traveled four miles through the bottoms and camped at a bridge that spanned Rock Roe Bayou. A few Chickasaws had fallen ill, but Dr. Keenan apparently treated them successfully.[17]

Travelers generally found the next leg of their journey much easier than what they had encountered since Memphis. From the White River bottoms, the road passed westerly across the Grand Prairie to Brownsville, just north of present-day Lonoke, west from there to present-day Jacksonville, where it joined the old Southwest Trail, turned south, crossed the Bayou Meto, which had been bridged, followed the old trail to the Arkansas River east of present-day North Little Rock, turned southwest, and followed the edge of the river bottom to the ferry opposite Little Rock.

Because of the heat, the Chickasaws traveled primarily at night through the Grand Prairie. A vast grassland dotted with groves of oak and other timber, it stretched north and south between the White River and the Bayou Meto watersheds. Though usually dry in summer, which made traveling easy, it was infested with green biting flies that plagued travelers and their animals during the daytime. Leaving Rock Roe Bridge at six in the evening of July 20, the Chickasaw party reached Mrs. Mary Black's before daylight the next day. In 1835, George

(95)

A. McCall described Mrs. Black and her place as follows: "I found Mrs. Black a widow of goodly proportions: I have seen fatter women, but not many. She had several sons and daughters growing up. She kept a public (being the half-way) house between Little Rock and White River. The house was a log building, a point of fine timber land stretching out from the south to within half a mile of the house, which was one of those structures called in the West *'two pens and a passage,'* which means two rooms from ten to twenty feet apart, the whole under one roof. One of these was the dining-room, the other the sleeping-room; the kitchen and other apartments occupied by the family, built likewise of logs, were in the rear." At Mrs. Black's, the Chickasaws found rations that the government had sent from Little Rock.[18]

The party continued to camp during the day and travel at night. By July 23, they were "encamped on a small bayou about ten miles east of Little Rock" at a place Millard called Camp Phillips. The following day, the train of thirteen wagons traveled by daylight, arriving at the north bank of the Arkansas River opposite Little Rock at 4:00 p.m., "after a warm drive." Others had joined them on the road so that the party numbered 516, and they were driving a herd of about 500 horses. Another group of about thirty Chickasaws who had not enrolled for removal with the party were still on the road and were expected to catch up.[19]

On July 26, the Chickasaws remained in camp on the north bank of the Arkansas, apparently preparing for the final leg of their journey, which Millard mistakenly thought would take them up the Military Road on the north side of the Arkansas River to Dardanelle Ferry, where they would cross the river and take the Military Road from there to Fort Coffee. That day, Lieutenant Gouverneur Morris arrived at Little Rock on his way from Fort Coffee to Pontotoc. Phillips appointed him disbursing agent to accompany the Chickasaws from Little Rock to Fort Coffee. Assuming that everything was in order, Phillips started back to Memphis.[20] However, problems developed. Late in the day, Morris came to Millard with news that rations had not been distributed along the road because of a lack of wagons. That mattered little to the Chickasaws, who had decided not to follow the road up the Arkansas anyway. Emmubbee, a chief of the nation, had told them that they should take the Little Rock-to-Washington road to the Red River country. That night Millard wrote, "The Indians after being twice in council concluded to disobey the wishes of the conductor and go as they had been directed by their chief. After much persuasion however they, by way of compromise, agreed that their women, children and infirm should go on board the steamer *Indian* and proceed to the Choctaw Nation by water, and that the young men with the chief Sealy should go by land with the horses."[21]

All was made ready for departure on July 27. Millard thought the affair of the previous day had been settled. However, he wrote, "The baggage was scarcely on board the boat when Sealy the chief came and informed me that about 300 of his men, would go with him by way of Fort Towson and would go no other way. They could not be persuaded from this intention by all the arguments and instructions of the conductors and such citizens of Little Rock as were acquainted with the Indian character and the country through which they were compelled to pass. They were told the comparative distance of the routes and the impossibility of procuring food on any but the Fort Coffee road, as the rations purchased for them were deposited at that place, but they could not be shaken from their determination." At three in the afternoon of July 27, Lieutenant Morris, Dr. Keenan, and Millard left for Fort Coffee in the steamer *Indian* with the baggage and about 150 Chickasaws. Assistant conductor W. R. Guy left Little Rock with a party of thirty-eight Chickasaws, fifty-eight horses, and three wagons by way of the Military Road toward Fort Coffee. The Chickasaws headed by Sealy, Millard wrote, "were determined to go to Red River and stop when and where they pleased."[22]

Though Millard, Phillips, and Morris were baffled at Sealy's actions, they might not have been if they had understood the respect commanded by Emmubbee. Phillips called him "an old and respected chief, recently killed." [23] He was, in fact, a respected warrior who had served under General Andrew Jackson in his campaigns and was councilor to Ishtehotopa, the last hereditary minko of the Chickasaw people.[24] Far from simply being recalcitrant, Sealy was following the advice of a respected leader. Of more significance, perhaps, is the identity of Sealy that Millard refers to. At Little Rock, Millard attributes the leadership to Sealy. Later in the journey, he calls Ehochetubby [Eiochetubby] the "principal" leader. This apparently was the same person as Eoichetubby, whom Emmubbee had called one of the "good" district chiefs during the period just prior to removal. Thomas Sealy, Jerry Sealy, and Josiah Sealy are the only Sealys specifically identified with the party. At any rate, both Eiochetubby and Thomas Sealy had been part of the Chickasaw exploring party in 1830 and had traveled the road from Little Rock to the Red River, both going and returning. Apparently, going to the Red River had been the plan from the start and may explain why Upshaw could not persuade the Chickasaws to travel by water from Memphis.

Of the trip upriver with the small party, Millard wrote, "We arrived at Fort Coffee Aug. 1st five days from the Rock without any accident—save the loss of one woman by drowning. She fell from the boat and was drowned before assistance could reach her. Every exertion was used but in vain." Interestingly, the drowning was the only death Millard recorded after the party left Memphis. Morris reported that the victim was fourteen years old and drowned on July 29. There was some sickness but all responded to medical treatment.[25] At Fort Coffee, Upshaw paid $1,500 to Simeon Buckner, the Louisville boat owner whose *Indian* had taken the Chickasaws up from Little Rock, and left the Chickasaws with Gaines P. Kingsbury, the newly appointed Chickasaw agent for removal in the West.[26]

Meanwhile, Guy's small overland party made its way along the Military Road. On July 30 they crossed Emzy Wilson's bridge over Palarm Creek; on July 31 Thomas Mathers' ferry over Cadron Creek near present-day Conway; and on August 2 Frederick Fletcher's ferry over Point Remove Creek. They crossed the Arkansas River on Samuel Norris's ferry at Dardanelle, and followed the military road south of the river to Fort Coffee.[27]

Upshaw's concerns at Memphis, that agents might not be available to receive the Chickasaws, proved unfounded. Captain Jacob Brown, disbursing agent for Indian removal stationed at Little Rock, had appointed Kingsbury Chickasaw agent on June 11, following Commissioner Harris's direction to find an agent for the Chickasaws. Kingsbury had reported for duty on June 14 to William Armstrong, superintendent of Indian affairs for the Western District, stationed at the Choctaw Agency West. Armstrong, who was sometimes authoritarian and often petulant, complained to the commissioner of Indian affairs that Brown should have consulted him before he appointed Kingsbury, and because no Chickasaws had arrived at the time Kingsbury reported for duty, Armstrong said there was nothing for the agent to do. Despite Armstrong's apparent displeasure at having Kingsbury on hand, the young man would prove a valuable agent to the Chickasaws. A former dragoon, he had served with his father-in-law Colonel Henry Dodge on a peace mission to the western Indians, commissioned in 1835 by Andrew Jackson, and had marched through, and was familiar with, much of the land the Chickasaws were to occupy. Armstrong's opposition to Kingsbury may have been political. Kingsbury had some strong family connections to people in political offices. Besides his connection to Dodge, he was also a brother-in-law of Senator Lewis F. Linn, known as the "Model Senator" of Ste. Genevieve, Missouri.[28] Or was Armstrong simply reluctant to share authority in his territory? Facts later showed that Armstrong had his hand in the fraud being perpetrated on the Chickasaws. On the other hand, it was clear from Harris's order to hire an agent that he intended the agent to have limited authority and report to Armstrong and Upshaw.

While Millard was traveling up river, the party headed by Thomas Sealy and Eiochetubby had started on their way toward Fort Towson. The entire party probably camped opposite Little Rock near the Woodruff and Mills Ferry, where they could take advantage of their free lots for horses, mules, and cattle. The ferry owners, as well, kept a supply of corn and fodder for sale.[29] The route that the Chickasaws took from Little Rock went through Saline, Hot Spring, Clarke, Pike, and Sevier counties before entering the Choctaw Nation. Unlike the terrain they had been through, this was hilly and heavily wooded.

After Millard and Morris left their group at Fort Coffee, they turned back to Little Rock to overtake the larger group on the road to Fort Towson and escort them along the remainder of the trail. Millard, who had been a removal agent for other tribes, was perplexed by the independent mood of the Chickasaws. He called them "the refractory and ungovernable Indians, who broke off from the main party in defiance

(99)

of every effort of the agents." With Millard and Morris went Daniel C. McCurtain, a Choctaw interpreter sent along at the insistence of Superintendent Armstrong. Morris, though angry at the Chickasaws, laid part of the blame for the "rebellion" on Phillips. After the fact, he criticized Phillips for deserting the party and returning to Memphis at the time of the difficulties, which he should have helped resolve before leaving Little Rock. Morris was at a disadvantage, he believed, because he was a stranger to the Chickasaws and could exercise little authority over them. Perhaps that is why he felt it his "duty" to go with Millard in pursuit of the Chickasaws on their way to the Red River, to help as he could to furnish supplies and see to their arrival on their new lands.[30] The two agents apparently did not realize that it was the Chickasaws, and not they, who were in charge.

When Sealy vowed that the Chickasaws under his leadership would travel at their own pace to the Red River country, he meant it. During the two weeks after the Chickasaws left Little Rock, the advance party traveled only thirty-five miles, with others trailing behind. On August 10, Millard and Morris overtook a group of seventy to eighty Chickasaws only five miles from Little Rock. A number of them were very sick, and Millard tried to persuade them to return to Little Rock and take a steamboat, where provisions had been arranged. However, Millard wrote, "They declared they would sooner die than change the way they had determined to go." Millard had little choice but to hire a wagon to carry the sick. The following day, he and Morris found about twenty more encamped eleven miles down the road. Here, too, was sickness. One woman had died and another woman and child were ill with bilious fever, the most common illness during the hot season in Arkansas. Morris procured medicine from a local doctor and hired another wagon to carry the sick and baggage. They took up the march once more in pursuit of the main group, whom they overtook on August 12. They were on the Saline River near the new village of Benton, established the year before. While Millard set about getting organized, he lodged at the well-known public house of Mrs. William Lockhert and at the house of Joseph Clift, from whom he bought fresh beef, corn, and salt. Because they found provisions scarce and difficult to purchase on the route, Millard and Morris hired wagons to go back to Little Rock to obtain supplies from the government warehouses. Thus they went into camp and spent a day bringing up the sick and the scattered Chickasaws to join the main party. On August 13, the entire party was united in their camp only thirty-five miles from Little Rock. That morning a little boy died.[31]

During the next four days, the Chickasaws made little progress, much to the consternation of Millard and Morris. On August 14, Millard wrote, "The Indians felt no desire nor could they be moved today, they gave the excuse, that they could not find their horses, that most of their men were engaged in hunting them, and that they had reason to believe a great many were stolen by the whites, which I think is very possible. The deer moreover, abounded in great numbers at this place and the hunters were very successful in killing them, which rendered them more reluctant than otherwise to remove." On August 15 they had gone only two-and-a-half miles when a heavy shower fell, and they refused to go on. Millard had hired teams of local residents to haul the sick.[32] Most of the sick were convalescing, but two who were extremely ill refused to ride a horse or be placed in a wagon and had to be carried on litters. The next day, the Chickasaws traveled only three miles and camped. "Five venison stopped their progress," Millard wrote; "they went early in the morning to hunt up their horses, and came in loaded with deer." On August 17, the supply wagons and a few of the Chickasaws traveled twelve miles to the Ouachita Crossing, at present-day Rockport, where they camped, waiting for the others to catch up. The followers went only two-and-a-half miles and camped, and remained in camp all the next day. On August 19, Millard and Morris retraced their trail from the Ouachita, and when they arrived at the camp, many of the Chickasaws were out hunting.[33] On that day, Millard bought fresh beef and supplied the sick with coffee, sugar, and chickens.[34]

The Chickasaws were clearly traveling slowly in order to hunt. They were passing through some of the richest hunting lands in the Southwest, and they were enjoying some of the best hunting that the older Chickasaws had experienced in years and better than some of the younger Chickasaws had ever seen. In 1830, a report to the secretary of war stated that game had declined in the Chickasaw country and that it could no longer support a hunting economy. Instead, the report said,

(101)

the Chickasaws were shifting to cotton culture and domestic herding. One historian has argued that the report may have been sugared by wishful thinking, for it had long been the argument of "civilization" theorists that a decline in hunting meant that Indians needed less land to support themselves by agriculture.[35] Wishful thinking or not, there can be little doubt that as more Chickasaw land was converted to agriculture, the game supply declined. The region through which the Chickasaws were traveling in Arkansas was not prime agricultural land. It was sparsely settled, and game abounded. Their ability to supply their daily needs with wild game demonstrated their independence. The government had not placed rations along this route, but for two weeks they had managed their own subsistence. There was no reason why they should stop hunting and depend on Millard, who, with Morris, was continually busy trying to procure goods and services from Arkansans along the way.

The slow progress of the removal party also worked against them. They were beset by horse thieves and whiskey sellers, who may have been one and the same. Because the Chickasaws had diverged from the original route, no forage for their animals was waiting. Forage was hard to find, forcing the Chickasaws to let their horses loose at night to graze, putting bells on the animals to help locate them in the mornings. Soon after they left Little Rock, they began to lose horses to thieves. On August 14, Millard wrote, "Found all the horses but five which had their Bells cut off, and from the appearance and direction of their tracks had been driven off and stolen in the night. Some citizens in spite of our exertions and demonstrances for a few days past in particular, and indeed during the whole route from the Rock had for a little base lucre, succeeded in selling ardent spirits to the Indians, occasioning dissatisfaction, riot and disorder among them."[36] These problems unfortunately plagued the Chickasaws as long as they were in Arkansas.

By August 19, Millard and Morris had run out of patience regarding the delays. They called for the camp to assemble and held a talk with the principal men. Millard told them in plain terms that their behavior was "unaccountable and singular" and that he expected them to change their ways and follow his orders. Morris read them a letter he had drafted to the commanding officer at Fort Towson, informing him that the Chickasaws had "refused to proceed, they throw their baggage out of the teams which have been provided for their transportation, say they will have their own time and manner to get to their country, and seem to take great satisfaction in disregarding all directions and orders they receive from us." Although the Chickasaws had not exhibited tendencies to be hostile, Morris said, "There is something behind their actions, something I cannot account for." He asked the commander at Fort Towson to dispatch two companies of infantry to force the Chickasaws along. After Morris read the letter, he addressed the Chickasaws, telling them that if they would promise to keep up with the supply wagons and march eight to ten miles each day, he would not forward the letter to Fort Towson. If they would not march, the troops would force them, at the point of a bayonet if necessary. At that, they agreed to comply with orders and march the required distance.[37] It was probably due to their own choice rather than Morris's threats, as Gibson has concluded, that the Chickasaws more or less complied with orders during the remainder of the trek. The weather was hot, the terrain was changing, and the good hunting grounds were playing out. Morris's language makes one point clear: it was the Chickasaws, not he and Millard, who were in charge of the group's movements.

On August 20, the entire party encamped at the Ouachita crossing, where the horses were allowed to graze on cane growing in the bottoms. The ferry keepers at Ouachita Crossing were likely some of the local suppliers of whiskey. Located at present-day Rockport, the business at the crossing had all of the earmarks of a public house on the well-traveled road from Little Rock to Washington and Fulton on the Red River. Formerly of Little Rock, Lorenzo and William R. Gibson sold dry goods, groceries, and liquors. They dealt in cash or traded "for cotton, peltries, furs, and the usual products of the country." They also maintained "a house of entertainment," they said, "for the accommodation of travelers, emigrants and others who may call on them, and will endeavor to keep it supplied with the best the country affords."[38] Whether the Chickasaws crossed on the ferry on August 20 or August 21 is uncertain.

Chickasaw progress during the next few days must have pleased Millard and Morris. On the morning of August 21, an infant died, and

(103)

after five miles most of the Chickasaws stopped to bury it while a few of them and three wagons continued on eight miles and camped. On August 22, the main group caught up, and the entire party continued six miles farther to Prairie Bayou. There the Chickasaws enjoyed the last good hunt of the journey, as Millard said, nearly all the camp being supplied with venison and turkey. There, too, the horse stealing began again, the Chickasaws losing "several fine horses." On August 23, the party reached Jacob Barkman's at the Caddo crossing, now known as Caddo Valley, where they remained two days, bringing up stragglers and procuring fresh beef.[39]

Barkman's place was as well known to travelers between Little Rock and Texas as Mrs. Black's was to those traveling between Memphis and Little Rock. Barkman, who had been in the area since 1811, was known widely for his annual horseracing season. He used two ancient Caddoan mounds that sat near the trail as a reviewing stand for his track. Rebecca, his wife, was a heavy, rough-talking, pipe-smoking woman who was prone to fist fighting with men who got out of hand. A former judge and state legislator, Barkman was wealthy by standards of the day. He supplied beef to the Chickasaws, so Millard hired him to transport the sick and also hired a local teamster to haul supplies.[40]

On August 25, the Chickasaws were two miles west of Antoine Bridge, near present-day Antoine, where they were able to purchase more fresh beef. There the horse thieves struck again. Millard wrote, "It appears that there were a gang of horse thieves who followed the Indians and robbed them when ever they could get an opportunity, notwithstanding all the precaution the Indians took to guard their camp." The next day at Cox's Stand, they lost more horses. The route the party took from Antoine diverged from the old Southwest Trail, which the Choctaws had taken a few years earlier to Washington before they turned west to Fort Towson. The road from Antoine to Fort Towson had been cut only two years earlier. From Antoine Bridge, it crossed the Little Missouri River; the Cossatot, the Rolling Fork, and intersected the road from Washington to Fort Towson.[41]

At Murfreesboro on August 27, they encountered the whiskey sellers again. That day they camped at the Little Missouri River, three miles west of the town. "The citizens of this place evinced great desire," Millard said, "to sell ardent spirits to the Indians. They followed the train three miles to the River with a large supply of whiskey and introduced it in camp the next morning at the very moment the Indians had mounted their horses to start, and in fact after about one half of them had taken the road." The following morning the wagons and a third of the Chickasaws went on to Brier Creek, where Millard procured beef for the party. Eiochetubby, whom Millard called the "principal" leader, and the rest of the party remained at the Little Missouri River with the whiskey peddlers. When they caught up to the lead party the next morning, several of them were still intoxicated.[42]

The party remained intact for the most part during the remainder of the journey. The country they passed through on August 29 and 30 was "a scrub oak barren" with little or no grass. Because so many Chickasaw horses had been lost or stolen, Millard directed the Chickasaws to keep their horses in camp, instead of letting them range, and procured fodder for them from local farmers. Good water was also scarce. On August 30 they camped on Holly Creek and the next day a mile and a half east of the Cossatot River, where they remained the next day because of the illness of Sealy's son. On September 2, they camped at a "big" spring within ten miles of the Choctaw line. Morris took the teams on to the line at Ultima Thule, where he discharged and paid the teamsters and purchased beef and corn. The party moved up to the line on September 3 and camped on Rock Creek, where they remained the next day to bury Sealy's child. On September 5, Millard and Morris went ahead to David Folsom's place, twenty-two miles west of the line, where the party was to assemble and receive rations and be enrolled. Morris made a contract with Folsom, a Choctaw, to provide subsistence for the Chickasaws. Because Agent G. P. Kingsbury was not there, Millard remained until September 9, when the last of the stragglers came in, and made a muster roll. On September 10, Millard and Morris started for Fort Coffee on their way to Pontotoc to assist Upshaw with removal efforts there. In reporting on the journey, Millard wrote, "This emigration has perhaps caused the Agents more exposure, and vexation and expense than any that has been made."[43]

Kingsbury was not at Fort Towson when the Chickasaws arrived because he had been preparing for settlement of the Chickasaws in

(105)

their new country. Immediately upon their arrival at Fort Coffee on July 31, the group of 170 that Millard had conducted from Little Rock by steamboat had wanted to go directly to the district set aside for them. However, two problems had to be overcome. First, it was impractical to transport provisions from Fort Coffee to the Chickasaw district in the western Choctaw Nation; the cost of transporting them would have been more than the provisions were worth. Kingsbury knew the country well. The group wanted to settle sixty miles from the Cross Timbers near the mouth of the False Washita, where General Leavenworth had established a temporary post in 1834. Though Leavenworth had ordered a road cut from Fort Coffee to Fort Towson and Fort Gibson, no road led to the lands the Chickasaws wanted to reach. Kingsbury suggested that if the Indians insisted on going to their country immediately, it might prove advantageous to exchange the provisions at Fort Coffee for beef cattle that could be driven to the Chickasaw country or to sell the provisions and buy corn and beef on the Red River, much closer to their destination.[44]

The second problem of concern to Kingsbury was that the Chickasaws were settling in areas remote from military posts and would therefore be exposed to raids by the Indians to the west. They would be open, he said, "to the predatory incursions of the wild Indians, the Comanches, Kiowas, and Pawnee Picts, and would in a short time have all their horses stolen from them, which might lead to more fatal result." Kingsbury believed that the post on the Washita should be reactivated and another built in the vicinity to protect the Chickasaws. Meanwhile, he urged the newly arrived Chickasaws to camp in the vicinity of Fort Coffee to let their horses recover from their journey and send parties out to explore all of the new country before they decided where to settle permanently. The Chickasaws took his advice and settled at a "good spring" near the Choctaw Agency.[45]

Whether the latter advice originated with Kingsbury or William Armstrong is uncertain, for Armstrong claimed he advised them the same. He was apparently still pouting about not being consulted about Kingsbury's appointment, and was clearly working to get Kingsbury out of his region. There was little need for a Chickasaw agent, he argued, and he suggested to the commissioner of Indian affairs that Kings-

(106)

bury be sent to the Red River. There he could be useful as an agent to both the Chickasaws and Choctaws, while Armstrong could take care of the Chickasaws that settled near the Choctaw Agency. Whether Armstrong really thought this the best plan or was simply jealous of his territory and his authority, he envisioned future Chickasaw settlement patterns differently from Kingsbury. He had little doubt, he said, that perhaps half of the Chickasaws would settle "promiscuously with the Choctaws." The wealthy ones who wanted to farm cotton would settle "on Red River below Towson in Oaklafaliah district," and those who wanted to raise livestock would "settle promiscuously through the nation." As evidence, he stated that a number of Chickasaws had already settled near Fort Towson and had bought improvements from the Choctaws.[46]

The anomalous position in which Armstrong attempted to place Kingsbury had prompted the latter to ask Commissioner Harris to clarify his duties and chain of command. Was he under the direction of Armstrong, Brown, Collins, Upshaw, Morris, or some other person?[47] This query was apparently in response to not only Armstrong's concerns but also the roster of the Chickasaws and the subsistence contract with David Folsom that Millard and Morris, respectively, had made at Fort Towson.

Fortunately, Kingsbury's quandary regarding the 170 Chickasaws at Fort Coffee was quickly resolved. By early September they had decided to settle on the Canadian near Pheasant Bluff, about thirty miles above Fort Coffee. Kingsbury hired teams to transport them and a month's provisions to their final destination. Shortly thereafter, he went to Fort Towson to deal with the remainder of the party.[48]

When Kingsbury arrived in the Red River country, he found the group encamped near Folsom's place about thirty-five miles below Fort Towson, where they had received rations since their arrival. He called the principal men together and told them what they already knew: that their decision to take the southern route from Little Rock had greatly increased the expense of removal because the northern route had been oversupplied, the surplus provisions would likely spoil, and new contracts for provisions had to be made in the south. On their part, the Chickasaws claimed that it had been their intent to take the southern route from the start and that the chiefs who made arrangements for the route to Fort Coffee had done so without their consent. In fact, it had not been the chiefs who had made the decision, but War Department officials in the West. Kingsbury found the Chickasaws anxious to go to their country on the False Washita. He promised to get them there as soon as possible and urged them to send out an exploring party to find desirable locations for settlement. Meanwhile, he arranged for Folsom to continue supplying them until December, and he again recommended to the commissioner of Indian affairs that a military post be established on the False Washita to protect them and to serve as a depot for provisions. He also said that when the time came to remove the Chickasaws farther west, a number of teams would be needed to transport them to the Washita. The government could make agreements with the Chickasaws who owned slaves to supply the drivers, and at the end of the journey, the government could likely sell the wagons for more than it paid for them because of the scarcity of such items in the west.[49] Although both Kingsbury and Armstrong expected the Chickasaws to move away from Folsom's, some of them, in fact, remained there.

After his meeting with the Chickasaws, Kingsbury and a few of them went back to Arkansas to see if they could retrieve some of the many horses the party had lost to thievery. At Murfreesboro, they found the people helpful in finding the thieves and recovering the horses. One man was jailed and sentenced to death, and seven horses were recovered. From there, they worked their way to Little Rock in search of others.[50]

The loss of horses was only one way the removal of the first party had been costly. The decision at Little Rock to take the southern rather than the northern route added costs to the supplies that had already been placed along the northern route. Rations that the government had expected the Chickasaws to consume continued to spoil at Fort Coffee. This removal made it clear that the Chickasaws were willing to pay whatever it cost to do things their own way, a point they made clear again and again as removal continued.

NOTES

1. "Chickasaw History According to Malcom [sic] McGee," *http://www. chickasawhistory.com/mcgee.htm*, retrieved January 1, 2004. According to Malcolm McGee, the Sealys descended from Ben Sealy, a Virginian who came to the Chickasaw Nation as a boy and died a very old man shortly after the War of 1812 at his home at the mouth of the Tippah on the Tallahatchie.

2. Joseph A. Phillips to C. A. Harris, July 4, 1837 (Chickasaw Emigration P151), National Archives Microfilm Publications Microcopy M234, Roll 143, hereafter cited as M234 followed by the roll number; M. B. Winchester receipt, August 31, 1837, 27th Congress, 3rd Session, *House Document 65*, p. 10, hereafter cited as *House Document 65;* "Muster Roll of Chickasaw Indians about to Emigrate West of the Mississippi River, under the Direction of John M. Millard in the Month of June, 1837," National Archives Microfilm, Special Filming, Chickasaw 1847 Census. Of the heads of households on the roll, only twelve bore English or part-English names.

3. Memphis story reported in *Army and Navy Chronicle* 5 (August 3, 1837), 75; Oliver E. Thorp Receipt, July 31, 1837, C. G. Kennan Receipt, July 31, 1837, Alexander Mizell Receipt, July 24, 1837, John L. Mizell Receipt, July 6, 1837, National Archives Record Group 217, Records of the U. S. Department of the Treasury, Accounting Officers of the Department of the Treasury, E524, Chickasaw Payments, 1833–66, Box 2, File 22, J. A. Phillips. E524 is hereafter cited as Chickasaw Payments.

4. A. M. M. Upshaw to Harris, July 4, 1837 (Chickasaw Emigration U14), M234-R143.

5. For details of the funding, planning, and construction of these roads, see Julia Ward Longnecker, "A Road Divided: From Memphis to Little Rock through the Great Mississippi Swamp," *Arkansas Historical Quarterly* 44 (Autumn 1985), 203–19.

6. "Military Roads," *American State Papers*, Military Affairs (1831), 4: 27. See also *Arkansas Gazette*, February 25, 1825; January 3, 1826; March 20, June 12, August 21, September 4 and 18, October 2 and 30, November 13, and December 4, 1827; January 8, 1828. For Gray's involvement in road and bridge construction, see Carolyn Yancey Little, "Samson Gray and the Bayou Meto Settlement, 1820–1836," *Pulaski County Historical Review* 39 (Spring 1984): 2–16.

7. Journal of Occurrences in J. M. Millard to Harris, September 23, 1837 (Chickasaw Emigration M220), M234-R143, hereafter cited as Journal of Occurrences; Arrell M. Gibson, *The Chickasaws* (Norman: University of Oklahoma Press, 1971), 183–84.

8. 23rd Congress, 2nd Session, *House Document 83*, 3, 4, hereafter cited as *House Document 83*.

9. Journal of Occurrences (Chickasaw Emigration M220).

10. *House Document 83*, 4.

11. Journal of Occurrences (Chickasaw Emigration M220); *Document 83*, 6.

12. Journal of Occurrences (Chickasaw Emigration M220); *Arkansas Gazette*, November 29, 1835, August 9, 1836, and April 18, 1837; William Strong receipt, August 29, 1837, *House Document 65*, 10, hereafter cited as *House Document 65*.

13. Journal of Occurrences (Chickasaw Emigration M220); S. Norris receipt, August 3, 1837, *House Document 65*, 7.

14. Journal of Occurrences (Chickasaw Emigration M220).

15. Alexander Mizell Memorandum of Expenses, July 24, 1837, Chickasaw Payments, Box 2, File 22, J. A. Phillips.

16. Journal of Occurrences (Chickasaw M220); Jo Claire English, *Pages from the Past: Historical Notes on Clarendon, Monroe County and Early Arkansas* (Clarendon, AR: J. C. English, 1976), 48. Parts of the road traveled by the Chickasaws are still visible. Some remarkable segments of it west of Strong's place are accessible to hikers in Village Creek State Park, and parts of the road near Zent where it entered present-day Monroe County have been placed on the National Register of Historic Places. The part of the journey west of Strong's took them along the approximate route of present-day Highway 306 to the vicinity of Hunter, and from there along Highway 49 to present-day Brinkley, passing through Zent, where a portion of the road is preserved today. From Brinkley, the route followed what is now Highway 70 and then 302 to Clarendon, the present name for Mouth of Cache.

17. Journal of Occurrences (Chickasaw Emigration M220), M234-R143. Rock Roe Bridge has been tentatively located at or near Hart Lake, and the road just north of Highway 79 that goes through Hart Hill; G. W. Ferebee receipt, August 24, 1837, *Document 65*, p. 10. See English, *Pages from the Past*, 21.

18. Journal of Occurrences (Chickasaw Emigration M220); M. O. Hogan Receipt, July 22, 1837, and P. McGraw Receipt, July 25, 1837, *Document 65*, 10, 25. McCall's statement is reprinted in *http://anpa.ualr.edu/trail__of__tears/indian__removal__project/people/Black__Mary.htm*, retrieved July 1, 2008.

19. Journal of Occurrences (Chickasaw Emigration M220); Gibson, *The Chickasaws*, 184; *Arkansas Gazette*, July 25, 1837; Phillips to Harris, July 30, 1837 (Chickasaw Emigration P167), M234-R143; *Arkansas Advocate*, July 31, 1837.

20. Phillips to Harris, July 30, 1837 (Chickasaw Emigration P167), M234-R143.

21. Journal of Occurrences (Chickasaw Emigration M220).

22. Journal of Occurrences, Phillips to Harris, July 30, 1837, and Gouverneur Morris to Harris, August 2, 1837 (Chickasaw Emigration M220, P167 and M180), M234-R143; *Arkansas Gazette*, July 25, August 1, and August 15, 1837.

23. Phillips to Harris, July 30, 1837 (Chickasaw Emigration P167), M234-R143.

24. Gibson, *The Chickasaws*, 188; *Army and Navy Chronicle* 5 (August 3, 1837), 75.

25. Journal of Occurrences, Millard to Harris, September 23, 1837 (Chickasaw Emigration M220), M234-R143.

26. Morris to Harris, August 2, 1837 (Chickasaw Emigration M180), M234-R143.

27. *Ibid.*; Emzy Wilson Receipt, July 30, 1837, Thomas Mathers Receipt, July 31, 1837, and Frederick Fletcher Receipt, August 2, 1837, Chickasaw Payments, Box 1, File 16, Summary: Receipts.

28. G. P. Kingsbury to Harris, June 14, 1837, William Armstrong to Harris, June 18, 1837, and Jacob Brown to Harris, August 2, 1837 (Chickasaw Emigration K24, A200 and B281), M234-R143; Armstrong to T. Hartley Crawford, July 29, 1839, http://www.chickasawhistory.com/CHICl__39.htm, retrieved November 1, 2004; Harris to Brown, May 5, 1837, Chickasaw Vol. 1, pp 159–60, National Archives Record Group 75, Records of the Commissary General of Subsistence, Entry 253, Chickasaw Removal Records.

29. *Arkansas Gazette*, October 18, 1836.

30. Journal of Occurrences, Millard to Harris, September 23, 1837, Journal of Emigration, September 17, 1837 (referred to hereafter as Journal of Emigration), and Morris to Harris, August 2, 1837 (Chickasaw Emigration M220, M225, and M180), M234-R143; *Arkansas Gazette*, July 25, August 1, and August 15, 1837.

31. Journal of Emigration, September 17, 1837 (Chickasaw Emigration M225), M234-143. F. A. McWilliams Receipt, August 11, 1837, John Millard Account, September 30, 1837, Joseph Clift Receipt, August 15, 1837, Chickasaw Payments, Box 4, File 25, Capt. Gouverneur Morris. Gibson, *The Chickasaws*, 185, says, "Whereas during the early phases of the migration only an occasional death, burial, and extended family mourning had occurred, by early August the number of daily burials had increased to as many as four or five in a single day." The statement leaves the impression that the mortality rate was high in this group. How

Gibson drew this conclusion is uncertain, for Millard's daily journal does not indicate a large number of deaths, as the following narrative shows.

32. *Ibid.*; Receipts, August 14 and 16, 1837, *House Document 65*, p. 7.

33. Journal of Emigration, September 17, 1837 (Chickasaw Emigration M225), M234-143. Grant Foreman, *Indian Removal* (Norman: University of Oklahoma Press, 1972), 213, says that on August 16, Morris issued rations at Hot Springs. The party was in Hot Spring County between present-day Benton and Rockport. This unfortunate error has led many local historians to conclude that the removal route went through Hot Springs. It was, in fact, many miles away from that site.

34. Receipts, August 19, 1837, *House Document 65*, p. 7.

35. Gibson, *The Chickasaws*, 138—40.

36. Journal of the Emigration (Chickasaw Emigration M225), M234-143.

37. *Ibid.*; Gibson, *The Chickasaws*, 185, leaves the erroneous impression that the Chickasaws decided to move on in response to the threat of troops.

38. *Arkansas Gazette*, May 30, 1837.

39. Journal of the Emigration (Chickasaw Emigration M225), M234-143.

40. Receipts, August 22, 23, and 24, 1837, *Document 65*, p. 8; J. Barkman Receipt, August 22, 1837, Chickasaw Payments, Box 4, File 25, Gouverneur Morris.

41. Journal of the Emigration (Chickasaw Emigration M225), M234-143; Foreman, *Indian Removal*, 211; *Arkansas Advocate*, December 4, 1835; T. O'Neal Receipt, August 25, 1837, and Samuel Hosley Receipt, August 25, 1837, Chickasaw Payments, Box 4, File 25, Gouverneur Morris.

42. Journal of the Emigration (Chickasaw Emigration M225), M234-143; J. Green Receipt, August 28, 1837, Chickasaw Payments, Box 4, File 25, Gouverneur Morris.

43. *Ibid.*; Receipts August 29, August 30, and September 2, *Document 65*, p. 8; C. Stewart Receipt, August 30, 1837, John King Receipt, September 2, 1837, and Joseph W. McKean Receipts, September 4 and 5, 1837, Chickasaw Payments, Box 4, File 25, Gouverneur Morris.

44. G. P. Kingsbury to Harris, August 8, 1837 (Chickasaw Emigration K35), M234-R143.

45. *Ibid.*; Armstrong to Harris, August 10, 1837 (Chickasaw Emigration A138), M234-R143.

46. Armstrong to Harris, August 10, 1837 (Chickasaw Emigration A138), M234-R143. Armstrong apparently refers to Chickasaws who removed on their own before Upshaw was appointed to remove them.

47. Kingsbury to Harris, September 28, 1837 (Chickasaw Emigration K46), M234-R143.

48. Kingsbury to Harris, September 23, 1837 (Chickasaw Emigration K43), M234-R143.

49. *Ibid*.

50. *Ibid*.

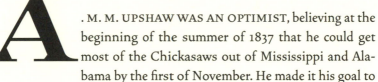

REMOVAL OF A NATION

A. M. M. UPSHAW WAS AN OPTIMIST, believing at the beginning of the summer of 1837 that he could get most of the Chickasaws out of Mississippi and Alabama by the first of November. He made it his goal to remove the entire Chickasaw Nation that fall, for, he said in retrospect, "I was convinced from what I had seen that if they remained until next fall they would be penniless and I therefore believed it my duty to leave nothing undone to get as many of them off as possible."[1] By the time Upshaw wrote these words, he knew that he had been overly optimistic because he began to confront obstacles almost immediately after his return from the West. He wanted to blame the Chickasaws themselves for the delays, expressing regret, as would other removal officials, that the Chickasaws had retained the money from the sale of their allotments. Economic independence, he believed, made them less pliable and more reluctant to bow to the demands of removal agents. However, it was matters of national economy and bureaucratic shortcomings, rather than Chickasaw money, which delayed removal. In addition, removal agents had learned some valuable lessons during the first removal, the most important being, perhaps, that it would be to the government's advantage to control more closely, if it could, the remaining removal parties and to send as many of the Chickasaws by water as possible. Once more, in the fall of 1837, they would learn that what the government wanted was not necessarily what the Chickasaws wanted and that the Chickasaws were willing to bear the expenses of doing things their own way.

The growing national banking crisis that had created problems in procuring Chickasaw rations also created fiscal difficulties for Captain J. A. Phillips at Memphis as he prepared to receive the Chickasaws and send them on the next leg of their journey. Finding the ready cash needed to conduct the removal was the problem. Because of the un-anticipated expenses during the first Chickasaw removal, Phillips estimated that costs would run $18,000 for every 1,000 removed in the fall, exclusive of subsistence. That would require a large cash flow. He urged the War Department not to deposit money in Mississippi banks. Kentucky and New Orleans paper was more current in Arkansas, where the longest leg of the Chickasaw journey lay; thus he continued to have warrants sent to Louisville where they could be more readily and safely cashed.[2] It was also convenient for him, for that was his home.

Travel conditions and Chickasaw temperament made Phillips consider a number of contingency plans as time for the removal approached. He reassigned Lieutenant Gouverneur Morris to his position as disbursing agent for Creek removal, which was still underway. Because the Chickasaws had indicated a preference to travel as far as possible by water, Phillips worked at arranging for light-draft steamboats as transport vessels because of the uncertainty of water levels above Little Rock. It would be more expensive than land travel, but it eliminated the hardships and fatigue of the overland trek. If the water was too low in the Arkansas, boats could always ascend the White River to Rock Roe, just below Mouth of Cache. The Chickasaws could go from there by land if the wagons could make it through the Mississippi Swamp, which in the fall was often impassable, even for empty wagons.[3]

(116)

After the first removal in the spring, Phillips had been concerned about the quality of the vast stores of rations on hand at Memphis, Little Rock, and Fort Coffee. Pork and flour would not likely keep through the hot, humid summer without spoiling, and sacked corn certainly would not. The government and the Chickasaw Nation, particularly the latter, stood to lose a great deal money. Even before the first removal was complete, agents at the various depots had begun to reduce the stores as Van Horne had done at Fort Smith in his agreement with John Drennen.

In early July, when it became obvious that no other Chickasaws would remove before fall, Commissioner Harris became concerned about the condition of the huge ration stores. He gave Captain Collins at Little Rock discretionary power to save the Chickasaws from as much loss as possible and to prevent any loss to the United States by selling the pork and corn likely to spoil "by exchanging them, or by some other expedient," hiring extra assistants or building buildings. However, he cautioned Collins to be mindful that these were Chickasaw expenses and to be careful not to blend them with the public accounts of the United States.[4] In short, no matter how grossly the matter of procuring rations had been mismanaged by the government, the Chickasaws would bear any resulting losses.

Phillips had similar discretionary authority at Memphis, where rations were held by commission merchant Marcus B. Winchester, who, as a highly connected merchant, was safe against loss. The younger Winchester established the first store there in 1819 and was an agent for the three founders.[5] Because forage was scarce along the route in Arkansas, Phillips had sent as much corn with the first party as they could conveniently carry, for corn was indispensable for teams to endure and perform such a long journey. Concerned that the remaining corn stored at Memphis would spoil before fall, he received permission from Harris to allow Winchester to sell the corn at the market price, from eighty cents to a dollar a bushel, "depending on the kind of money paid." In the fall, the disbursing agent would buy corn for the removal at perhaps thirty-seven to fifty cents a bushel, for corn crops in the region looked good and the harvest promised to be abundant. By the end of July, Winchester had sold about one-half of the corn at Memphis for $1.25 to $1.50 a sack and expected to sell the remainder at forty-seven to eighty-seven cents per sack. By then, too, Phillips had begun to solicit proposals for contractors to furnish the Memphis depot with 2,000 bushels of sacked new-crop corn by October 10.[6]

Phillips' and other officials' belief that corn would be readily available in the fall of 1837 was based in part on reports of economic recovery coming out of Indian Territory. Jacob Brown, Collins' predecessor at Little Rock, for example, had reported that summer that Choctaw recovery had begun with the harvest of 1833, when the Choctaws had not only supplied their own needs but also produced a surplus for the market, the government buying some 40,000 bushels to feed newly arrived removal parties. "Since then, to the present time," he wrote, "those people have been equally prosperous in their agricultural pur-

(117)

suits." Prospects also looked good for the Creeks who removed in 1836 and who anticipated a good crop and were beginning to establish herds of cattle and hogs.[7]

In late August, Commissioner Harris gave Brown, Collins, and Armstrong authority over the rations in Indian Territory and approved the transactions they had made to dispose of the stores at Fort Coffee.[8] By October, much of the corn had been sold or exchanged for a promise of corn to be delivered in the fall. What remained was largely spoiled. The flour and pork had been of superior quality when they were purchased, and they remained stored. To William Armstrong, the way to protect the government from loss was to force all of the Chickasaws to remove by way of Fort Coffee. Apparently thinking of the party from Sealy's district, he asked the commissioner to order removal agents to prevent the Chickasaws from crossing the river at Little Rock and going to the Red River. "I have had some little experience in emigrating Indians," he said, "and if they are permitted to travel what road they please, there cannot be much regulating in the party." When they reached Little Rock, he argued, the parties should go on by water if the river was high enough. If forced to go by land, they should go to Fort Coffee. Even those who wanted to settle near Fort Towson would travel no more than forty miles out of their way, he claimed, by going through Fort Coffee. Forcing them to go to Fort Coffee would ensure consumption of the rations already on hand. If they went to Fort Towson, they would have to be supplied, and because of the migration of Americans to Texas along the road from Little Rock, corn prices in that region had risen to one to two dollars a bushel, while corn was still cheap on the road up the river.[9]

On this recommendation, Harris directed Upshaw to prevent the Chickasaws from deviating from the route prescribed for them by their conductors. If at any point along the route they insisted on going another way, as the party from Sealy's district had done, the conductor, disbursing agent, and other officials were to abandon them and withdraw all aid or relief.[10]

Meanwhile, Phillips faced obstacles in preparing for a mass removal of the Chickasaws. He bought wagons and placed provisions on the various routes leading through the Chickasaw Nation into Memphis.

He arranged transportation of the Chickasaws by boat from Memphis to Fort Coffee. Money problems, however, continued to plague his efforts. Costs were going over original estimates, and as the national banking panic spread along the Ohio and Mississippi, he abandoned the Louisville banks and asked for his funds to be deposited in more reliable New York or Philadelphia banks. The commissioner of Indian affairs challenged his estimates of costs. Phillips said, "Given conditions out here, it is impossible to estimate accurately," and just as the Chickasaws were arriving in Memphis, Phillips threatened to resign. Upshaw supported him: "It will take a very large sum of money to move the Chickasaws, a much larger sum than I had any idea of."[11]

While Phillips struggled with money matters, bureaucratic problems plagued Upshaw and threatened to slow down removal. He had returned to his home in Pulaski, Tennessee, after his trip to the West, concerned about the pay for his assistants. The office of Indian affairs not only questioned the amount of their salaries but also denied their daily expense reimbursement, and Upshaw was afraid that all of them would quit, even Millard and Vanderslice. Inflation had hit the economy of Mississippi, and he predicted it would cost them three dollars a day "for board of the commonest kind." Refusal to pay would retard removal, he argued. Phillips, too, was having similar problems with his employees. Convinced by their arguments, Harris supported them before Secretary of War Joel Poinsett. Millard apparently wanted to leave the Chickasaw removal anyway, and from his home at Belville Farm near Leonard Town, Maryland, he offered to take on removal of the remaining Choctaws in Mississippi. "I am confident," he said, "if any one can get them off I can. I know most of the principal men among them, many of whom I can manage as I please."[12] Millard may not have known the Choctaws as well as he thought, for he had miserably misjudged his ability to "manage" the Chickasaws earlier that year.

(119)

Because of the debate over pay, Upshaw was slow getting back into the field. In late September he planned to set up four camps and stay at each about ten days to enroll Chickasaws before setting out for the West. His assistants included William Guy, Dr. Keenan, Millard, Brooke, Langtree, W. J. Wilburn, and Dr. James Walker.[13]

The Chickasaws were slower to gather for removal than Upshaw had anticipated. In late October he visited all of the encampments and planned to start 2,500 to 3,000 the following week. Chickasaws gathered at, and started their journey from, various places such as Luksihoma, Gray's Camp, Houlka, Tippoo Village, Vanderslice's Camp, Chickasaw Old Fields, Pontotoc, Carrollville, and Bryant's Camp, where wagon trains formed and took to the roads feeding into the main road from Cotton Gin Port to Memphis. The road went diagonally through the heart of Chickasaw country. It led from Cotton Gin Port on the Tombigbee River, located between what is now Okalona and Amory, Mississippi, where Highway 41 crosses the river, one branch going to the vicinity of Monroe Mission and then rejoining the northern branch before it reached Toccopola, and then to Lafayette Springs. From there the road went northwest, passing east of Holly Springs and, finally to Memphis.[14]

Removal was a major logistical undertaking. Both Chickasaw and American teamsters made money by hauling baggage, foodstuffs, and animal forage to supply the people and livestock awaiting removal. J. L. Mizell was the principal interpreter, and others such as J. Foster and James McLish served as well. When the removal began, many Chickasaws drove their own wagons, carrying personal belongings. Wagon drivers hired on at each camp. Some of the American teamsters made round trips from their starting points to Memphis, Little Rock, and Fort Coffee, collecting a flat salary of four dollars a day on the outward journey, and from forty-four cents to a dollar or actual expenses per diem on the return trip. The popular image of one huge removal train is false. Groups set out at various times in October, November, and early December and gathered at Memphis. Once on the road, the *Memphis Enquirer* said, the movement of the Chickasaws "was sufficiently slow to enable the Indians living near the line of march, to join the party, and gave them time to place their baggage in the wagons, thereby saving the strength of their horses." By November 9, nearly 4,000 were either at Memphis or within ten miles of town, and Upshaw estimated that no more than 500 or 600 remained in the old nation. Upshaw's plan was to send them all by water, except those needed to take care of the horses and wagons overland.[15]

Phillips had made a lucrative contract with Simeon Buckner to take the Chickasaws by steamboat from Memphis to Fort Coffee. Buckner, a steamboat owner from Louisville with Arkansas and Memphis business ties, agreed to take the Chickasaws in steamboats and towed keels for $14.50 per person from Memphis to Fort Coffee or $9 to Little Rock, and their baggage at $2.50 or $2 per hundred for each respective destination. Buckner was guaranteed $100 per day demurrage for four boats should they become idle while en route or have to wait for the Chickasaws to arrive at Memphis. This latter scenario proved a boondoggle for Buckner, who had four boats ready at Memphis at the time projected for the Chickasaws' arrival, but in actuality, a month before they got off. Although the contract called for four boats, Buckner had six that he would use in the removal: *Kentuckian, Cinderella, DeKalb, Fox, Cavalier,* and *Itasca.* The estimated number to be removed was 5,662.[16]

There were delays in getting the boats off. The Chickasaws apparently were reluctant from the start to board them. To convince them, Buckner took a large group for a ride up the river. Said the *Memphis Enquirer,* "They very soon became accustomed to the noise and novelty of the steamboat."[17] All was in readiness, and the baggage had been loaded, when about 1,000 of the Chickasaws refused to board. Word had come that the *Thomas Yeatman*, which had been used in earlier removals of other tribes, had blown a boiler and killed a number of crewmen. When word came about the wreck of the *Monmouth* on October 31 and the loss of more than 300 Creeks, the Chickasaws balked, and Upshaw had to plan for large overland parties. As a result, the first contingents did not leave Memphis until late November. By the twenty-fifth, five boats had been dispatched. The *Fox, Itasca, DeKalb, Kentuckian,* and *Cavalier* took advantage of a rise in the Arkansas and reached Fort Coffee in eight to ten days. The *DeKalb*, with an estimated number of 500 aboard, stopped overnight on November 22 at Little Rock and continued up the following morning. The *Cavalier* passed by Little Rock on November 23, and the *Itasca,* with an alleged 800 aboard, passed on November 24. The *Kentuckian*, with a reported 800 aboard, arrived at Little Rock on November 27.[18] The *Fox* apparently went by unnoticed. Evidence later surfaced to challenge the number of Chickasaws who were reported to have traveled aboard the boats. Without question, a much larger number went by land than by water.

(121)

Despite the Chickasaws' resistance to the boats, the local Memphis press praised not only the removal agents but the boats as well: "The boats were commodious, and of the best description, and commanded by able and experienced men." By the time of their departure, it reported, there had been only "ten or twelve deaths," all children. After the Chickasaws had all departed from Memphis, the *Memphis Enquirer* said, "Upon the whole, the emigration has been conducted more to the credit of the government, and the agents employed than any previous one coming under our observation." The credit went to Upshaw and Phillips, whom the editor called "gentlemanly and polite" and who had made "judicious arrangements" for the removal.[19] But resistance to the boats had already brought into question how "judicious" the arrangements were, and subsequent events would raise more questions.

Because so many had determined to go overland, Upshaw and Phillips had to make hasty arrangements. Additional teams and drivers had to be hired. Dr. C. G. Keenan of Pontotoc was the physician assigned to the removal. Dr. J. P. Irvine was hired at Memphis to attend the passengers on one of Buckner's steamboats. J. L. Mizell was the principal interpreter, but it became necessary to hire others. W. H. McBride was hired to serve as pilot through the Mississippi Swamp, and his four men cut a new road from Blackfish Lake to the St. Francis River. William Garson and crew cut a road to a new ferry, especially for the use of the Chickasaws at the White River crossing at present-day Clarendon, Arkansas. Simeon Buckner transported corn from Memphis to the ferry across the St. Francis aboard the *DeKalb* and a flatboat, which he had to buy for the purpose and for which the Chickasaws were later billed.[20]

While the Chickasaws were encamped at Memphis, local merchants, teamsters, and physicians found markets. Corn brought fifty cents to a dollar a bushel, and fodder a dollar a hundred weight. Fields were let for Chickasaw horses at an exorbitant seven dollars a day. Merchants supplied corn mills and devices such as half-bushel measures, balances, and steelyards. A storehouse was rented, and apothecaries supplied medicines to Dr. Keenan.[21]

The Chickasaws who intended to go by land took several days to cross the Mississippi River. Marcus B. Winchester ferried Chickasaws, horses, wagons, and provisions. Buckner used one of his steamboats to ferry horses and oxen. J. McMahon supplied the Chickasaws with a flat boat to take them across.[22] Upshaw blamed the slow crossing on the "immense quantity of baggage," the "fine waggons [sic] and teams" that many Chickasaws had, and the vast herd of horses, which he estimated to number 4,000 to 5,000. "I have used all the influence that I had to get them to sell off their horses," he said, "but they would about as leave part with their lives as to part with a horse. I have ordered that each horse should be given two quarts of corn per day and their work horses and steers to have one peck per day. I also give them a small portion of fodder or hay when it can be had. In the removal of the Chickasaws, I have used the greatest economy that I could without letting the Indians or horses suffer. They complain very much about the small allowances that I give their horses, and very frequently say to me that they are moved at their own expense, and I ought not to starve their horses."[23]

Upshaw's concern for the horses most likely grew out of John M. Millard's earlier recommendations because of his experiences with Arkansas horse thieves and lack of forage during the removal the previous summer. He had stressed to the commissioner the importance of issuing forage so that the horses would remain in camp. "They would be always strong and in good condition," he said, "enabled to perform long marches every day, actually prevent great delay and expense in the emigration, and at the same time the Indians would not lose their animals by being stolen or broken down from famine and fatigue."[24]

While preparations for land travel were being made, the *Fox* returned to make its second of three trips. On December 3, Upshaw departed Memphis with 227 Chickasaws aboard and arrived at Fort Coffee on December 12. "Nothing of any importance occurred except the death of one negroe who was considered dying when he was put on board, but he lived for twenty-four hours."[25] Later criticized for having taken such a small party when so many were en route, Upshaw said he did it "to satisfy the Indians, for it was the wish of them all that I should go and I promised them early in the fall that I would do so, and complied with their request."[26]

The government's plan continued to disintegrate. Instead of large

(123)

parties, small contingents continued to travel in Buckner's boats. Captain Phillips accompanied a group of about 200 aboard the *DeKalb*. His plan was to go to Fort Coffee and return as far as Little Rock to take charge of a land party, conducted by Millard, which he expected to meet there. But the *DeKalb* made a fast trip, and Millard's party had not reached the north bank of the Arkansas at Little Rock by the time Phillips returned. On learning that there were Chickasaws at Memphis awaiting a steamboat, he returned there, and on December 28, started west again aboard the *DeKalb* with "a small party of Bear Creek Indians," with plans to accompany them as far as Little Rock and from there go on to Fort Coffee with Millard's land contingent. Phillips reported that only one accident had occurred during the removals by water, and that due to "carelessness on the part of the individual." The favorable river conditions had resulted in rapid and trouble-free transportation. In contrast, the land contingents had been slow, and, of course, Millard's party was not at Little Rock. "The Mississippi swamp has been so very bad for the last month that it is almost impassable," he wrote. "The circumstance has delayed the emigration by land very much." He blamed the delays on the Chickasaws themselves: "And such is the obstinacy of some of the Indians to carry their own baggage & by land, that I would not be surprised if some of them were to remain in the swamp all winter. It were much better for themselves, and less trouble for the agents, if these people had less money; for then they would be more disposed to adopt the advice of those appointed to remove them."[27]

Without question, the Chickasaws' determination to take their property with them slowed down the overland parties. But it was they, and not the government, who were in charge. Time after time during removal, they set their own pace in moving, and because they were paying for removal themselves, they asserted their right to take with them what they chose. Clearly, their concern was less for how convenient their property was to removal agents than their fear of reaching the West as paupers.

While the removals by steamboat continued, the overland parties finally got underway. These parties, with their equipage, baggage, and vast herds of horses and oxen, were remarkable scenes for travelers and residents. Bowes Reed McIlvaine, a Louisville merchant, crossed the

(124)

Mississippi with those headed overland. Imbued with the romanticism of his day, he described them as they marched to the river. He wrote, "I do not think that I have ever been a witness of so remarkable a scene as was formed by this immense column of moving Indians, several thousand, with the train of Govt wagons, the multitude of horses; it is said three to each Indian & beside at least six dogs & cats to an Indian. They were all most comfortably clad—the men in complete Indian dress with showy shawls tied in turban fashion round their heads—dashing about on their horses, like Arabs, many of them presenting the finest countenances & figures that I ever saw. The women also very decently clothed like white women, in calico gowns—but much tidier & better put on than common white-people—& how beautifully they managed their horses, how proud & calm & erect, they sat in full gallop. The young women have remarkably mild & soft countenances & are singularly decorous in their dress & deportment. There were some white women, wives of Indians & they were decidedly the least neat of the party."[28]

Once across the Mississippi, they presented a picturesque sight. "I shall never forget," he wrote, "the singular picture the whole party presented, when all were got across the Miss[issippi]—& in one mass covered the whole open ground on the bank. It was a scene to paint, not describe with words—civilized society is as uniform & tame in the dress & manner & equipage that a crowd has no life in it. Here however no one man was like another, no horse caparisoned like another. Their clothing was of all the bright colors of the rainbow & arranged with every possible variety of form & taste—but all *flowing* & fantastic & *untailorlike*. I wish I could have sketched that scene, as they stood each above the other from the water's edge to the top of the ascending ground. They seemed grouped there, to present one grand display of barbaric pomp."[29]

The Chickasaws did not move overland in one great body. On December 3 before he left Memphis by boat for Fort Coffee, Upshaw had sent two overland parties on their way and directed a third to follow them shortly. The first was conducted by Caleb Langtree, the second by W. J. Wilburn, and the third by J. M. Millard. Langtree left on November 16 with 276 Chickasaws, their animals, and 28 wagons. Wilburn

(125)

started on November 22 with 379 Chickasaws. How many Chickasaws made up Millard's group at the outset is uncertain.[30] Travel conditions and the arrival of late parties that followed Millard's group caused the size of contingents to change along the route.

In addition to his vivid descriptions of the land contingents on the west bank of the Mississippi, though thoroughly romantic, McIlvaine offers some detailed vignettes of the Chickasaws' camp life on the trail. "It was a striking scene at night—," he wrote, "when the multitudes of fires kindled, showed to advantage the whole face of the country covered with white tents & white covered wagons, with all the interstices (between them) filled with a dense mass of animal life in the shape of savages, uncouth looking white hunters, the picturesque looking Indian Negroes, with dresses belonging to no country but partaking of all, & these changing & mingling with the hundreds of horses hobbled & turned out to feed & the troops of dogs chasing about in search of food—& then you would hear the whoops of Indians calling their family party together to receive their rations, from another quarter a wild song from the Negroes preparing the corn, with the strange chorus that the rest would join in—& then the waggoners & hunters round their fires would get up their odd singing—& this would set a thousand hounds baying & curs yelping—& then the fires would catch tall dead trees & rushing to the tops throw a strong glare over all this moving scene, deepening the savage traits of the men, & softening the features of the women."[31]

He continued, "It was my delight to wander at will, wherever anything strange led me, going into the tents—making friends with the men by shaking hands & with the women by playing with the little fat naked wild children—dividing apples among them, to their great satisfaction. Great pains were taken by the agents to keep liquor from the men, & few were drunk—the women neither drink nor smoke—but mostly were seated on skins sewing or doing some kind of work—singularly calm & composed—& contrasted with the incessant galloping about of the men. Only the poorest of the squaws carried burthens—nearly all had ponies for that purpose, which they led, riding (on good side saddles) other horses. The women make their own clothes remarkably well. The fondness for dogs was the most prevalent & amusing.

(126)

One old woman who had lost her pony was carrying a heavy load on her back with a belt across her forehead—to balance which, she had a basket in front suspended round her neck in which were nine fine puppies; the respectable mother of which, trotted contentedly—though doggedly behind, to see that none were dropped by the way. Some had their cats & litters of kittens—others their favorite chickens ducks & turkeys."[32]

The decision of so many Chickasaws to go by land from Memphis forced government officers to act quickly to provide subsistence for such a large number of people. Phillips hired Buckner's boat *DeKalb* to haul food and forage from the Memphis storehouse to the St. Francis River and White River crossings. Langtree and Wilburn were well on their way from Memphis on December 5 when Captain R. D. C. Collins at Little Rock made contracts with farmers and merchants along the route to provide corn, fodder, salt, and beef.[33]

At Little Rock, in anticipation of the second and third groups, Collins not only purchased provisions but hired teamsters to haul them from Little Rock, east along the road as far as the White River. There, the ferryboat had to be repaired, and the rations were ferried across the river and stored in a house used to issue rations to the Chickasaws from December 7 through December 16.[34]

By the time the first two parties reached Little Rock, they were scattered along the line of travel and thus broken apart as identifiable parties. In addition, a party of 112 followed the others, crossing the White River on December 7 with their livestock and wagons. Langtree's party had reached Little Rock by that day, when he sent fourteen of his party upriver aboard the steamboat *Fox*. By the time he arrived opposite Little Rock, nearly 2,000 Chickasaws and more than 4,000 horses and oxen had gathered, which probably represented a combination of his, part of Wilburn's parties, perhaps others who had followed them and caught up, and some who had ridden Buckner's boats as far as Little Rock.

From there they began the last leg of their journey up the Military Road toward Indian Territory. On December 10 an overland party of 1,938 with 4,098 horses crossed Emzy Wilson's ferry near the mouth of Palarm Bayou a few miles north of Little Rock. Chickasaws were scattered along the road to the east. The main party of Wilburn's contingent had begun arriving at the Arkansas River opposite Little Rock on December 15. Three days later, 236 left upstream aboard the *Cavalier*, while the *Kentuckian* waited to take others. Meanwhile, the large overland party—apparently a combination of Langtree's, Wilburn's, and other parties—that was moving up the Military Road had begun to scatter along the road. On December 18 the small group that had followed them reached Little Rock and moved up the Military Road under the direction of William Love, reaching Fort Coffee on January 2, 1838.[35]

Millard's party was about two weeks behind Langtree and Wilburn. Charles Johnson was Millard's assistant conductor. At nineteen, Johnson had come to America from England. A member of a musical and theatrical family, he was a trained Shakespearean actor. He joined an itinerant acting company that toured the South, but gave up acting and became a trader in the Chickasaw Nation, where he married Rebekah Courtney, a Chickasaw. He had been hired to supply rations to Chickasaws encamped in preparation for removal, and his work so impressed Millard that Millard made him an assistant conductor. According to Johnson's family story, when Millard's party reached the Mississippi Swamp, Johnson organized companies of men who cut poles and built corduroy roads through portions of the swamp, helping the party through the boggy land. As a result, the story goes, "the Chickasaws, in Indian fashion, gave him the name 'Boggy,' which he used for the rest of his life." Decades later, Johnson, writing under the name Boggy, recalled the journey, providing eyewitness details of the Arkansas part of the trek. He had been with a group who left Chickasaw Old Fields, he said, on October 8 and arrived at Memphis about October 20 in a train of wagons drawn by oxen, horses, and mules. Boggy wrote, "It took many days to cross the Mississippi, during which time bad weather had set in, with rain nearly every day. By the time we were ready to take up the line of march from the west bank, the roads through the swamp were in fearful condition, frequently nearly every wagon of the command was stalled at the same time; consequently the progress was very slow."[36]

This was, without question, the hardest part of their journey. They crossed H. N. Ferguson's ferry at Blackfish Lake and William Strong's ferry over the St. Francis River, and reached Strong's place on the west side of the St. Francis on December 10 with 300 Chickasaws, their wagons, and animals. The road through the Mississippi Swamp had been so bad that about 800 Chickasaws were still there and not expected to catch up for some days. Millard estimated that seventy to eighty horses had bogged and died in the mud. He crossed the White River on December 24 with 1,220 Chickasaws, their wagons, and more than 1,000 animals. By then, cold weather had set in. Normally, the route between the White River bottoms and Little Rock was easily traveled. However, Boggy wrote, "The prairies between the White River and Little Rock were covered with water, which would freeze during the night and make it difficult for the horses and oxen to break through. Opposite Little Rock, large quantities of supplies were stored, which we were anxious to reach. During the march through the swamps and ice covered prairies, the Indians became so scattered that it was impossible at times to issue them rations." Millard decided, Boggy said, that when the group reached Little Rock, he would wait for all the stragglers to catch up.[37]

To meet their needs on this next leg of the journey, Captain Collins had hired teamsters to haul provisions and forage to the Grand Prairie and White River during the last two weeks of December and the first week of January. Millard's contingent had continued to grow after he left Memphis, and many remained on the road. The last group to follow him out of Memphis crossed the White River on January 6 with 979 Chickasaws, their wagons, and over 900 animals. Millard's party of 1,000 to 1,500 began to arrive at the Arkansas River opposite Little Rock on January 1, 1838.[38]

(129)

Millard had decided to hold the party at Little Rock and regroup for the last leg of the journey while he waited for all the stragglers to catch up. He believed that the struggle through the swamps and ice might have convinced the Chickasaws of the advantages of traveling by steamboat. Thus he had sent word ahead to Captain Collins, who had two of Buckner's boats waiting on the north side of the river opposite Little Rock when the party arrived. Boggy wrote, "A few hundred, mostly women and children, took passage, the remainder preferring the overland route. The Chickasaws were well to do; they had good horses and plenty of money." [39]

The river party departed on January 5, 1838, on board the *Itasca* with two keel boats in tow and aboard the *Cinderella*, which left on January 7. Millard went with them, leaving those remaining encamped to go on to Fort Coffee by land, once the stragglers came in. Captain Phillips, who had taken the Bear Creek Chickasaws to Fort Coffee, had just returned down river and assumed the job of conducting the overland contingent in Millard's absence. Upshaw, who was returning down river from Fort Coffee in "a small open skiff," was camped on the riverbank about sixty miles above Little Rock when Millard's boat passed. He hailed the boat and got a report from Millard as it passed. At Little Rock, he found the remainder of Millard's party camped on the north side of the river and found that they "were well pleased with the agents that were with them," he said. "There was a great loss of horses in passing the Swamp. On account of the fatigue and falling off of the horses, I directed Captain Phillips to give them 1 gallon of corn per day. I had previously given them ½ gallon." [40]

By the time Upshaw arrived at Little Rock, the Chickasaws had begun to experience what other removal parties of Chickasaws and members of other tribes had experienced before them. Whenever removal parties had remained in one place for an extended time, they were beset by horse thieves and whiskey peddlers. In this case, local merchants and whiskey peddlers began to separate them from their cash. Boggy wrote, "After the steamers had left for Fort Coffee, the warriors commenced having a high old time; flats, skiffs, and dug-outs took them across the river." They had cash. The merchants were happy, and the whiskey shops did a thriving business. "On the east bank [i.e., the bank opposite the town]," Boggy wrote, "enterprising persons replenished their stocks of wine and whiskey; the old Malaga was a favorite drink with the Chickasaws, and for days it was hard to find a sober Indian." [41]

Simeon Buckner, always the opportunist, added to the party mood. "Wishing to show his appreciation for the efforts of the officers of emigration to get the Indians on board his boats, 'he gen a treat,' a dance and supper at the City Hotel then kept by Capt. Jeffries," wrote Boggy. "It was a 'big thing,' nearly all the elite of the City o' Roses were there.

The supper tables were filled with delicacies brought expressly from New Orleans. The bright particular star of the occasion was Major Buckner's lovely daughter, afterward the wife of the lamented Lambert Reardon."[42]

While the merchants were happy, others in Little Rock began to complain. For two or three days running, people were fighting and yelling in the streets. Captain Collins decided to enlist the help of Millard, who had returned from Fort Coffee, to put a stop the Chickasaws from crossing the river and to get those in town back to camp. "The major took several of the leading chiefs over," wrote Boggy, "and as I was beginning to talk very good Chickasaw I was pressed into service on such occasions." The party gathered up the Chickasaws in town. "Some had to be tied and carried on the boats, and it was dark before all was quiet."[43]

That took care of matters in Little Rock, but the problem remained on the north side. Millard had been trying to get underway for two or three days, "but whiskey had control," according to Boggy. Whiskey boats regularly crossed the river, and a canal boat with a bar serving the American teamsters with the removal party was tied on the north side. In addition, there were saloons. In the evening after Collins, Millard, and the Chickasaw leaders had cleared out Little Rock, they met in council and decided that all river crossings should stop, and all boats except the canal boat with the teamsters' bar, were taken to the Little Rock side and the canal boat placed in the control of a removal officer. They notified the saloon keepers to stop selling whiskey or have their saloons destroyed, but they refused. The Chickasaw leaders then decided to organize a group of warriors and destroy them. Boggy was pressed into service to head the group, he said, "the chiefs fearing if no white man was along trouble might ensue," and he got ready, he said, "by dressing and painting his face like the Chickasaws." To make his act more convincing, he took Richmond, a black slave, with him to act as "interpreter."[44]

The following is Boggy's narrative. "We started about 8 o'clock. It was a beautiful moonlight night. We quietly made our way to the canal boat and cut her loose. The river was high, and away she went down stream. Some two or three of the party who were on her jumped overboard and swam ashore." [45]

Boggy continued. "We next visited one of the saloons, and without any attempt at prevention, took part of two barrels, all there was there, knocked in the heads and let the whiskey run out; the next was the same. On reaching the third and last one, we were confronted by a very respectable looking woman. By this time there was a great crowd following us, both white and Indians. She wished to know what we wanted. 'Whiskey' was the reply. She said, 'You can't take ours without you pay for it, or I will shoot some of you.' During the parley some of our party got into the house. She stepped back, and came toward us with a large, old-fashioned horse-pistol. It did look ever so large. Some one caught her arm and took it from her. Through an interpreter (for I was acting Indian) I told [her] we did not wish to hurt her, and she might as well remain quiet and let us take the whiskey. Looking at me, and holding a candle up to my face, she said, 'You are no Indian, and should be ashamed of yourself to take what belongs to me.' And truly I did feel so, and wished myself out of the scrape. We took one full barrel and two half barrels. When we knocked in the head of the full one, and was about tipping it over, the Indians remarked that there was too much waste of a good thing, proposed it should be drank by the crowd. Vessels of all kinds and sizes were dipped in, and a big drunk was the consequence. Next morning, however, all were sober and serene, and preparations for leaving camp were commenced."[46]

(132)

But the affair was not finished. About noon, Collins warned the camp that authorities had issued a warrant for Boggy's arrest and that he should go to the next supply station at Emzy Wilson's on the Military Road at Palarm Bayou. Boggy quickly saddled up and left. About bedtime he received word from Millard that the whiskey had been paid for and the legal proceedings had stopped. Boggy returned to the camp that night, and on the following day, the party started up the military road toward Fort Coffee.[47]

Nothing of interest occurred, Boggy reported, until they reached Norristown opposite Dardanelle Rock. Millard planned to cross to the south side of the river and take the road directly west to Fort Coffee rather than follow the Military Road on the north side of the river. Crossing was tedious: "We had only two small flats to ferry with, and it took us a week to cross the river," Boggy wrote. Samuel Norris charged twelve and one half cents for each of the 1,796 Chickasaws and 3,095 horses to cross. The seventy wagons and teams cost $1.50 each and the three small wagons a dollar. "The day we left Dardanelle," Boggy said, "the dreaded 'Schokwah' small pox broke out, and there our real trouble commenced." [48] They did not reach Fort Coffee until sometime in February. [49]

The great smallpox epidemic of 1838 was raging at the time in the trans-Mississippi West. While they were in Arkansas, Chickasaws aboard Buckner's *Itasca* had contracted the disease and spread it among the other tribes. Four hundred to five hundred, primarily Choctaws, died. Concerned about the cholera rather than smallpox, they had refused vaccination. The Chickasaws did not suffer high mortality rates for two basic reasons. First, under the Indian Vaccination Act of May 1832, agent Benjamin Reynolds sought to vaccinate them, but they were scattered over the whole nation and the rank-and-file Chickasaws did not trust American doctors, holding their medical practice in contempt. Thus Reynolds believed an official program of inoculation would fail and urged the commissioner of Indian affairs to give thirty lancets and small quantities of vaccine matter to a few intelligent "half breeds" and others throughout the nation, letting the "common" Chickasaws see the effect, and perhaps they would change their minds. How many vaccinations occurred and "took" is uncertain, but it is likely that some of the Chickasaws were immune. The Chickasaws were also spared because doctors began vaccinating immediately, and their efforts were effective because the Chickasaws were still concentrated, for the most part, in camps and were vaccinated first. At the end of April 1838, the disease seemed confined to a few families who were living in isolated areas. The next month, orders went out to vaccinate the entire Choctaw Nation population. [50]

Meanwhile, the removals continued. After increasing the rations for Chickasaw horses at Little Rock in January, Superintendent Upshaw started back to Mississippi to organize more Chickasaws for removal. On his way from Little Rock to Memphis, he stopped at Helena on January 15, where he learned that some 250 Chickasaws were camped about seven miles from town. They had crossed the river at

(133)

Helena at their own expense and were determined to make their own way to the West. With Upshaw was Robert B. Crockett, his brother-in-law who was returning from Fort Gibson, having escorted a party of refugee Creeks that had been removed from the Chickasaw country. Upshaw directed him to enroll the Chickasaws and accompany them to the West, but they refused to be enrolled or to accept an agent. Their plan was to go south from Helena, cross the Arkansas River at Arkansas Post, and travel overland to Fort Towson, taking their time, hunting through the winter, and arriving at Fort Towson in the summer. Therefore, following the commissioner's orders to removal officials to refuse assistance to "refractory" groups, Upshaw left them to their own devices and sent orders to Captain Collins at Little Rock not to furnish them or other such parties any provisions and to refuse assistance to any party that chose to travel by way of Fort Towson.[51]

At Memphis, Upshaw and Crockett learned that Kin-hi-che's group, known as the "Clean House Indians," were on their way west. Traditionally a Chickasaw identified himself or herself by a house name, which once referred to camps, but in more recent times to local dwelling areas. Each house was identified with a specific clan. The Chickasaws supposedly had an old saying "that each person must know his own house name and his own clan name." John Swanton identified more than fifty houses and argued that there had probably been many others that had died out. The Clean House, however, was not among the Chickasaw house names. According to Cyrus Harris, about 1830 the name was given by white people to four Chickasaw families "who kept their houses so neat, and their yards so free of all grass, weeds and rubbish of all kinds. . . . Three of the heads of the four families were brothers, and the other a brother-in-law to the three." Harris identified the head man as "Chikasah nana ubih (pro. *Chik-a-sah nar-nar-ub-ih*, and sig. *A Chickasaw who kills anything*)." His brothers were "Ishkitahah (pro. *Ish-ke-tar-hah* and sig. *No mother* or *mother gone*)." and "Innihtawa (pro. *In-nih-to-wah*, sig. *Warm the ball*)." Their brother-in-law was "Aiyuka ubih (pro. *Ai-yu-kah-ubih* and sig. *Each one kills* or *to kill each one*)." By the time of removal, Kin-hi-che was apparently leader, even though Chickasaw Nahnubbee was among the group. Kin-hi-che, who formerly resided in what is now Itawamba County, Mississippi, had

(134)

been to the West and knew the route. However, Crockett joined them as conductor a few miles east of Memphis, where they arrived on January 18.[52]

Because the Mississippi Swamp was impassable at the time, on January 28 Crockett put the 175 Chickasaws aboard Simeon Buckner's *Itasca* and their 206 horses and oxen aboard flatboats, which the *Itasca* towed to Arkansas Post, where the livestock was unloaded. They also brought with them 499 bushels of corn, 2,353 pounds of bacon, and 7,000 pounds of hay. Crockett's plan was to take some of the Chickasaws with him to drive the livestock and send the majority of the party on to Little Rock aboard the *Itasca*. However, the majority of the Chickasaws got off, determined to go overland with Crockett. Only about 15 remained on the *Itasca*, which arrived at Little Rock on February 1 and anchored on the north side of the river opposite Little Rock, waiting for a rise in the river. At this turn of events and not having sufficient public funds available to him, Crockett borrowed money from Chickasaw Nahnubbee and one of his brothers and hired his wagon and Kin-hiche's for four dollars a day on promise to pay at Little Rock or Fort Coffee. Leaving Arkansas Post on that same day, Crockett and the overland party took the road toward Little Rock, stopping at farmers' houses and supplying themselves with corn, fodder, and hay along the way.[53]

Crockett had left Arkansas Post in a disgusted mood. The captain of the *Itasca*, upon learning that most of the Chickasaws would leave his boat, tried to get Crockett to sign a receipt that stated the opposite. Through a heated argument, Crockett stood his ground. At Little Rock, he was to learn that not just the captain but the boat owner, Simeon Buckner, was avaricious, dishonest, and determined to commit fraud to get what he could of the Chickasaw fund. Buckner himself met Crockett at Little Rock and tried to get him drunk and persuade him to sign the receipt. Other removal personnel had already experienced such tactics and had learned how dishonest Buckner's operation was. William Guy, who had been on board the *Fox*, said that on arrival at Fort Coffee, the captain of the *Fox*, one of Buckner's boats, wanted Guy to certify that they had carried 125 tons of baggage, but Guy refused. Then the captain bargained for 100, but Guy countered and later said that he "ignorantly" signed for 75. An eyewitness aboard the *Fox* said that it could not possibly have been 20 tons. There were only about 260 people, the baggage, and some 16 wagons.[54]

Friedrich Gerstacker, the German traveler, found Crockett and the Clean House Chickasaws on the river opposite Little Rock when he arrived there on February 9, 1838: "Long after sunset on the 9th I arrived on the Arkansas river; the lights of Little Rock shone from the opposite bank, but a strange fantastic scene presented itself on this side of the river, on which I stared with astonishment. An Indian tribe had pitched their tents close to the banks of the river. A number of large crackling fires, formed of whole trunks of dry fallen trees, which lay about in abundance, offering good shelter against the wind; over the fires were kettles with large pieces of venison, bear, squirrels, raccoons, opossums, wild-cats, and whatever else the fortune of the chase had given them. Here young men were occupied securing the horses to some of the fallen trees, and supplying them with fodder; there lay others, overcome by the firewater, singing their national songs with a mournful and heavy tongue. I stood for a long time watching the animated scene."[55]

The whiskey peddlers at Little Rock preyed on this group just as they had done earlier contingents. Gerstacker continued, "A tall powerful Indian, decked out with glass beads and silver ornaments, came staggering towards me, with an empty bottle in his left hand and a handsome rifle in his right, and, holding them both towards me, gave me to understand that he would give me the rifle if I would fill his bottle. The dealers in spirituous liquors are subject to a heavy fine if they sell any to soldiers, Indians, or Negroes. The poor Indians have fallen so low, and become so degraded by the base speculations of the pale faces, that they will give all they most value, to procure the body and soul-destroying spirits. Though I had but little money left, only twelve cents, I declined the exchange; he turned sorrowfully away, probably to offer the advantageous bargain to some one else, in which case I thought it best to indulge the poor savage, and save him his handsome rifle; I took the bottle out of his hand, filled it, and gave it back to him. On my refusing to accept his rifle, he laid hold of me, and dragged me almost forcibly to his fire, obliged me to drink with him, to smoke out of his pipe, and eat a large slice of venison, while his wife and three children

(136)

sat in the tent staring with surprise at the stranger. He then stood up, and in his harmonious language related a long history to me and to some sons of the forest who had assembled round us, and of which I did not understand a word. At last as the noise became annoying, I stole away quietly to seek a berth for the night."[56]

David Vanderslice met the Clean House Chickasaws at Little Rock and went with those that were aboard the *Itasca* on to Fort Coffee, while Crockett continued overland with the remaining Chickasaws and the livestock. Before leaving, they obtained supplies of corn and corn meal from local suppliers. They left the north bank of the Arkansas on February 12 and reached what is now Pottsville in ten days. Leaving there on February 22, they crossed the river at Dardanelle Ferry. On this leg of the journey, Crockett acquired beef from farmers along the way and hired teams and wagons to transport Chickasaws, baggage, and supplies for the remainder of the journey. Leaving Dardanelle on February 24, they reached Fort Coffee in early March. There being no contractors to supply rations, Crockett remained some time longer, going into the surrounding region and buying beef from the Choctaws to supply the party's needs.[57]

Upshaw's efforts to remove the entire Chickasaw Nation in 1837 and 1838 ran into a major obstacle in the form of Chickasaw independence. Refusal to ride on Buckner's boats, choosing their own routes, and a willingness to strike out on their own for the western country without organized government support demonstrated again and again what the first removal party had made clear to government officials. Because they were spending their own money, the Chickasaws were determined to remove however they wished. With Crockett's arrival in the west with the Clean House Chickasaws, the major part of Chickasaw removal was over. Estimates varied regarding the number of Chickasaws who remained in Mississippi and Alabama. Those who remained would continue to be an abiding concern to the Chickasaw leadership, and there would be attempts to get the remaining Chickasaws to remove before the government "officially" closed removal.

NOTES

1. J. A. Phillips to C. A. Harris, September 20, 1837, and A. M. M. Upshaw to Harris, July 21, 1837, September 22, 1837, and November 9, 1837 (Chickasaw Emigration P208, U18, U21, and U25), National Archives Microfilm Publications Microcopy M234, Letters Received by the Office of Indian Affairs, Roll 143, hereafter cited as M234 followed by the roll number.

2. Phillips to Harris, July 4 and 30, 1837 (Chickasaw Emigration P151 and P167), M234-R143.

3. Phillips to Harris, October 1, 1837 (Chickasaw Emigration P211), M234-R143.

4. Harris to R. D. C. Collins, July 6, 1837, 27th Congress, 3rd Session, *House Report 271*, 72, hereafter cited as *Report 271*.

5. "The Family of General James Winchester, Part Two," *http://www.rootsweb.ancestry.com/~tnsumner/winch2.htm*, retrieved November 12, 2004. Winchester was the son of General James Winchester of Revolutionary War fame, who with Andrew Jackson and Judge John Overton of Nashville, founded Memphis. The same source says that during the late 1830s and early 1840s, Winchester bought more than 3,000 acres of land in Crittenden County, Arkansas. Overton was much admired by Jackson, who was succeeded by Overton as superior judge in Nashville.

6. Phillips to Harris, July 4 and July 30, 1837, and Upshaw to Harris, July 7, 1837 (Chickasaw Emigration P151, P167 and U15), M234-R143.

7. Jacob Brown to Harris, July 18, 1837, *Report 271*, 71.

8. Harris to Collins, August 31, 1837, and Harris to Armstrong, August 31, 1837, *Report 271*, 72–73.

9. William Armstrong to Harris, October 4, 1837 (Chickasaw Emigration A261), M234-R143.

10. 27th Congress, 2nd Session, *House Report 454*, 10, hereafter cited as *Report 454*.

11. Phillips to Harris, September 11 and 20 and November 17, 1837 and A. M. M. Upshaw to Harris, November 9 and 25, 1837 (Chickasaw Emigration P204, P208, P232, P233, U25, and U26), M234-R143.

12. Upshaw to Harris, July 31, 1837; Phillips to Harris, August 8, 1837; Harris to Joel Poinsett, August 16, 1837; and Millard to Samuel J. Potts, undated (Chickasaw Emigration U19, M168, W273, and Frame 129, respectively), M234-R143.

13. Upshaw to Harris, September 22, 1837 (Chickasaw Emigration U21), M234-R143.

14. Upshaw to Harris, October 30 and November 9, 1837 (Chickasaw Emigration U22 and U25), M234-R143; John Wilson, *Old Monroe Presbyterian Church and Cemetery, 1821–1823* (Algoma, MS: n. d.), 12.

15. Various Receipts, October, November, and December 1837, 27 Congress, 3 Session, *House Document 65*, pp. 11–17, hereafter cited as *Document 65*; Upshaw to Harris, October 30 and November 9, 1837 (Chickasaw Emigration U22 and U25), M234-R143.

16. *Report 454*, 1–2, 8, 9, 11.

17. *Army and Navy Chronicle* 6 (January 18, 1838), 44; *Arkansas Gazette*, January 10, 1838.

18. Upshaw to Harris, November 25, 1837 (Chickasaw Emigration U26), M234-R143; Arrell M. Gibson, *The Chickasaws* (Norman: University of Oklahoma Press, 1976), 186–87; *Arkansas Gazette*, November 28, 1837, and *Arkansas Advocate*, December 4, 1837.

19. *Arkansas Gazette*, January 10, 1838; *Army and Navy Chronicle* 6 (January 18, 1838), 44.

20. See Receipts to the above men, *Document 65*, pp. 13–14; Receipt No. 3, January 20, 1838 (Chickasaw Emigration C816), M234, R143.

21. See Receipts to these men, *Document 65*, 16–17.

22. Receipts, November 28, 1837, March 8 and August 31, 1838, *Document 65*, 16, 24.

23. Upshaw to Harris, November 25, 1837 (Chickasaw Emigration U26), M234-R143.

24. Journal of Emigration, September 17, 1837 (Chickasaw Emigration M225), M234-R143.

25. Upshaw to Harris, December 1 and 7, 1837, January 26, 1838, and April 10, 1838 (Chickasaw Emigration U27, U28, U32, and U45), M234-R143.

26. Upshaw to Harris, August 1, 1838 (Chickasaw Emigration U54), M234-R1.27. Upshaw to Harris, December 1, 1837 (Chickasaw Emigration U27), M234-R143; *Arkansas Gazette*, December 24, 1837; *Arkansas Advocate*, December 18, 1837; Phillips to Harris, December 28, 1837 [two letters] (Chickasaw Emigration P253 and P254), M234-R143.

28. John E. Parsons, ed., "Letters on the Chickasaw Removal of 1837," *New York Historical Society Quarterly*, 37 (1953), 280.

29. *Ibid.*, 281–82.

30. Upshaw to Harris, December 1, 1837, and August 1, 1838 (Chickasaw Emigration U27 and U54), M234-R143; in March 1848

31. Parsons, ed., "Letters," 280–81.

32. Parsons, "Letters," 281.

(139)

33. See, e. g., Subsistence Receipts (1837) No. 7, 8, 14, 15, 17, 18, and 22 (Chickasaw Emigration C816), M234-R143; Receipts, National Archives Record Group 217, Records of the U. S. Department of the Treasury, Accounting Officers of the Department of the Treasury, E524, Chickasaw Payments, 1833–66, Box 2, File 22, J. A. Phillips. E524 is hereafter cited as Chickasaw Payments.

34. See Subsistence Receipts (1837), No. 7, 10, 14, 15, and 22, and Transportation Receipts (1837) No. 2, 3, and 4 (Chickasaw Emigration C816), M234-R143. John Barkloo, owner of the stage company at Little Rock, made the round trip in six days, and James Pitcher of the Little Rock mercantile company of Pitcher and Walters made it in seven.

35. Subsistence Receipts (1837) No. 7, 8, 14, 15, 17, 18, and 22 and Transportation Receipts (1837) No. 1, 7, 20, 38, 39, 40, and 41 (Chickasaw Emigration C816), M234-R143; Receipts, Chickasaw Payments, Box 2, File 22; *Arkansas Gazette*, December 19, 1837; *Arkansas Advocate*, December 11 and 18, 1837.

36. Neil R. Johnson, *The Chickasaw Rancher*, Revised ed., C. Neil Kingsley, ed. (Boulder, CO: University of Colorado Press, 2001), xii, 8, 11; Boggy, "A Reminiscence," *Van Buren Press*, February 1, 1879. Charles "Boggy" Johnson was in the Indian Territory a few months before the article appeared in the *Van Buren Press*. A note appended to the story indicates that Johnson later lived in Boggy Depot: "The interpreter on the occasion of my acting Indian, was Richmond, a negro of remarkable intelligence, of whose tragic fate, in my room at Boggy Depot, I may, some day write about." Johnson continued writing to various newspapers, until his death in the 1890s.

37. Receipt, November 17, 1837, *Document 65*, 14; Boggy, "A Reminiscence."

38. Transportation Receipt (1837), No. 7, 10, 13 and Upshaw to Harris, January 2, 1838 (Chickasaw Emigration C816 and U31), M234-R143; *Arkansas Gazette*, December 19, 1837; *Arkansas Advocate*, January 8, 1838.

39. Boggy, "A Reminiscence."

40. Upshaw to Harris, January 26 and August 1, 1838 (Chickasaw Emigration U32 and U54), M234-R143.

41. Boggy, "A Reminiscence."

42. *Ibid*. Lambert Reardon was mayor of Little Rock, 1845–46.

43. Boggy, "A Reminiscence."

44. *Ibid*.

45. *Ibid*.

46. *Ibid*.

47. *Ibid*.

48. *Ibid.*

49. *Ibid.*; Receipt No. 27, March 15, 1838 (Chickasaw Emigration C816), M234-R143.

50. Grant Foreman, *Indian Removal: The Emigration of the Five Civilized Tribes of Indians*. New ed. (Norman: University of Oklahoma Press, 1972), 221–22; J. Diane Pearson, "Lewis Cass and the Politics of Disease: The Indian Vaccination Act of 1832," *Wicazo Sa Review* 18 (Fall 2003), 9–35; Benjamin Reynolds to Elbert Herring, December 9, 1832, M234-R136, Frame 340; Armstrong to Harris, April 30, 1838 (Chickasaw Emigration A367), M234-R143.

51. Upshaw to Harris, January 26 and August 1, 1838 (Chickasaw Emigration U32 and U54), M234-R143; Foreman, *Indian Removal*, 216.

52. John R. Swanton, *Chickasaw Society and Religion* [Forty-second Annual Report of the U. S. Bureau of American Ethnology] (Lincoln: University of Nebraska Press, 2006), 31–41. Harris is cited in H. B. Cushman, *History of the Choctaw, Chickasaw and Natchez Indians*. Angie Debo, ed. (Norman: University of Oklahoma Press, 1991), 414.

53. *Arkansas Advocate*, January 8, 1838; Upshaw to Harris, January 26 and August 1, 1838 (Chickasaw Emigration U32 and U54), M234-R143; Receipts, Chickasaw Payments, Box 2, File 22. Kin-hi-che and Chickasaw Nahnubbee were listed among the Chickasaw leaders during the post-removal period. The debts Crockett had with them for use of their wagons languished for years. Malinda Kin-hi-che was attempting to collect her father's money a decade later. See Upshaw to Medill, April 29, 1848 (Chickasaw Emigration U 34), M234-R144; Ethan Allen Hitchcock, *A Traveler in Indian Territory: The Journal of Ethan Allen Hitchcock*, Grant Foreman, ed. (Cedar Rapids, IA: The Torch Press, 1930), 170. Their claims were not paid until the summer of 1849. Chickasaw Nahnubbee's claim for use of his wagon was not filed until June 1, 1842. Crockett swore that he hired the wagon for 35 days at $5 a day. Armstrong to Crawford, June 1, 1842 (Chickasaw Emigration A1258), and Upshaw to William Medill, April 3 and July 26, 1849, Chickasaw Emigration U61 and U91, M234-R144.

54. Hitchcock, *A Traveler*, 175.

55. Friedrich Gerstacker, *Wild Sports in the Far West* (Boston: Crosby Nichols and Company, 1859, 91–92

56. *Ibid.*, 92–93.

57. Upshaw to Harris, August 1 and 31, 1838, Subsistence Receipt (1838) No. 6, 8, 11, 12, 13, 23, 30 and Transportation Receipt (1838) No. 24, 31, 32, 33 (Chickasaw Emigration U54, U55, and C816), M234-R143; Statement of Robert B. Crockett, February 11, 1842, *Report 271*, 115.

W HEN UPSHAW RETURNED FROM the West in January 1838, he was convinced that Chickasaw removal was nearly completed. He dismissed all of his agents except Brooke, Millard, and Vanderslice, whom he asked to meet him in mid-March or early April to gather the widely scattered Chickasaws that remained in Mississippi and Alabama, estimated to number 250 to 300. He told a Nashville, Tennessee, newspaper, in language typical for removal agents, that the Chickasaws who had already removed had arrived safely in the West and "express themselves satisfied in their new abode." He had told the Little Rock press the same thing.[1] Nashville was far enough distant from Fort Coffee to make Upshaw's statement believable there, but people in Little Rock knew better. Removal was not over. It was simply winding down, and years would pass before it was completed. Chickasaw leaders were determined to get all of the Chickasaws to the West, and as subsequent events showed, the effort would go on at least until 1850. The leaders were willing to expend as much of the Chickasaw invested funds as necessary to get the late-removing Chickasaws to the West, insisting that they be paid the same commutation, or self-removal, amounts that had been paid others. The leaders' insistence that each Chickasaw deserved the same treatment as any other reflected the remarkable unity of the Chickasaw people that had characterized their endurance of the trauma of removal from the start.

On March 20, 1838, Upshaw set out from Nashville to begin his last effort at removal, arriving at Pontotoc on April 6. On the way, he had spent several days in the northwestern part of the Chickasaw Nation, where he claimed that he saw "several half breeds" who had decided to stay until fall. Optimistic as always, he believed he might change

(143)

their minds. Ishtehotopa and his people had also planned to stay but agreed to leave in the spring. Upshaw returned to the field to persuade others to remove. For a month, he and W. A. M. Brooke rode throughout the old Chickasaw Nation, urging removal, but, he concluded, the Chickasaws were "very uncertain people." He designated Ishtehotopa's home eighteen miles north of Pontotoc as a starting point and set May 7 as the assembly deadline for those planning to leave. Upshaw went to Ishtehotopa's place at the appointed time and went into camp, but after two weeks "but few" had come in.[2]

While Upshaw's work dragged on in Mississippi, groups of Chickasaws who had moved on their own arrived in the West. Gaines P. Kingsbury, the Chickasaw Agent, estimated that by April 1838 nearly 1,000 Chickasaws had made their way to the West without escort, "dropping in a few families at a time during nearly the whole winter" of 1837–38. It was often hard to tell when they arrived, when their year of rations should begin, or even who qualified for rations. In some cases, part of a family came by water and other members by land, bringing their horses and arriving several months later. Similarities of names caused additional confusion to Kingsbury and others.[3] A group of eighty-six who had managed their own subsistence as far as Little Rock arrived at Fort Coffee on May 13. On May 18, Kingsbury reported the arrival of sixteen at Fort Coffee aboard the *Liverpool* and twenty aboard the *Itasca*. They had gone overland to Little Rock, where Captain Collins arranged their passage. According to Kingsbury, small parties like these had arrived during the spring; how many, he was unsure, because some of them had not tried to draw rations. He expected an overland group of about 150 in late May. "They have come by themselves all the way from the old nation paying their own expenses on the route," he said. He had received no instructions regarding such groups, but he believed that they should be reimbursed for their expenses. In addition, "Several of those who came by land under the charge of a conductor," he said, "made use of their own teams for the transportation of their baggage and I think it but just that some allowance should be made them."[4]

During the spring of 1838, Chickasaws continued to remove on their own in large groups and single families. About mid-May, a group of more than 300 arrived at the Arkansas River opposite Little Rock, where they intended to cross and go to the Red River by way of Fort Towson. These were, in part, the group that Upshaw and Crockett had seen near Helena in January, and in part, Glover's party that had left the old nation on their own. The *Arkansas Gazette* said that they had "been loitering along the roads on this side of the Mississippi, for some months past." They remained at Little Rock for almost a week, and about half had crossed the river when Millard reached Little Rock on his way back to Mississippi. He and Captain Collins convinced eighty of them to cross back to the north side because the government would assist them if they went southwest, and Collins persuaded them to accept Millard as an agent. Those who refused to re-cross the river left Little Rock and started southwest on their own. Millard hired teams and wagons and left for Fort Coffee on May 29 with those who remained on the north side. They crossed Samuel Norris's ferry at Dardanelle with their wagons, horses, cattle, and oxen on June 8, and went west along the Military Road.[5]

Meanwhile, in Mississippi, Upshaw had finally gathered a small group that he started west in June, with Minko Ishtehotopa and his family among them. On June 22, the group of 133 Chickasaws with their train of 11 wagons and 243 horses crossed the Mississippi at Memphis. On the following day, 45 people crossed,[6] likely Chickasaws who were removing on their own resources. On June 24, Upshaw and the Chickasaws, including Ishtehotopa and his family and four slaves, left their camp on the west bank opposite Memphis and began their march toward Little Rock. They were followed on June 25 by one of Ishtehotopa's slaves and two horses, and on June 26 by another slave with seven horses.[7]

Upshaw blamed stories of smallpox, other diseases, and scarcity of provisions that travelers had brought back to Mississippi for the small number of Chickasaws who were willing to remove during the previous three months. As his group had approached Memphis, they met John Moore, who was returning from the West to Holly Springs. Moore's reports of sickness among the Chickasaws in the West so alarmed Upshaw that he became convinced that he might lose half of his party if he went to Fort Coffee. Three of his party deserted at that point, a Mrs. Allen and her two male slaves.[8] Moore's warnings were in a way pro-

(145)

phetic. He had determined to remain in Mississippi, but he soon died and left his widow, Delilah Love Moore, to remove to the West a few years later, after the family means had declined.

Ishtehotopa's party began their trek to Little Rock, which took them less than two weeks. Their passage through the Mississippi Swamp was fast. The road was in good shape no doubt because of the severe drought the South was experiencing in the summer of 1838. By June 26 they crossed Blackfish Lake, reached William Strong's on the St. Francis on July 1, a week later reached the White River ferry at present-day Clarendon, Arkansas, and arrived at the Arkansas River opposite Little Rock on July 15, where they remained in camp for two weeks because of illness. They had lost 4 people since they left Memphis, and of the 129 remaining in the party, 70 were down with fever at one time. While they camped opposite Little Rock, they lost two more. According to Upshaw, "One of the two was the King's wife, who was Queen of the Chickasaw Nation." The other casualty was a child about two years old.[9]

Choctaw historian Muriel Wright suggests that the Queen might have been Pakaunli, the "old, revered Queen," who had received a life pension in the Treaty of Pontotoc in 1832. Wright also speculates that she was probably the mother or aunt of Ishtehotopa.[10] However, Pakaunli (or Pakarnli) does not appear on the muster roll of Ishtehotopa's party, and Upshaw clearly identified the woman who died at Little Rock as Ishtehotopa's wife, who is presumably buried somewhere near the river crossing.

Although departmental policy had denied assistance to those who took the Red River route, Upshaw considered taking this group that way for several reasons. He had learned that the smallpox was raging between Fort Coffee and the Blue and Boggy Rivers and that provisions had become scarce between Little Rock and Fort Coffee. On the other hand, the roads were "good" to Fort Towson, provisions were plentiful, the distance to the Blue River, their final destination, was only seven miles farther than the Arkansas River route, and the southern route was free of the smallpox, which had become epidemic among the Indians on the Arkansas.[11]

On August 1, the Chickasaws crossed the Arkansas River in preparation for their journey to Fort Towson. A number of their group were still ill, requiring one wagon to make two trips across the river to carry them. Another made two trips carrying provisions.[12] John M. Millard and David Vanderslice accompanied the party. When they arrived in the Choctaw country is uncertain.

Although Chickasaws remained scattered throughout the old nation in the summer of 1838, their absence in some areas was conspicuous. With the great body of Chickasaws now on the other side of the Mississippi, white residents who had displaced them could romanticize their leaving. On July 5, 1838, Miss Nancy Fontaine wrote her friend, who was a student in Paris, about the Fourth of July celebration in Pontotoc. After relating the events of the celebration in the midst of the gossip of the town, she wrote: "Since you left, our village presents a different appearance. The Indians are all gone; it was melancholy to see the poor creatures leaving the land of their birth and the graves of their fathers. A deep sadness was imprinted on their countenances."[13] Her youthful sympathy for the Chickasaws was probably not shared by most whites, who were undoubtedly glad to see the Chickasaws go.

Upshaw had thought to make one final effort to get the remaining Chickasaws out of Mississippi, but with removal of Ishtehotopa's group, he considered Chickasaw removal essentially completed. So did Commissioner Carey A. Harris. In June Harris directed Upshaw to settle outstanding accounts against Chickasaw removal. However, accounting had become a nightmare, primarily because of the number of self-removals and straggling groups that had characterized removals during the preceding months. Harris turned his criticism on Upshaw, who countered that he had no way of estimating how many Chickasaws had removed themselves. He had a roll of a group that Pitman Colbert had taken west with him and one of a group headed by George Colbert, who had moved "a small number of Indians and several negroes on their own expenses," with expectations that they would be reimbursed. In the summer of 1838, Pitman Colbert returned to "the old nation to wind up some business" and asked for his reimbursement because he was short of money[14] Vanderslice, too, had worked during the spring, assisting Chickasaws who had been stopped on the road by sickness in getting to Fort Coffee. And Upshaw was still receiving complaints that there were "straggling parties" of Chickasaws between the Mississippi

(147)

and Fort Coffee, but most of those, he thought, had already reached the west.[15] By August 1838, most of the accounts had been settled.

Removal efforts east of the Mississippi were also winding down. J. A. Phillips, disbursing officer at Memphis, asked to be relieved of duty in the Indian Department so he could return to his military unit and leave any final disbursements for Chickasaw removal to Captain R. D. C. Collins at Little Rock, which, as events later demonstrate, may have been a mistake. When Phillips sought to settle accounts, he found that funds were unavailable. "To be a disbursing officer without funds and . . . with applications for money, is not a very desirable position to be placed in," he complained.[16]

In mid-August, Upshaw was still in Little Rock, winding up affairs. All outstanding accounts had been paid, and he had instituted a pay-as-you-go policy for new accounts. His plan was to muster Millard and Vanderslice out of service as soon as they returned to Little Rock and settled their accounts. He kept Brooke on and returned with him to Pontotoc to make one more try at taking the remaining Chickasaws west.[17]

Harris tried to blame Upshaw for the high expense of Chickasaw removal. From the start he had questioned Upshaw's hiring practices and challenged the salaries he had set for some of his assistants. While Upshaw was at Fort Coffee in March 1838, the Chickasaw leaders had complained to William Armstrong about the number of assistant agents Upshaw had hired.[18] Upshaw defended his actions. Because the Chickasaws had gone in several steamboats at different times, he had not wanted to leave them to the captains and their crew. "I well knew how the Captains and crew of small steam Boats treated white passengers at times," he said, "and I was confident that the Indians might suffer, if they did not have an Agent along, and since it is over I know it." In response to Harris's criticism in the summer, Upshaw blamed the high costs on the Chickasaws' insistence on taking so much personal property with them.[19]

Upshaw left Little Rock in late August, believing his affairs were in good order. However, at Memphis he found the unsettled Simeon Buckner claim for transporting Kin-hi-che's party of Clean House Chickasaws. Phillips had left Memphis, directing the post office to forward the long-awaited funds to Louisville. Upshaw had counted on those funds to reimburse his expenses, for he had paid for much of the cost of removing Ishtehotopa's party out of his personal funds and what he could borrow from others, not having access to any other funds at the time. With Phillips gone and his personal financial situation dire, he could not settle accounts with his lenders, and he had no operating funds as he set out to try to bring another group of Chickasaws out of Mississippi. He accused Phillips of having had the funds sent to Louisville solely to facilitate payment of his Louisville friend, Buckner. Phillips was officially relieved of duty in the Indian Department on September 6, making any debate over his actions moot.[20]

A month later, Upshaw was financially embarrassed, preparing to leave his camp forty miles southeast of Pontotoc on October 10. He would start with about 200 Chickasaws and expected to be joined by perhaps 100 more by the time they reached Memphis. He had enough money to get them that far, but no farther. He believed that this group would end "the whole of the business" of Chickasaw removal, as he called it. He and Brooke, he said, had "rode ourselves and horses down" in gathering the scattered people from all over the old nation, enrolling a larger group than he had anticipated.[21] Fortunately for Upshaw, he and Harris mended their fences before the party moved out. Nearly all accounts had been settled. Only two assistants remained, Brooke and Vanderslice, whom Upshaw brought back into service because, he said, "really I do not think it entirely safe with only two persons to manage the Indians."[22] His plan with this party was to pay his accounts as he went, and all future disbursements would go through R. D. C. Collins at Little Rock.[23]

(149)

Three groups of Chickasaws began arriving in Memphis on the last day of October 1838. Upshaw was with the advance party who were "all in good health," he said. The second party arrived on November 1 and the third, from near Tuscumbia, Alabama, the next day. They began crossing the Mississippi on November 3 with more difficulty than was usual because the river was very low and the banks were bad, and they had difficulty getting on and off the ferry boat.[24] The *Memphis Enquirer* reported this removal in the journalistic style of the day: "The last of the Chickasaw Indians, 300 in number, are now crossing the Mississippi at this place, on their way to their new western home, under the superintendence of Col. A. M. M. Upshaw, to whom the Indians have become much attached, from his humanity and attention to their wants. They appear very cheerful and comfortable, and are the finest and most decent looking Indians we have seen. Many of them are quite wealthy."[25]

This group was on the road between Memphis and Little Rock almost twice as long as Ishtehotopa's party the previous summer. The drought that had gripped the South had broken in October, and this party was larger. The train consisted of 299 Chickasaws, their horses, cattle, wagons, and carriages. Their sixty-six wagons suggest that the Chickasaws were taking as much personal property as possible in what Upshaw considered the last removal party. They crossed Blackfish Lake on November 6, reached William Strong's on the St. Francis on November 10, arrived at the ferry on the White River on November 19, and reached the bank of the Arkansas opposite Little Rock about November 24.[26]

The group had decided to go southwest from Little Rock. On November 27, they crossed the Arkansas River. On November 28 the *Arkansas Gazette* reported: "A party of about 300 Chickasaw Indians, with their baggage, wagons, ponies, cattle &c.,... has been crossing the river at this place since Sunday morning, and will probably be ready to resume their journey to their country high up on Red river, to-day or to-morrow. The party appear to be in good health, and look cheerful and happy."[27] Upshaw confirmed their "fine health and spirits" when he reported their crossing the river and departure that day for Fort Towson.[28]

G. P. Kingsbury, the Chickasaw agent, met the party at Doaksville, Choctaw Nation, where they had encamped in December. Some wanted to go to Boggy Depot, and others to remain near Doaksville. Kingsbury arranged for subsistence for those at Doaksville, and Upshaw continued with the others to Boggy, where Kingsbury planned to follow. They reached their destination on January 1, 1839.[29] This was the only Chickasaw removal party that went directly from their homes in the old nation all the way to their final destination in the West.

As far as Upshaw was concerned, Chickasaw removal had officially ended. At Fort Towson on February 2, 1839, he dismissed his remaining assistants: Vanderslice, Brooke, and Dr. James Walker. He made a roll of the Chickasaws who were in the West in 1839. There were 7,968, including slaves, consisting of 2,549 households. Of those heads of household, only 241, or 9%, bore English or a mixture of English and Chickasaw names. Of the total population, 1,171, or 15%, were listed as slaves. Upshaw reported that there were perhaps 18 or 20 families who had approximately 300 slaves yet to remove. Although he believed they were competent to remove themselves, he also believed that they would claim to need an agent to remove them, presumably to make money. However, he said, "I have no doubt but what they would suffer greatly on the road by the intrusion of the whites had they no one with them who was authorized to protect them."[30]

History would prove Upshaw wrong about the Chickasaws' desire for a removal agent. In fact, they would be adamant to the contrary. One way Chickasaw removal differed from removals of the other tribes was Chickasaw independence. Having observed the removals of the Choctaws and Muscogees, the Cherokee forced roundups, and Seminole armed resistance, the Chickasaws wanted as much control over removal as possible and rebelled against the idea of a removal agent to make decisions for them or to have disbursing authority.

The Chickasaws were also determined to get all of their people to the West, whatever the cost. Upshaw submitted muster rolls of Chickasaws who had removed themselves, some before he had been appointed and some after. The latter were perhaps those that Armstrong claimed in 1837 had settled near Fort Towson and bought improvements from the Choctaws. Those who moved after that had traveled with the George Colbert and Pitman Colbert families. The Colberts had been allowed thirty dollars per person, and Upshaw recommended that the others receive the same amount, given the cost of transportation and rations.[31] The War Department, in subsequent years, accepted his recommendation.

Many Chickasaws were perfectly capable of removing themselves and did so. Among the many small groups of Chickasaws who had struck out for the West on their own were Chickasaw leaders like McGilivray and Greenwood. McGilivray and Captain Greenwood had left

(151)

Coonewah campground in Mississippi on October 26, 1837, and arrived at Fort Coffee with their families on February 6, 1838. Also moving west on their own in 1837 were Billy Wellington and Chahicha, also known as George Waters. They first went to the enrolling camp run by F. G. Roche about eight miles south of Pontotoc. They enrolled for removal, but after a day or two in camp they struck out with their families for the West, about three weeks before Roche's party left. Wellington had seven in his household. Two children died shortly after they departed, but he took in two orphaned girls on the route. Chahicha had seven in his household as well, but he took Unatoonba into his household.[32] The households of Caton Nelson, James McCoy, Edmund Perry, John Cravat, Daniel Harris, and Mishoyo arrived in the West on March 8, 1837. The household of Levi Thomas arrived west in April, those of Dickson Frazier and Adam Perry arrived on November 2, and those of Ishtefelachee, Yockapache, Cooper, and Captain Mahatah arrived on December 15 of that year. Richard Overton and his family arrived in January 1839.[33]

Those who went west after the removal had "officially" ended were for the most part Chickasaws who had decided to remain in Mississippi but later chose to join their people in the West, usually for social or economic reasons. As early as 1831, the missionaries had expressed fears that allowing some Chickasaws to remain in Mississippi would undermine their attempts to Christianize the nation. They became convinced that the Chickasaws they considered "civilized" would take reservations and remain east of the Mississippi, while those they considered "heathen" would "be consigned to the dark forests of the west." A report from Martyn Mission in 1831 claimed all of the Chickasaws in that neighborhood intended to stay. The missionaries had not encouraged them to do so, they said, "for we are convinced that it will be most disastrous to the nation to have the most civilized portion remain behind."[34]

The missionaries' fear that the Christianized Chickasaws would remain seems to have been well founded. By the time removal took place, Chickasaw membership in the Presbyterian church, which had never been large, had significantly declined. A handful of members of the Monroe church received letters of transfer and recommendation to take with them to the West: James and Elizabeth Perry, Tennessee Bynum, and slaves Harry, Sally, Bob and Amy, Abram and Delilah, Agnes, Manuel, Juda, Apphia, Billy, Titus, Sally, Fanny, and Lilphia, all dismissed on September 16, 1837. On October 10, 1837, Samuel Cunningham, his wife, William Cunningham, and Jack also received letters.[35]

Missionaries' remarks about those Chickasaws near Martyn clearly referred to members of the extended Love family. The Loves included the most influential Chickasaws in the Holly Springs area of what had become Marshall County, Mississippi. It was apparently the Love family's interest in education that resulted in the establishment of Martyn Mission near them in 1825. At one point, shortly after the mission school opened in 1826, ten of twenty-four students bore the name Love. On the eve of the treaty of 1832, the area on Pigeon Roost Creek about six miles southwest of Holly Springs was known as Love Village, sporting not only the mission and its school but a grist mill and blacksmith shop as well.[36]

Henry Love and Benjamin Love, sons of Thomas, had figured prominently in pre-removal Chickasaw affairs. Benjamin, who had been educated in Washington, was the Chickasaw interpreter at the Treaty of Pontotoc in 1832. He and Henry were members of the delegation of five sent to Washington in 1834 and who negotiated a supplemental treaty that modified the earlier one.[37] The new treaty made both Henry and Benjamin two of the seven commissioners who oversaw the sale of Chickasaw allotments. Under the new treaty, allotment size depended on the size of family and the number of slaves that the household held. The Loves qualified for thousands of acres, which promised to prove lucrative.

Henry Love had two tracts, one near Martyn Station and another located about six miles south of Holly Springs—the latter consisting of 2,560 acres. The former plot was located where the road from LaGrange, Tennessee, intersected the Memphis to Cotton Gin Port road. Mahota, the widow of Thomas Love, lived just north of Henry on the LaGrange road. Love sold his property near Martyn in 1836 and moved to the other, which later white residents referred to as the "Indian Reserve" and which became the center of Love family concerns. Near an ancient mound on the tract, Love built a six-room log house.

(153)

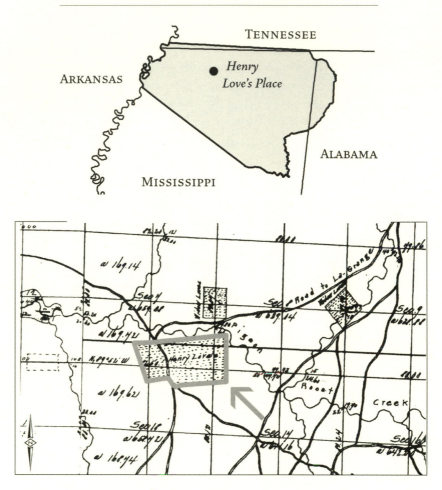

Henry Love's Place. From the Cession Surveys of 1832.

His brother Benjamin bought part of the reserve, where he owned a log house and farmed extensively with slaves. John B. and Delilah Love Moore, Henry's sister, owned a plantation nearby. When John B. Moore died in 1839, his estate held forty-two slaves.[38]

For a time, the economy of the region boomed despite the economic downturn in other parts of the United States. Marshall County, established in 1835, became a significant cotton-producing area. The northernmost navigable point on the Tallahatchie River was at Wyett, a boomtown now extinct, that was located only a mile south of the southern boundary of Marshall County. Located on the former allotment of Slone Love, son of Henry Love, during the 1830s it had at one time fourteen mercantile establishments and a hotel. From it, steamboats carried the cotton of the area to market in New Orleans. In 1838, some 10,000 bales left the port.[39]

From the wealth generated in the boom years of the cotton economy, the Loves prospered. They embellished their homes with an elaborate style by any standards of the day. For example, a Marshall County woman recalled having attended a wedding in the mid-1840s at the house formerly owned by Benjamin Love. The ceremony took place in a room "with French wallpaper depicting 'Indians on ponies and on foot, with tomahawks, bows and arrows, and wild animals in trees and woods.'" The Loves educated their children. After he resettled in the Holly Springs area, Henry Love sent his sons to the Holly Springs Academy. Benjamin Love's wife and three servants became members of the Holly Springs Presbyterian Church, established in 1836, as did James Colbert, kinsman of the Loves, who also sent his son Holmes to the local academy. In 1839 Mrs. Charlotte Love and two slave women, Nancy and Jenny, moved their membership from the Monroe church to Holly Springs.[40]

The land speculation boom caused Holly Springs to materialize rapidly. By 1837, Marshall County had the largest white population of any county in the state, and Holly Springs was next only to Natchez and Vicksburg in size. Before Chickasaw removal began, it had churches, a male academy, and a courthouse under construction. It claimed the first bank established in northern Mississippi. By 1838 two newspapers appeared there. Because of land speculation, the town had more than forty attorneys. There were debating societies, dramatic clubs, a female academy under construction, and fraternal societies, and a charter for a university had been granted. In 1839, the citizens enjoyed professional theatrical troupes, a racing season, and an additional bank.[41]

But signs of the panic of 1837 had begun to appear. The court dockets were crowded, and newspapers carried advertisements for forced sales of land to satisfy creditors.[42] The early 1840s brought hard times to the Loves. Heavily invested in slaves and cotton culture, they fell victim to the economic decline. In 1840, Henry Love had twenty-three slaves. The heirs of John B. Moore, who had died in 1839, inherited forty-four, and Benjamin Love had sixty-six. The cotton market collapsed in 1840. The Loves began to think that their future was better cast with the Chickasaws in the West and began to sell off their property.[43] They formed parties and headed west, some of them taking large numbers of slaves with them.

Late arrivals like the extended Love family were welcomed in the West, for during the decade following removal, there was a growing effort by the Chickasaw leadership to consolidate the Chickasaw population and reestablish a separate Chickasaw Nation. Although those who removed late faced the same hardships in the West as others who had gone earlier, they did not have the same access to subsistence rations that earlier parties had. Most removed after 1840, when the full effects of the banking panic of 1837 were felt. Chickasaws who might have been considered well off for the day and had fair prospects to be able to compete in Mississippi society found themselves low on resources. However, in the West, the subsistence ration period had passed for most of them, the large rations firms had moved on, and the straggling groups were not large enough to create profitable contracts. Added to these problems was the fact that the Chickasaw fund was invested, and at times there had accrued insufficient interest to pay for removals. Early on there seems to have been no settled per capita amount to reimburse those who removed themselves, yet there was an understanding that reimbursement was due them.

Late removals began in earnest in 1840. Susan Allen Guest arrived at Fort Towson with her household of thirty-eight in January. Her husband was killed the following July, and she remarried and was known thereafter as Susan Wall. Sometime during February and April of that year, fifty-three arrived in the West, including Tushkioway, Imnooklombe, Pahshekishi, Ekoonokatubby, Tishchopla, Tahluchetubby, Ahthutubby, Chimmenah, Isaac Alberson Jr., Ishtimmahcoyea, Enoalutkey and one other in the family, Allecoche, Pallis Sealey, Nookachubby, Enoquiche, Abijah Colbert, Morgan Colbert, and John T. Roach.[44] In late 1840 another party consisting of the households of Lottie Davis and Robinson James, emigrated and arrived in January 1841. Because there was no money in the Chickasaw fund to pay for their subsistence, Superintendent William Armstrong made a contract with Charles Johnson to provide them with rations for a year with an understanding that he would be paid when funds became available. The James family, he said, were educated and "every way qualified to receive their own rations, and to attend to their own business." Johnson had supplied the corn, and Armstrong attended the beef issue himself. The contract, of course, was "expensive and troublesome" because the group was so small. Martin Colbert's widow, Sarah, and her household, accompanied by her nephew William F. Stuart arrived at Fort Coffee on January 10, 1842, and went directly to the Chickasaw district. She had asked for subsistence, but the number was so small Armstrong said he could do nothing for her and suggested that she might be included in a contract when another group arrived. The small parties were troublesome to U. S. officials, yet the Chickasaws were often without funds to buy the provisions they needed.[45] And there were many still to come. Early in 1842 Chickasaw Commissioner Slone Love estimated that about 300 Chickasaws remained in Mississippi and Alabama.[46]

(157)

From that point on, nearly every removal season, that is, October through March of each year, saw stragglers arriving in the West. Experiences of the earlier groups such as Colbert and Stuart caused others to resort to different tactics to find the means to remove. In July 1842, for example, Charles F. Eastman, S. M. James, and Pitman Colbert Jr. appealed to the government for money to move west in the fall, using as a model George and Pitman Colbert, who had removed in 1838 and received $30 per person in their parties. Without similar help, Eastman and the others claimed, they would realize nothing for their Mississippi lands, and others would have to make sacrifices for them. They refused to consider having an emigration agent because "most of the Chickasaws and those that are connected with the Chickasaws are as capable to move as any set of people." They sent along a petition in their behalf from prominent white men of Holly Springs, calling for assistance.[47] The following month, James Colbert Jr. appealed to the secretary of war for help in moving in the fall. "But from the extreme hardness of the times many of us will not be enabled to realize money from the sale of our lands & some of us will be compelled to sacrifice our lands & other property to procure money to remove without we can procure the assistance of the government." Like Eastman, they were adamant in not wanting to travel under a removal agent: "Our objections arise from the fact that speculation & corruption appear to be the order of the day." And like Eastman, they cited the precedent of Pitman and George Colbert to request funds. Alexander B. Lane of Holly Springs, who supported James' appeal, claimed that about 350 Chickasaws wanted to remove in the fall and argued that $30 per person would be less than a removal agent's salary and removal costs if the government removed them.[48]

In late October 1842, the Chickasaw commissioners in the West heard rumors that a large group of more than 100 would arrive there shortly and asked Armstrong to make arrangements to supply subsistence to them. The commission—Ishtehotopa (the King), Isaac Alberson, Slone Love, and James Wolf—said, "They are Chickasaws and therefore entitled to a fair participation in the benefits arising under the late treaty."[49] This party consisted of the households of Delilah Love Moore and, primarily, her children and their families, and other relatives. The party of 188, of whom 138 were slaves, traveled from Holly Springs directly to the Chickasaw District. Like her brothers Henry and Benjamin Love, Delilah Moore had suffered economic setbacks, in her case caused by the death of her husband and the decline of the cotton economy.[50] This group, who arrived in December 1842, received rations of corn and pork for five months, the pork delivered on the hoof in season so that they could put it up for bacon. Even though Armstrong said that "the party are intelligent, educated men just as capable of receiving their rations as any other set of men," he sent an assistant to monitor the rations issues. Disaster struck Moore's party shortly after they arrived west. They, like other Chickasaws and Choctaws along the Red river, were devastated by a flood that raised the water level fifteen feet higher than ever known. "A large number of horses, cattle and hogs have been destroyed, leaving many Choctaws and Chickasaws where they commenced in a pecuniary point of view," wrote Armstrong.[51]

The Moore party also raised an issue regarding free blacks. During earlier removals, slaves received rations equal to those received by Chickasaws. After the ration period ended and compensation for removal became policy, owners were paid an amount for slaves equal to that for their own family members. Among the Moore party were eight or ten free blacks. Commissioner Isaac Alberson and Slone Love protested against the Chickasaws' paying for their removal. However, Commissioner of Indian Affairs T. Hartley Crawford rejected their complaint in 1843, saying, "If the Chickasaws who removed chose to take free negroes to the number of 8 or 10 with them, as members of their community and to recognize them as members of their families, I see no reason why any expense they have incurred by permitting these negroes to go with them should not be paid. It was their own voluntary act."[52]

As the removal season of 1842 wound down, Armstrong began to prepare for the next. Late in 1842, under instructions from Commissioner T. Hartley Crawford, he advertised proposals for subsisting other Chickasaws who might arrive for "more or less a year." The bids, which were to be opened on February 1, 1843, would be paid when the Chickasaw fund contained sufficient funds to pay.[53] Daniel Saffarans, Tennessee land speculator and trader who had already made a fortune from Chickasaw assets, but, like other speculators in Mississippi had lost money in the panic of the late 1830s, saw the removals as a way of getting at more Chickasaw funds. He had already sponsored some of the Chickasaws who had removed late and found the arrangement lucrative. In early 1843, he made arrangements that effectively sped up the removal process. In February, he received affirmation from the War Department that any Chickasaws who removed on their own would be allowed $30 per person.[54] He meant to get his share of the money.

The Chickasaw leaders likewise anticipated continued removals and, in fact, encouraged them. From July 12 to 15, 1843, a council of the whole Chickasaw people met at Boiling Springs, where the chiefs, commissioners, and warriors agreed unanimously that Agent A. M. M. Upshaw should go back to Mississippi and Alabama to move all of the remaining Chickasaws. When they made their request to Commissioner Crawford, they argued that Chickasaws remained involuntarily in the east. Some were poor. Others had property, but in some cases, widowed women had court-appointed administrators of estates, whose apparent object was to keep the Chickasaws there until the property was gone. Orphaned children had guardians who controlled their property. In one case, the father had died, the mother had moved to the West, and the children and the property, which was considerable, were "kept." The children were left at "the mercy of the unfriendly person to live out a miserable existence." Every day they stayed, their property wasted, so that every day they became more impoverished. Ishtehotopa wrote, "We want you to hear us, those people that are left are of our blood, and we love them and we want them with us." The Chickasaw leaders asked Crawford to appoint Upshaw to help their people get to the West. "We must ask you," they said, "once more not to turn a deaf ear to us but hear us." [55]

In August 1843, additional members of the Love family arrived in the West from Holly Springs. These included Benjamin Love, who brought thirty-three slaves, traveling first to Fort Coffee and then to the mouth of the False Washita in the Chickasaw District. Love's wife and family remained in Mississippi, to follow him with another party of fifteen or twenty in the fall. Overton Love, brother of Benjamin, brought fifteen slaves belonging to their father, Henry, who planned to follow in the fall. Jackson Frazier came alone. Others of the Love family followed as planned. They arrived at Fort Coffee and remained there briefly before going on to Fort Washita in the Chickasaw District, where they arrived without money and applied, but had to wait, for rations. [56] Subsequent events showed that those who turned to Daniel Saffarans, rather than relying on reimbursement or assistance from the government, fared better.

Saffarans found the late removal a good opportunity to make more money. He had financed the large group of 188 who had arrived in the West in late 1842. In October 1843, he agreed to remove the Love party from Fort Towson to the Chickasaw district.[57]

Saffarans could count on the newly arrived having to face hard times. Crops had failed during the summer of 1843, and the poor were facing a hard winter. James Colbert Jr. and S. M. James appealed for an additional seven months' subsistence for households that had come in their group, just as other late-arriving groups had received. But they did not like Saffarans. They complained about his claim of being an emigration agent. If he had been appointed, James said, he did not act like an agent, nor did any of the emigrants know him in that capacity. James pointed out how he, C. F. Eastman, and James Colbert Jr., had protested against having an agent in 1842. Apparently concerned that they had not received all that was due them per capita for self-removal, James wanted to know how much was being allowed Saffarans for each person and horse from Holly Springs to the Chickasaw district. James also alleged that a firm (apparently Saffarans and all those allied with him) had been established in the Choctaw country to buy up orphan claims. However, James was not averse to making money off the claims himself. He told Jacob Thompson, "If you can put me on the track I can buy them and they can be bot [sic] for goods at a mear [sic] song."[58]

Appeals came from others. Eastman made inquiries similar to those James had made. He knew that Saffarans had collected for some of those who had gone west in his party, and Eastman wanted to know how much. Benjamin Love applied for the expenses of removing himself, his family, and Sally Love. He claimed hardship, arguing that the move had cost him a good deal and that he had run out of money on the way and had had to borrow. Meanwhile, emigrant Chickasaws in Love's party were subsisted by George W. Knox.[59]

(161)

In early 1844, removals continued and went on until late spring. A. W. Jones, Josiah Fisher, and David Burney and their families arrived in the West in January. Of these, Jones had been supported by Daniel Saffarans. In late February or early March, George Waters and his family and effects arrived in "a large wagon drawn by mules." Henry Love and his family arrived in May.[60]

From the "official" end of removal, the Chickasaw leadership had constantly urged the removal of all Chickasaws from Mississippi and Alabama and was insistent that they be treated like all others who had removed earlier. Once more, in early December 1844, Ishtehotopa and commissioners Isaac Alberson, Benjamin Love, Slone Love, Joseph Colbert, and James Wolf requested an extension of George Knox's ration contract to accommodate the late-arriving parties. During the previous two years, groups under Benjamin Love's and James Colbert's direction had emigrated, been subsisted for twelve months, and then had an extension of seven months like earlier emigrants. Without governmental approval, the Chickasaws had asked Knox to provide pork because his prices were low and the season was right for slaughtering and curing meat. They sought only an extension of the contract based on the trust they had in Knox. In a separate appeal, Ishtehotopa asked the secretary of war for his approval.[61]

When they urged this policy, the removal season was under way once more. In November 1844, William Love, Mahotey [Mahota] Love, J. T. Roark, George W. Colbert, and John H. Rice removed. Samuel Love and William Simpson removed in December, arriving at Fort Towson.[62]

By the beginning of 1845, the subsistence system, which had been in place since 1837, practically failed the Chickasaws. Faith placed in Knox was misplaced. He failed to deliver the seven months' provisions the leaders had authorized for the Loves and others. Armstrong had authorized an extension of his contact in the fall, and Knox agreed to deliver the pork early. However, pork prices rose suddenly, and Knox could not buy and deliver it at his contract price. By April, Armstrong pressed for cash payments, instead of rations, equal to those given others who had arrived late. Under these conditions, most of the late-arriving Chickasaws apparently sought out Saffarans, or he sought them out. Others worked through Upshaw that winter. Still others appealed to the leadership. In June 1845, Ishtehotopa and the commissioners forwarded to the government a list of those Chickasaws who had paid for their own removal in 1844 and 1845, but who had not been given self-removal money.[63] By the end of 1845, subsistence rations were a thing of the past. Knox, the last subsistence contractor for the Chickasaws, had not only failed, but had left a large unpaid account with Berthelet, Heald & Co., who filed their claim that fall. By early 1846, Armstrong urged newly arrived Chickasaws to ask for money rather than rations because it was too difficult to find contractors for such small numbers.

(162)

Apparently, Chickasaws preferred money to rations anyway.[64]

Throughout 1846, inquiries about removal continued, and small parties arrived in the West. In May, Saffarans filed a claim for Sarah A. Colbert, who had arrived in March with her household of forty-five, including thirty-two slaves. They settled near the mouth of the Washita. In June, Upshaw filed a claim for Parmelia Reynolds, who had thirteen in her party, including seven slaves. They arrived from Alabama in April and settled in Pushmataha District of the Choctaw Nation near Fort Towson. Removing with her were Harvey Bacon and his household of eleven, including four slaves. In October, George Washington and Thomas McKinny, both with two in their households, removed from Mississippi.[65]

Evidence suggests that by 1847, removal was about finished. Only three small family groups arrived in the West that year. In late April, George G. Allen, his family of five, and his fifteen-year-old sister Mourning Allen removed and settled near the mouth of the False Washita. The Allens may have been the minors that Ishtehotopa and the other commissioners had in mind when they spoke earlier about those being "kept" in Mississippi. In July, the households of Lewis L. Brown and his family of five removed and settled near Fort Smith just inside the Choctaw Nation. That same month, Susan Perry, with a household of twenty-seven, including thirteen slaves, removed and settled near the mouth of the False Washita.[66]

(163)

The Chickasaw leadership continued to insist on equal treatment of their people. Because of the approaching end of removal, in May 1847 the Chickasaw leadership under James McLaughlin and James Wolf sought to reduce removal compensation to the value of twelve months' subsistence rations instead of nineteen months that the leadership under Ishtehotopa, who had relinquished his position as minko by then, had insisted upon for years. However, this reduction caused some discontent among the Chickasaws. Thus following the subsequent general election in the Chickasaw District, the leadership under McLaughlin, Wolf, Benjamin Love, Jackson Frazier, Isaac Alberson, and others reversed the earlier position and, in March 1848, asked for a reinstatement of the nineteen months' ration value. The reduction of the value to twelve months for future removal parties had been unfair, the leaders concluded: "Denying them would create hard feelings among our people. Those who remained so long behind are principally families who had lost their husbands shortly after we emigrated, had large families or were unwillingly detained. It would therefore look very hard, if they were not to receive so good treatment, as those more fortunate." The Chickasaw leaders also asked that the rations be valued at three cents and four-and-a-half mills each. Upshaw endorsed the request: "That has proved best, as they are nearly all half breeds they could purchase stock as would suit them."[67]

In August 1848, thirteen Chickasaws removed, the only ones known to have gone west that year. Peter M. Fletcher's family of five settled near Fort Smith just inside the Choctaw Nation. Lake Erie McKinney with seven in her family, including two slaves, settled in the Chickasaw District near the mouth of the Washita. She had a third slave who died just as they reached the Indian Territory line. And Malcolm McGee settled near the Chickasaw line at Boggy Depot. Fletcher and McKinney had been advanced money by the firm of Johnson Strain and Company of Mississippi to pay their way. Others recently arrived had turned to Saffarans.[68]

Finally, a group enrolled for removal in early 1850. Those were apparently four people—Isham Matubby and one slave, Untahcunneubby, and Ebenezer Pitchlynn—who received $37.50 per person plus 3 cents, 4.5 mills for daily rations for 19 months.[69] Theirs was apparently the last recorded Chickasaw removal.

Chickasaw removal, which Upshaw had declared officially over in 1839, had perhaps finally come to an end. The Chickasaw leaders had been insistent: all of those left in Mississippi and Alabama must join their people in the West. Their decisions had been costly, but they were willing to use whatever amount of the Chickasaw fund was necessary. Like those who removed earlier, those who went west later went through a number of years of hard times. Unfortunately, they had to turn to merchants and others like Daniel Saffarans, who, like merchants in Mississippi, accepted their indebtedness with assurance that the government would pay them out of the Chickasaw national fund. For the Chickasaws, however, it was a price they gladly paid to have their people together once more.

NOTES

1. A. M. M. Upshaw to C. A. Harris, January 2 and 26, 1838 (Chickasaw Emigration U31 and U32), National Archives Microfilm Publication M234, Roll 143 (hereafter cited as M234 followed by the roll number); *Army and Navy Chronicle*, 6 (February 15, 1838), 111; *Arkansas Gazette*, February 19, 1838.

2. Upshaw to Harris, March 20, April 20, April 21, and May 18, 1838 (Chickasaw Emigration U44, U45, U47, and U48), M234-R143.

3. G. P. Kingsbury to Harris, April 20, 1838 (Chickasaw Emigration K93), M234-R143; Simeon Buckner receipt, May 5, 1838, National Archives Record Group 217, Records of the U. S. Department of the Treasury, Accounting Officers of the Department of the Treasury, E524, Chickasaw Payments, 1833–66, Box 2, Bundle 12. Entry 524 is hereafter cited as Chickasaw Payments.

4. Kingsbury to Harris, May 18 and June 22, 1838 (Chickasaw Emigration K101 and K106), M234-R143.

5. Upshaw to Harris, August 1, 1838, and Kingsbury to Harris, June 22, 1838 (Chickasaw Emigration U54 and K106), M234-R143; *Arkansas Gazette*, May 18 and 30, 1838; Transportation Receipts (1838) No. 35, 47, and 48, and Subsistence Receipts (1838), No. 16 and 19 (Chickasaw Emigration C816), M234-R143; Receipts, Chickasaw Payments, Box 1, Bundle 16.

6. Upshaw to Harris, June 5 and 7, 1838 (Chickasaw Emigration U49 and U50), M234-R143; Chickasaw Payments, Box 1, Bundle 16.

7. Upshaw to Harris, June 24, 1838 [two letters] and J. A. Phillips to Harris, July 14, 1838 (Chickasaw Emigration U51, U52, and P398), M234-R143; Chickasaw Payments, Box 1, Bundle 16.

8. Upshaw to Harris, June 24, 1838 [two letters] and J. A. Phillips to Harris, July 14, 1838 (Chickasaw Emigration U51, U52, and P398), M234-R143.

9. Chickasaw Payments, Box 1, Bundle 16; Upshaw to Harris, August 13, 1838 (Chickasaw Emigration U53), M234-R143; *Arkansas Gazette*, July 18, 1838.

10. Muriel Wright, *The Indian Tribes of Oklahoma* (Norman: University of Oklahoma Press, 1951), 87–88. The woman named in the Treaty of 1832 was probably the widow of an earlier minko, but her identity has not been confirmed. Cushman, who calls her "Pakarli," which he says means "Blossom," was the widow of Tuskaapela, which he translates as "Warrior-Helper," whom no other source lists as a minko. He says that Tuskaapela was a former Chickasaw king, but was made an invalid for life by an accident that rendered him unable to walk in an upright position, but slowly crawled about my means of a buck's horn in each

hand extended behind him, and his feet thrust forward, presenting an object of great compassion. H. B. Cushman, *History of the Choctaw, Chickasaw and Natchez Indians*, ed. Angie Debo (Norman: University of Oklahoma Press, 1999), 404.

11. Upshaw to Harris, June 5 and 7, 1838 (Chickasaw Emigration U49 and U50), M234-R143.

12. Transportation Receipt (1838) No. 49 (Chickasaw Emigration C816), M234-R143; *Arkansas Gazette*, July 4, August 8, and September 12, 1838.

13. "Infant Pontotoc celebrated Fourth in patriotic fashion in 1838," *Journal of Pontotoc County Historical Society* 1 (Summer 1999), 71. Miss Fontaine was the daughter of Patrick Henry Fontaine, Andrew Jackson's appointment as manager of the land office when the Chickasaw lands opened for sale.

14. Upshaw to Harris, January 26 and August 31, 1838 (Chickasaw Emigration U32 and U55), M234-R143.

15. Upshaw to Harris, August 1, 1838 (Chickasaw Emigration U54), M234-R143.

16. Phillips to Harris, August 7 and 19, 1838 (Chickasaw Emigration P381 and P388), M234-R143.

17. Upshaw to Harris, August 13, 1838 (Chickasaw Emigration U53), M234-R143.

18. Upshaw to Harris, April 10, 1838 (Chickasaw Emigration U45), M234-R143.

19. *Ibid.*; Upshaw to Harris, August 1, 1838 (Chickasaw Emigration U54), M234-R143.

20. Upshaw to Harris, August 31 and September 1, 1838, and Adjutant General R. Jones, Special Orders No. 61 (Chickasaw Emigration U55, U56, and A421), M234-R143.

21. Upshaw to Harris, October 9 and 12, 1838 (Chickasaw Emigration U57 and U58), M234-R143.

22. Upshaw to Harris, October 12, 1838 (Chickasaw Emigration U58), M234-R143.

23. Upshaw to Harris, November 2, 1838 (Chickasaw Emigration U59), M234-R143.

24. *Ibid.*

25. Quoted in *Arkansas Advocate*, November 12, 1838.

26. Chickasaw Payments, Box 1, Bundle 16.

27. *Ibid.*, 16; *Arkansas Gazette*, November 28, 1838.

28. Upshaw to Harris, November 28, 1838 (Chickasaw Emigration U61), M234-R143.

29. William Armstrong to T. Hartley Crawford, January 1, 1839, with enclosure, and Upshaw to Crawford, February 2, 1839 (Chickasaw Emigration A521 and U64), M234-R144.

30. Upshaw to Crawford, February 2, 1839 (Chickasaw Emigration U64), M234-R144; 1839 Chickasaw Census, National Archives Microfilm, Special Filming, Roll entitled Chickasaw 1847 Census. Following the Treaty of 1866, the Chickasaw Nation steadfastly refused to adopt its former slaves and free blacks. One of their major arguments was that they had not had a long relationship with their African-descended people, and that the Nation as a whole had not been in the slave business very long. Travelers among the Chickasaws during the late eighteenth century reported the presence of African slaves. By the time of the Treaty of Pontotoc, slavery was institutionalized because the treaty made provisions for larger land allotments for slave owners. However, for the rank-and-file Chickasaws, the statistics of Upshaw's census of 1839 seem to bear out Chickasaw claims that slave ownership was new for the Chickasaws at the time of removal. For example, of the 258 slave owners listed in the census, 210 owned 5 slaves or fewer, and 35 owned between 6 and 10. These statistics reflect the absence of slave families, present in slave communities of the Cherokees, Creeks, and Seminoles, who had a long-standing relationship with African-descended people. See Records Relating to Indian Trust Funds, Ledger for Trust Funds of Chickasaw Incompetents and Minors, 1837–43.

31. Upshaw to Crawford, February 25, 1839 (Chickasaw Emigration U65), M234-R144.

32. Chickasaw Payments, Box 4, Bundle 36.

33. E. A. Hitchcock to J. C. Spencer, June 1, 1842; Armstrong to Crawford, April 9, 1843; and Roll of Chickasaw Indians in Upshaw to Crawford, April 9, 1844 (Chickasaw Emigration H1048, A1430, U158), M234-R144. Greenwood died before he received payment for his expenses. They were collected by his widow, Ishtimihachah and other heirs: Uslachah, Samah, Elizabeth, Vicy, Tiyehoya, and Jefferson. See Chickasaw Payments, Box 4, Bundle 32 and Box 5, Bundle 66.

34. *Missionary Herald* 27 (1831), 45, 251.

35. John Wilson, *Old Monroe Presbyterian Church* (Algoma, MS: n.d.), 14, 15.

36. Herbert H. McAlexander, *A Southern Tapestry: Marshall County Mississippi, 1835–2000* (Virginia Beach: The Denning Company, Publisher, 2000), 8.

37. *Ibid.*, 10.

38. *Ibid.*, 9, 24; Betty C. Wiltshire, *Marshall County, Mississippi, Probate and Will Records* (Carrolton, MS: Pioneer Publishing Co., 1996), 70.

39. McAlexander, *A Southern Tapestry*, 26.

40. *Ibid.*, 16, 24; Wilson, *Old Monroe*, 15.

41. McAlexander, *A Southern Tapestry*, 15–16.

42. *Ibid.*, 16.

43. *Ibid.*, 24.

44. Roll of Chickasaw Indians, in Upshaw to Crawford, April 9, 1844, and Upshaw to William Medill, February 3, 1846 (Chickasaw Emigration U158 andU197), M234-R144; Chickasaw Payments, Box 5, Bundles 59, 60, and Box 4, Bundle 37. Joseph Bryan filed claims for these Chickasaws on behalf of Daniel Saffarans in February 1846. Bryan to Medill, February 23, 1846 (Chickasaw Emigration B2648), M234-R144.

45. See Muster Rolls in Armstrong to Crawford, April 22, 1842 (Chickasaw Emigration A1233), M234-R144. See also Armstrong to Crawford, April 9 and 22, 1843 (Chickasaw Emigration A1430 and A1233) and Hitchcock to Spencer, June 1, 1842 (Chickasaw Emigration H1048), M234-R144.

46. Ethan A. Hitchcock, *A Traveler in Indian Territory*, ed. Grant Foreman (Cedar Rapids: Torch Press, 1930), 169.

47. Jacob Thompson to Secretary, August 13 and 24, 1842 (Chickasaw Emigration T972 and T980), M234-R144.

48. James Colbert to Secretary of War, August 1, 1842, and W. B. Campbell and R. L. Caruthers to Spencer, with enclosure, August 15, 1842 (Chickasaw Emigration C1771 and C1772), M234-R144.

49. Ish to ho to pi [Ishtehotopa], et al., to Armstrong, October 28, 1842 (enclosed in Chickasaw Emigration A1356), M234-R144.

50. Second Auditor to Medill, July 17, 1848 (Chickasaw Emigration A233) and Armstrong to Medill, July 17, 1848, and Armstrong to Crawford, April 29, 1843 (Chickasaw Emigration A233 and A1430), M234-R144. Moore's extended family included Joseph G. Mitchell, Moore's son; R. B. Willis, who married her daughter Harriett Moore Mosby; Everet M. James; Susan Colbert, Samuel C. Colbert; Charles F. Eastman; Dougherty Colbert; Untombee; Moley Colbert, Colbert Carter, and Mitchell Frazier. The commutation for subsistence during removal and for forage for her party's 171 horses from Memphis to the Chickasaw District, plus interest before the money was finally paid in the summer of 1843, was $9,040.62.

51. Armstrong to Crawford, April 9 and February 20, 1843 (Chickasaw Emigration A1430 and A1407), M234-R144.

52. T. H. Crawford to J. M. Porter, June 26, 1843, National Archives Record Group 75, Records of the Bureau of Indian Affairs, Entry 252, Indian Removal, Chickasaw Removal Records, Letters Sent, 1832–61, 2: 305–09.

53. Armstrong to Crawford, December 1, 1842 (Chickasaw Emigration A1356), M234-R144.

54. D. Saffarans to Crawford, February 14, 1843 (Chickasaw Emigration S3334), M234-R144.

55. Ish to ho to pa [Ishtehotopa], et al., to Crawford, July 15, 1843 (Chickasaw Emigration I1269), M234-R144.

56. Armstrong to Crawford, September 11, 1843 (Chickasaw Emigration A1516) and Upshaw to Crawford, September 20 and December 30, 1843 (Chickasaw Emigration U146 and U149), M234-R144; Chickasaw Payments, Box 4, Bundles 28, 29, 30, 38. Among this group were the families of R. B. Willis, with a party of eleven, including seven slaves, James L. Tyson with eleven, including eight slaves, Reuben Bourland with eleven, including nine slaves, having had one death on the road, and Molly Gunn with two, James Bird with ten, James H. Neal with three, and Benjamin Love's wife and four children.

57. Saffarans to Crawford, June 6, 1843 (Chickasaw Emigration S3410), G. Loomis to Crawford, November 12, 1842, and February 24, 1843 (Chickasaw Emigration L1799 and L1894), and Contract, February 23, 1843, in Saffarans to Crawford, June 6, 1843 (Chickasaw Emigration S3410), M234-R144.

58. Armstrong to Crawford, November, 1843, with enclosures (Chickasaw Emigration A1558), and J. Thompson to Crawford, January 19, 1844 (Chickasaw Emigration T1147), M234-R144.

59. C. F. Eastman to Thompson, January 16, 1844, enclosed in J. Thompson to Crawford, February 21, 1844 (Chickasaw Emigration T1166), Upshaw to Crawford, February 4, 1844 (Chickasaw Emigration U150), and Armstrong to Crawford, September 26, 1844 (Chickasaw Emigration A1713), M234-R144.

60. Upshaw to Crawford, February 25 and May 20, 1844 (Chickasaw Emigration U153 and U161), Bryan to Crawford, April 15 and May 6, 1844 (Chickasaw Emigration B1998, 2013, and 2012), Armstrong to Crawford, March 11, 1844, with enclosure (Chickasaw Emigration A1612), M234-R144. See also Upshaw to Crawford, May 25, 1844 (Chickasaw Emigration U164), M234-R144.

61. Armstrong to Crawford, with enclosures, December 7, 1844 (Chickasaw Emigration A1773), M234-R144.

62. Muster Rolls in Upshaw to Crawford, December 26, 1844, and January 15, 1845 (Chickasaw Emigration U173 and U174), M234-R144; Chickasaw Payments, Box 4, Bundles 42, 46, 47.

63. Armstrong to Crawford, April 10, 1845 (Chickasaw Emigration A1802), Bryan to Crawford, February 18, March 7, and June 16, 1845 (Chickasaw

(169)

Emigration B2338, B2358, and B2470), Bryan to William Medill, December 15, 1845 (Chickasaw Emigration B2606), and Upshaw to Medill, December 24, 1845 (Chickasaw Emigration U196), M234-R144. In February, Saffarans submitted claims in his name from John P. Roark, Robertson James, Davis James, John H. Rice, and William Simpson. In March, he filed claims for Lotty James and family and, in June, Isaac Love, May Simonds, and S. W. Lewis. These were followed in July by Richard Overton and family and, in December, by William Love and family. In June 1845, Ishtehotopa and Chiefs Isaac Alberson, Benjamin Love, Slone Love, James Gamble, and James Wolf forwarded a list of Chickasaws who had removed themselves, apparently in 1844 and 1845 but had never been paid. See Upshaw to Crawford, July 1, 1845 (Chickasaw Emigration U186), M234-R144.

64. Berthelet, Heald & Co. to Medill, October 17, 1845 (Chickasaw Emigration B2582), and Upshaw to Medill, May 20 and November 20, 1846 (Chickasaw Emigration U202 and U4), M234-R144.

65. Thompson to Medill, May 20, 1846 (Chickasaw Emigration T1453), Bryan to Medill, May 8, 1846 (Chickasaw Emigration B1694 ½), and Upshaw to Medill, June 8, September 11, October 13, and November 20, 1846 (Chickasaw Emigration U207, U211, U213, and U3), M234-R144; Chickasaw Payments, Box 5, Bundles 63 and 67 and Box 6, Bundles 82, 83, and 92.

66. Upshaw to Medill, May 5, June 25, and July 20, 1847 (Chickasaw Emigration U16, U20, and U22), M234-R144; Chickasaw Payments, Box 6, Bundles 85, 89, 90.

67. Upshaw to Medill, May 5, 1847, with enclosures, and March 15, 1848 (Chickasaw Emigration U17 and U29), M234-R144.

68. Upshaw to Medill, August 18, 1848 (Chickasaw Emigration U45), and Bryan to Medill, September 7 and November 15, 1848 (Chickasaw B290 and B319), M234-R144; Chickasaw Payments, Box 6, Bundles 95, 96, 97, 99, 114, and 127.

69. G. W. Long to Commissioner of Indian Affairs, June 20, 1850 (Chickasaw Emigration L663), M234-R144; Arrell M. Gibson, *The Chickasaws* (Norman: University of Oklahoma Press, 1971), 189; Luke Lea to P. Clayton, August 6 1850, and A. S. Landry to Gabriel W. Long, September 27, 1850; National Archives Record Group 75, Records of the Bureau of Indian Affairs, Entry 252, Indian Removal, Chickasaw Removal Records, Letters Sent, 1832–61, 3: 106, 111.

(170)

Privation, Fraud,
and Attrition
of the
Chickasaw Fund

ANYONE WHO TRAVELED INTO THE INTERIOR of the continent in the late 1830s understood the rigors they faced. The Chickasaws were no exception. However, their journey, either by land or water, was less demanding and less debilitating than that of any of the other tribes, except perhaps the Seminoles. The reasons were partly circumstantial, for example, in the form of mild seasons, both summer and winter. Perhaps more significant was the control they exerted over the removal process—their willingness to strike out for their western nation on their own and to abandon initial plans and follow their own judgment. Unlike many of the Choctaws, Creeks, and Cherokees, they did not give up their property, especially their horses. Instead of settling for the thirty-pound limit for baggage set by the government and instead of walking like others such as the Choctaws did, the Chickasaws took what they wanted with them, many riding in their own carriages and wagons, others riding steamboats, and the remainder riding horseback. For many, their time of trial began upon arrival at Fort Coffee, the Choctaw Agency, or Fort Towson. These were not their final destinations, only their points of entry into the Choctaw country. They still faced two major problems: making their way to the places where they wanted to settle and the government's handling of rations that were supposed to sustain them until they could reestablish their family economies. Unfortunately, for years after 1837, the Chickasaw people not only endured privation, but they were subjected to the fraudulent practices of rations contractors and traders, whose activities, as later investigations showed, had created great waste of the Chickasaw national fund.

When the Chickasaws began to arrive at Fort Coffee in great numbers in November and December 1837, Superintendent for the Western District William Armstrong seemed surprised that they were more anxious to settle in the Chickasaw District than he had anticipated. Armstrong first used the remoteness of the district from supply stations to discourage settlement there. Beyond the Blue were very few, if any, settlements in the Chickasaw district. It would be difficult to get supplies to them even though there was a "tolerable good" road from Fort Towson to the Washita. Armstrong had perhaps been misled by the actions of some of the wealthier Chickasaws, who had settled in the Choctaw country near Fort Towson in order to raise cotton. But the new arrivals had what they needed to settle a new country. They had large quantities of personal property, tents, farming tools, teams, and wagons. Armstrong hoped to get them to their new homes in time to put in a crop in the spring of 1838. But he could not tell them the best route to take from Fort Coffee to their country, for he had not had a road built, claiming a lack of horses, and justified delaying the exploration of a route until the Chickasaw horses arrived overland.[1]

Finally in late December, Armstrong authorized construction of a road from Fort Coffee to the area where the Chickasaws wanted to settle on the Boggy. On December 21, Chickasaw agent G. P. Kingsbury and four Chickasaws, including Ishtakekatubby, left to establish the route. Also in the party were a Shawnee guide named Jonathan and a Choctaw named David. They took the road from Fort Coffee south toward Fort Towson for about twenty-five miles and then turned to the southwest, following a course that took them over the prairie and timbered lands between the San Bois and Jack Fork Mountains and across tributaries of Brazil Creek and the Fouche Maline, Gaines Creek, Brushy Creek, the Little Boggy, the Muddy Boggy, and the Clear Boggy to the Blue River. The route they followed had few steep grades and promised to create little difficulty in road building. On the Clear Boggy they found good range for horses and cattle, as well as cane brakes and even green grass that late in the year. Kingsbury believed the range was sufficient to provide for the Chickasaw horses all winter. Fertile land, timber, and good water caused him to recommend a place on the lower Clear Boggy to establish a subsistence depot, at which the Chickasaws could draw their provisions before going out to select settlement locations within easy distance of the depot.[2]

Meanwhile, the large body of the nation remained in the vicinity of Fort Coffee, where they could receive subsistence rations until they could go on to their district. Much of the provision that had been stored since the previous spring remained unused. Because provisions were scarce and costly in Arkansas and in the Indian country, Armstrong proposed that the old provisions that had been stored since the spring of 1837 be used by the Chickasaws at Fort Coffee rather than sold at a loss and that new provisions be purchased for shipment to the Chickasaw district. He also suggested that if the pork were exchanged for beef on the hoof, the cattle could be driven and the expenses of hauling the pork could be avoided.[3] By the time Armstrong proposed these actions to the commissioner of Indian affairs, he had already decided to exchange part of the pork rations. Although the commissioner approved his action, it reflected a kind of free-wheeling attitude that Armstrong at times exhibited, and later made those who were investigating fraud in the ration system of the Chickasaws and other tribes think that Armstrong was too cozy with local contractors.

Armstrong and R.D.C. Collins, at Little Rock, contracted with Lorenzo N. Clark of Arkansas on December 8, 1837, to take off the government's hands all of the salted pork rations still in storage at Fort Smith and Little Rock. In return, Clark agreed that upon thirty days' notice, he would obtain and deliver, at his own expense, a quantity of beef of whatever quality the government required. For every barrel of pork he received, Clark was to deliver 266 2/3 pounds of fresh beef or, in lieu of that, "stock cattle, cows, and calves on the hoof, upon just estimates," when required by the government. Clark agreed to deliver the beef to the Chickasaws at places designated by U. S. agents no more than seventy-five miles from the Choctaw Agency.[4]

Meanwhile, the number of Chickasaws to be subsisted continued to mount. By January 1, 1838, Upshaw had accounted to Kingsbury for 3,538 Chickasaws who had removed that winter. Upshaw was expecting "upwards of a thousand" more in J. M. Millard's party to arrive in a few days. In total, he counted 4,329, but with Millard's anticipated group were a large number that had joined after they crossed the Mississip-

(173)

pi.[5] In reality, Upshaw had underestimated the latter group, which by the time it reached Little Rock, numbered between 1,000 and 1,500.

The old rations that were issued to the Chickasaws at Fort Coffee were hardly fit to use. The party of about 200 who had been conducted by William Guy and arrived at Fort Coffee in November 1837 had remained near the post for about a month. They received pork and flour out of the old rations. The sacks of corn, supposedly containing two bushels, in reality held only a bushel and a half. It was weevil-eaten, and most of the flour was sour, "some of it entirely unfit to eat."[6] Slone Love arrived at Fort Coffee on December 5, 1837, captain of 100 Chickasaws, and was appointed to oversee the issue of their rations during the month they remained there. The pork, flour, and corn were so damaged that many in the party refused it, and the salt was issued irregularly. The corn appeared to have been shelled green and had mildewed, some of it so bad that the horses would not eat it. Only an occasional barrel of flour was good. "The pork was so bad," Love said, "that Doctor Walker told me that, if the emigrants continued to use it, it would kill them all off. It gave those who eat it a diarrhea, and it was always my opinion that many of our poor people died in consequence of it."[7]

As they did regarding many matters, Kingsbury and Armstrong disagreed over the timing of Chickasaw removal from Fort Coffee to the proposed supply depot on the lower Boggy. Kingsbury recommended immediate removal for several reasons: the Chickasaws wanted to get to their new lands as soon as possible, the route was much easier to travel than he had earlier thought, and the teams would require little forage because there were large quantities of cane for grazing every ten to fifteen miles. During his expedition to mark the road, he had been out fifteen days without corn for the horses, which had "returned from the trip but little worsted."[8] Armstrong had sent a party out immediately following Kingsbury's return to begin cutting the road, and parties of Chickasaws started for the Boggy. Yet Armstrong pointed out obstacles to a quick removal. The road went through uninhabited country; thus all provisions must be hauled from Fort Coffee. To him, Chickasaw livestock was problematic. Removal had taken a tremendous toll on the horses and oxen. Large numbers had died between Memphis and the

Arkansas River at Little Rock. Those that survived were in such poor condition that Upshaw had ordered their corn rations increased. At the time Armstrong expressed these views in January 1838, he was expecting a group that had lost 500 to 600 horses and oxen. Those that were left would be very poor upon arrival at Fort Coffee. Another obstacle to Armstrong was transporting the large quantities of personal property that the Chickasaws had brought by steamboat to Fort Coffee. Armstrong believed that it would be "tedious, laborious and expensive to get them to their country." Finally, it was winter. Still, Armstrong realized that they must move soon. His plan was to supply them well with provisions when they set out and have a small supply sent out to sustain the Chickasaws until the contractors could begin their issues.[9]

Chickasaws elsewhere in the Choctaw Nation fared better than those at Fort Coffee. The group of 340 from Sealy's district who had removed the previous summer received subsistence rations at David Folsom's. Folsom, a Choctaw, had received a contract to supply them with rations of one pound of fresh beef or three-fourths pound of salt pork or bacon, a pint and a half of corn or corn meal, and one gallon of salt per one hundred rations. Armstrong expected those Chickasaws to go to the Boggy as soon as a depot was established.[10] The firm of Doak & Tim contracted to furnish complete rations for twelve months after January 1, 1838, to about 200 Chickasaws who had settled at Doaksville and to all who should join them. They also contracted to furnish forage rations of "good sound merchantable corn" for no more than 200 horses for a period of six months.[11]

Not until the middle of January 1838 did Armstrong begin to negotiate contracts for supplying the Chickasaw district, opening the door to opportunities for fraud. At Little Rock, Captain R. D. C. Collins accepted a proposal from the firm of Glasgow & Harrison of St. Louis to take all of the Chickasaw stores of corn and pork at Fort Coffee to sell, and in turn, to furnish rations of fresh beef or pork and corn in the Chickasaw district. The firm would supply the Chickasaws after February 1 for fourteen cents a ration—a high price. Armstrong approved those terms for a number of reasons. The distance to the Chickasaw district was from 100 to 120 miles, and the expense of hauling the corn would be great. There were such great quantities of pork in store

(175)

that even after a year of subsisting the Chickasaws, large amounts remained, which by then would certainly be spoiled. Glasgow & Harrison
owned wagons and a steamboat "or two," which better qualified them
to perform the service than anyone else. Although fourteen cents per
ration was high, it would cost that much for the Chickasaws to have
the stores delivered that far. Given the scarcity of goods in the region,
Armstrong argued that it could not be done for less than that, and in
his words, "the Chickasaws are well pleased with the arrangements, for
they will lose little of the provision deposited at Fort Coffee."[12]

Glasgow & Harrison had an inside advantage in making the agreement. A co-partnership in the company name had been formed at Little
Rock in early 1837 to trade and to furnish rations and subsistence to
Creeks and Seminoles. Company contracts were tended to by James S.
Conway, the Arkansas governor, at Little Rock, who was their "authorized agent." In partnership with Glasgow, Harrison, and Conway was
Thomas T. Tunstall. Tunstall, a steamboat captain, had purchased the
steamboat *Harp* at New Orleans for the company's use. It went into
regular trade on the Arkansas River, but its primary purpose was to
haul provisions for the recently emigrated Creeks. The firm of Glasgow
& Harrison also owned the *Tecumseh*, which was being used in removal
of the Seminoles and others.[13]

On February 1, Armstrong and Collins confirmed the proposal in
a contract. Glasgow & Harrison agreed to take the supplies of salted
pork and corn at Fort Coffee. They would replace the pork whenever
required, at the rate of 266 2/3 pounds of fresh beef or 200 pounds of
salted pork per barrel or, in lieu of these, beef on the hoof. In return for
each bushel of corn received, Glasgow & Harrison agreed to provide
the Chickasaws with 42 2/3 rations of "good sound corn; the rations
to consist of three-fourths of a quart of corn, and to be delivered at the
rate of 32 quarts, dry measure, to the bushel." They would deliver rations to points no more than 125 miles from Fort Coffee. For every meat
and corn ration the firm delivered, they would receive two cents and
five cents, one-and-one-third mills, respectively. If the number of rations required of Glasgow & Harrison from February 1, 1838, to January
31, 1839, exceeded the number received from the stores at Fort Coffee,
Glasgow & Harrison agreed to deliver the necessary standard rations.

(176)

Exceptions to this provision were rations the Chickasaws received at Doaksville from Doak & Tim and those issued at David Folsom's near Fort Towson. For the extra rations they furnished, Glasgow & Harrison would receive six cents, five mills for meat and seven cents, five mills for corn. If the firm failed to deliver the quantity or quality of subsistence required by the contract, the U. S. would make up the deficiency and Glasgow & Harrison would remunerate the expenses. On the same day they made this contract, Glasgow & Harrison made a similar one to receive the spoiling provisions in storage at Fort Gibson and to distribute them to the Creeks. Under the Chickasaw agreement, Glasgow & Harrison received 1,663 barrels of salt pork, 512 bushels of salt, 257 barrels of flour, and 3,064 bushels of corn.[14] All of these goods had been paid for out of the Chickasaws' fund, and all they received in return was a promise by Glasgow & Harrison to deliver rations sometime in the future.

These contracts looked suspicious to outsiders. Luther Chase, sutler at Fort Gibson for Glasgow & Harrison, later claimed that the Chickasaw contract of February 1, 1838, was issued without competitive bids as required by law. Chase, formerly a clerk for Collins, was probably in a position to know. Ethan Allen Hitchcock, who later investigated the possibility of fraud, wrote, "I *suspect*, and am to examine in Washington, that neither that contract, nor the other of the same date for issues to Creeks was ever put upon record. Look well to this."[15] Chase said that Armstrong and Collins had made both contracts at the same time at Fort Coffee. Although earlier contracts had gone for eight cents a ration, these not only gave up the rations held by the government but nearly eight cents more, as well as more than twelve cents for any rations above the amount handed over to Glasgow & Harrison. "Chase assures me the provision for the general depot greatly exceeded that purchased for the Chickasaws, yet it appears that of some $950,000 in provision, some $745,000 was charged to the Chickasaws and thus attempted to be covered up because the Chickasaw fund appeared to be available."[16]

The question of possible fraud was apparently a touchy subject at Fort Gibson because of the strong presence of Glasgow & Harrison. Seaborn Hill, who lived in the Creek Nation near there, claimed that he had once said something about fraud in the presence of James Harrison. Harrison, "a tremendous man with 'a hand as big as all out doors,'" Hill claimed, "collared" him and "wrung" his face. Hill challenged Harrison to a duel, but the fight was stopped by a dragoon officer at the fort.[17]

By the time the Glasgow & Harrison contracts were drawn, the Chickasaws who had moved on to the Chickasaw district were in dire need of supplies. The group that had arrived with Guy early in the previous November had split, part of them going to Pheasant Bluff on the Canadian, where some of the first removal party had gone in 1837. The remainder went southwest to the Blue River. They packed a month's supply of rations but only corn enough for four or five days because they were promised that corn would be sent after them. Because there was no road at the time from Fort Coffee to the Blue River, the party was on the route for more than a month because of "heavy sleet and other causes." No corn supplies, as promised, reached them. Local supplies were scarce. Richard McClure, a Kentuckian who had a Chickasaw family and had gone west with the party, managed to buy ten bushels from a Choctaw named Pickens at the exorbitant price of two dollars a bushel. That purchase allowed him to reach the Blue, but all of his horses eventually starved. "Every horse I had," he said, "was killed off by hard work and want of feed."[18]

The weeks following their arrival at the Blue were, without question, hard times. About forty bushels of corn reached them sometime in March. McClure received two sacks, but the corn was so rotten "that the horses would not eat it." For a period of six weeks to two months, they received nothing. Because corn was not to be had in the region, during that period they had no bread. "I bought buffalo meat and venison from the Delawares," McClure said, "and got bears' oil, &c., and made out with that." When rations finally reached them, the contractors refused to give the Chickasaws the back rations that were due them.[19]

Meanwhile, the road Armstrong had ordered from Fort Coffee to the Boggy, where a supply depot was to be established, was being cut. By mid-February 1838, about 500 Chickasaws had arrived at the Boggy, about that many were near Pheasant Bluff, and about 400 remained on the Red River near Fort Towson. The remainder were still in the vicinity of the Choctaw Agency and Fort Coffee. The weather had been unusually cold for about a month but was bitter in mid-February, so that the Arkansas was frozen over sufficiently for people to walk across it. Armstrong waited for the weather to break to send the remaining Chickasaws on to the southwest. He had a way of shading the truth to serve his own interests. He wanted officials in Washington to believe that the delay in their going to the Boggy was the Chickasaws' fault. "The Chickasaws are inclined to be very idle," he said, "and it requires starving to get them off. They have been doing nothing but drinking and are much indisposed to work. This with the loss of their horses and the great quantity of baggage they have brought with them makes it very difficult and expensive to move them." Armstrong would also have had officials believe that there were no problems with rations. The contractors Glasgow & Harrison had moved a herd of 250 cattle toward the Boggy, he reported, and planned to keep them on the range until the Chickasaws then at the agency arrived there, at which time they would be issued to the people. "I hope in a few days to get the Chickasaws started," he said; "the contractors have ample means to subsist them."[20] Subsequent revelations would prove Armstrong a liar.

By late April, the migration to the Chickasaw district was waning. On April 20, Kingsbury reported that 700 to 800 had settled, another large party was on the way, and another 800 were waiting on an issue of corn before departing. The season was growing late, so an estimated 1,500 had decided to remain near the Choctaw Agency and make a corn crop to supply themselves during the next year because it was too late to remove and get settled in time to farm. The number settled on the Red River near Fort Towson had reached about 500, some of whom planned to move to the Chickasaw district the following year.[21]

Although, as Armstrong had said, the contractors may have had the means to deliver subsistence to the Chickasaws, they failed to do so in a timely fashion. A part of the Chickasaw corn purchased in the spring of 1837 had been loaned to the partnership of Thompson and Drennen of Van Buren, Arkansas, the previous year. John Drennen was a man of growing influence. By 1835 Drennen and David Thompson, brothers-in-law, had a trading house at Columbus Landing near present day Van Buren, and Drennen had represented Crawford County at the Ar-

(179)

kansas Constitutional Convention the following year. In 1836 the two moved their trading house to Van Buren nearby, purchasing the town site. Upon receiving the Chickasaw corn, they were under bond to re-supply the Chickasaws upon proper notice. Although they had been notified in the fall of 1837 to replenish the supply by January 1, 1838, by April they had returned only a small amount. By then, the Chickasaw settlements on the Boggy had no corn, Kingsbury reported, and argued that Thompson and Drennen should forfeit their bond.[22] Conditions were equally bad in the settlements on the Blue. The household of R. J. Humphreys, a Tennessean with a Chickasaw family, was among those who suffered through the spring of 1838 for lack of provisions. They received no rations for two months, "during which time," Humphreys said, "the contractors had no provisions at the depot for us, and I was compelled to take my family out into the buffalo country for subsistence." When the contractors finally brought provisions, Humphreys and his family did not receive the rations that had been due them during the starving months. Richard McClure, who settled his family on the Blue, was reluctant to blame the contractors because the roads at that time were impassable. However, he thought it wrong for the contractors to be paid for rations the Chickasaws were entitled to but did not receive.[23]

William R. Guy, who served as issuing commissary at Boggy Depot from its establishment in February 1838 to September 1839, confirmed the problems with rations during the spring of 1838. The first rations sent to Boggy Depot came from Fort Coffee. Guy said the pork was good, but the flour was damaged. After that, issues were made in fresh meat and corn.[24] In May 1838, he wrote to Upshaw, who was at Pontotoc preparing other parties for removal, about the suffering of the Chickasaws at the Blue and Boggy. He had no rations to issue: "I am here starving with the Chickasaws, by gross mismanagement on the part of the contractors; and when our situation will be bettered is hard for me to say, for it is one failure after another without end. You or Colonel Armstrong are very much needed here at this time, for there is such a propensity to play faro at Fort Coffee, that I begin to think we shall have to starve to death or abandon the country. There has been corn within forty miles of this place for four or five days without moving a peg to relieve the sufferings of the people of Blue or Boggy."[25]

Conditions were little better at Fort Coffee and vicinity. When the Clean House group reached there on March 9, 1838, there was no subsistence for them or other Chickasaws who had remained encamped nearby since their removal the previous fall. Still others were scattered throughout the country between Fort Coffee and the Red River. Glasgow & Harrison was not prepared to issue rations because the river had been too low to bring corn up, the contractors said, and the cattle being brought from Missouri had not arrived. Chickasaw agent Kingsbury authorized Robert B. Crockett, Upshaw's brother-in-law who had accompanied the Clean House party, to go through the Choctaw Nation to see if he could procure corn and beef for his group. He obtained a little beef at $3.50 per hundred weight but was not able to find any corn. His party went into camp about thirty miles from Fort Coffee, where he issued the beef.[26]

They were still waiting for corn in early April, but none came. In its place, Glasgow & Harrison sent about thirty barrels of flour, presumably part of the old Chickasaw stores the company had earlier received from the government to issue to the Creeks. But the flour was sour, Crockett said, "so much damaged or spoiled that, when the hoops were knocked off, and the staves fell away, the flour would remain standing in a cake, and I saw hogs smell to it, and go away without eating it. There was in some of the barrels a small quantity out of the centre of the barrels that the Indians could use; but a good deal of it the Indians left, and the hogs would not eat it. There might have been about one-third of the flour that could be used by people in a starving condition." Crockett also reported that he had seen pickled pork issued that was so bad that the Chickasaws threw the largest quantity of it away, and some of the corn that was issued was so bad that the horses would not eat it.[27]

(181)

The Chickasaws were desperate for corn. At times, they paid as much as four dollars a bushel to the older settlers in the country when they could find it for sale. Crockett recalled issuing corn about fifty miles from Fort Coffee on their way to the Boggy. The teams or some of the other horses had been fed overnight, he said, "and in the morning, before the issue was made, the Indian women came about and picked up the kernels of corn that had been left upon the ground where the horses had been fed."[28] While some of the wealthier Chickasaws could purchase supplies when they could find them, the so-called "incompetent" as well as many of the "competent" Chickasaws were not that fortunate. The money they were supposed to have received for the sale of their allotments in Mississippi and Alabama had been invested by the government or remained with their "agents" east of the Mississippi. Said Kingsbury, they were "now very much in want of it for the purpose of purchasing stock and the necessaries and conveniences of life." There would probably not be a time when they needed it more than the spring of 1838, he said. By the middle of May, he reported that all of the Chickasaws that had been at Fort Coffee had removed to the Chickasaw district. Those with means had "erected comfortable houses & have large fields already planted with corn." However, he said, "many of the poorer and incompetent Indians say to me that they are very desirous to obtain the money, or a portion of it, that they have deposited in Mississippi."[29]

Armstrong steadily defended the contractors. He continued to blame the Chickasaws themselves for the subsistence problems that persisted throughout the spring of 1838. They were settling 50 to 120 miles from Fort Coffee, creating problems in transporting the "unusually large amount of baggage" that they had brought with them. The "scattered situation of the Chickasaws," as he called their settlement patterns, had required the establishment of more ration stations than usual: near Fort Towson, at Doaksville, at Boggy, at Brushy Creek, and on the Canadian.[30]

Kingsbury was the only official on the scene to admit that some Chickasaws had suffered that spring from lack of corn, especially on the Brushy and Boggy where the suffering had been great. However, like Armstrong, Kingsbury believed the distances that goods had to be hauled explained the failure of contractors to deliver corn to the Blue and Boggy. Glasgow & Harrison failed to get corn there in time for the April issue, but by early May, the wagons laden with corn had started moving again. The contractors had also sent a "large supply" up the Red River, leading Kingsbury to believe that there would be no more failures. The beef supply, he had to admit, had not been a problem because it was delivered on the hoof. Many Chickasaws, he claimed, had even received "stock cattle several months in advance."[31]

Armstrong's and Kingsbury's arguments might have been stronger if failure to supply had been the only problem with ration issues. When corn was available, the Chickasaws were given short rations. R. J. Humphreys attended an issue at the Boggy depot below Walls' settlement in May 1838 and received what he claimed was short ration. The Glasgow & Harrison agent used a square box rather than a "proper half bushel measure" to issue corn. Humphrey did not know how much the box held, but it looked too small to be a half bushel.[32]

In June 1838, Richard McClure's settlement on the Blue heard that the contractors had delivered corn to the Boggy depot, which was about fifty miles away. The contractors offered fifty cents a bushel to anyone who would haul corn from the Boggy to the Blue settlement. Because they were needy, McClure and others organized a five-team train. McClure rode ahead to the place where the agent was issuing corn for Glasgow & Harrison. Apparently distrustful of the company agents, McClure had with him a half-bushel measure that he had brought from Mississippi. It carried a Mississippi state seal, verifying a true volume. When he arrived, he said, "I saw the issuing commissary, a young man named Hughes, issuing corn to an Indian in a square box in place of a proper half bushel measure; and I heard Hughes tell the Indian to strike it close; for, he said, the box holds about a pint more than half a bushel. I told him it would not hold a half bushel, and he said it was a pint over. I said that it did not look larger than a hobbing miller's toll dish, and that I could tell when my wagon came up; for I had a half bushel measure in it. When the wagon came up, I measured what the box held, and, after pouring its contents into the proper half bushel measure, it lacked just seven large tin cupfuls of corn—that is, fourteen to the bushel. The tin cup was a large pint cup." McClure refused to have his corn measured by Hughes' box. Hughes finally agreed to give McClure an issue in the measure he provided but said that those who had come with him would have theirs measured by the contractors' measure. "I answered," said McClure, "by saying, that those who came with me, must fare as I did; that we had come a long way for corn by the bushel and were not going to take three pecks." The difference was too great, Hughes said, but he would issue by weight, for he knew that

(183)

fifty-two pounds of corn made a bushel. McClure agreed and, later, when he measured a bushel with his own measure, he found it weighed forty-eight pounds. "It was light corn," he said, "'rather chaffy,' and I was well pleased to have the fifty-two pounds in place of forty-eight; for the difference in weight made up for the inferior quality of the corn." The privation of the Blue settlement was later relieved when an issuing depot was established only eighteen miles away.[33]

William Guy and others supported McClure's charges. Hughes, it appears, was a thorough scoundrel and in some ways typified the men who worked for Glasgow & Harrison. It appears that Hughes and another white man "harbored" two slaves in the swamps near a corn crib below the well near Boggy Depot. Hughes and his partner were captured by the Choctaws and taken to Fort Towson. "Facts" could not be proved against them, and they were released. "They talked loud and threatened the Choctaws, who tied them up and whipped them in the woods." A Choctaw named Walls was supposedly involved in the affair, and as the two men later passed Walls' place, they fired randomly at some Choctaws working in a field, killing one and wounding another. The Choctaws went in pursuit, and Hughes was not heard from again. His partner hid out in Texas.[34]

There had also been problems with the beef issues, despite Kingsbury's assertions. At Fort Coffee in April 1838, Robert B. Crockett observed an issue of cattle on the hoof by Charles Johnson, "Boggy," who had been John Millard's assistant removal conductor in the winter of 1837–38 and who now was both the government issuing commissary and an agent for Glasgow & Harrison. Crockett had had some recent experience issuing beef to the Clean House Chickasaws. He had had steers of different ages killed and weighed to get an estimate of weight. The largest was a six-year-old steer that weighed no more than 550 pounds. In Johnson's issue, none were killed; weight was estimated. They were far inferior cattle to those Crockett had issued and were very poor from having been driven a long distance. Johnson issued them at estimated weights about one-third higher than those Crockett had issued. In Crockett's issue, three-year-olds averaged 350 pounds; four-year-olds, 450; and five- and six-year-olds, 500 and 550. Johnson's estimate for the largest in his issue was 800 to 900 pounds "and the younger ones at a less rate, but in proportion." Crockett believed that the Chickasaws did not receive two-thirds of the amount due them.[35]

Charles Johnson had been involved in making money off Chickasaw removal in Mississippi. In the fall of 1837, N. A. Bryant was the contractor who supplied rations to the Chickasaws until they reached Memphis. His man in charge of rations at Coonewah campground was Johnson. John M. Millard was named as conductor for the group from Coonewah and was so impressed with Johnson's work that he asked Johnson to go with the Chickasaws as far as Memphis. Once there, Millard appointed him as his assistant conductor. Although he may have had the good favor of Millard and others officials, there was an undesirable quality about him. He was later a clerk for William Armstrong and was described by Ethan Allen Hitchcock as "a forward pert flippant conceited young fop, and heartless too; for when Mr. Love spoke of having had a negro boy drowned and expressed a proper feeling on the subject, Johnson closed the subject by saying 'there is $400 gone.'"[36] Unfortunately, Johnson was typical of many of the agents employed by Glasgow & Harrison.

Richard McClure, who had complained about the short measure and poor quality of corn rations, reported more favorably about the meat rations. He knew that the contractors without question overestimated the weight of cattle on the hoof. He received two young and poor steers estimated at 700 pounds each, which McClure estimated at exactly half that much. The remainder of his beef issue satisfied him. He took cows and calves at 450 pounds each instead of 450 pounds of butchered beef and also took some young heifers to begin his livestock herd.[37]

(185)

In the midst of the contractors' failures and the reports of suffering by the Chickasaws in the spring of 1838, War Department officials became concerned about the rising cost of Chickasaw removal. They began to question the accounts of Captain Joseph Phillips, Upshaw, and other disbursing agents and asked them to explain certain of their expenditures. At the heart of their concern with Phillips' accounts was the lucrative contract he had made with steamboat owner Simeon Buckner. Phillips, like Armstrong, blamed the high expense on the Chickasaws themselves: "The Chickasaws previous to their removal purchased many heavy articles of comfort as well as convenience, both weighty & expensive; which they were unwilling to leave behind them." The Chickasaws had four times the baggage that the Choctaws had when they removed. Hence, higher freight costs. In addition, Phillips argued, the Chickasaws delayed removal at a time when inflation made prices about double what they had been during removal of the Choctaws and other tribes. And it had been the chiefs who asked to travel by water. Phillips, Upshaw, and others, he argued, had simply accommodated them. Although it had cost more, the Chickasaws had enjoyed the "comforts & conveniences" of steamboat travel.[38] However, Phillips knew when he wrote those words that more Chickasaws had traveled by land than by Buckner's boats and that Buckner had inflated the numbers of Chickasaw passengers. Neither did Phillips account for the waste that had gone with the overstocking of rations at the outset of the removal, the spoilage, and the agreements with local merchants and contractors to take the rations, at no charge, off the government's hands.

Like Phillips, Upshaw blamed the expense of Chickasaw removal on the Chickasaws themselves. He said, "In the first place, they had a great deal of money, that is, their own private funds which they spent very freely. They bought a great many valuable articles, for themselves, to take west, believing their wants could not be supplied after getting to their homes. In fact, some of them bought as high as a thousand dollars worth of goods of various kinds which it was impossible for me to prevent, even had I been present." Mississippi merchants pressed them to buy. Upshaw said that he had seen two women buy $700 worth of merchandise in two hours. Getting the Chickasaws and their personal property to Memphis had been expensive. In addition to the necessary public wagons, a large number of Chickasaws had their own wagons. "Some had three or four wagons. In fact Col. James Wolf sent to Memphis, besides two wagons of his own, six wagons loaded with baggage. In addition to the wagons that they brought loaded, they brought about seven thousand ponies and horses, all packed as long as an Indian could pack them, and they can pack more on a horse than any other people I ever saw. Well, sir, all this came to Memphis. What had I [to] do?"[39]

What he did was to complain to the Chickasaw leaders, telling them that they could not take so much personal property. To that they replied, "'We are moved out of our own money. This is our property. We want it. It is valuable to us. Were we to attempt to sell it, we could not for a hundred dollars worth get five dollars. Will you make us burn or throw our property in the river? We are the friends of the whites. We have ever been and wish ever to be. In our Treaty with our Great Father, it does not say that we shall not carry our baggage with us.' Under the Circumstances," said Upshaw, "what could I say? I tell you what I did say. 'Put your baggage in the boat.' If I was wrong, it was in not obeying the Regulations. Feelings of kindness and justice compelled me to take the course I did. It was too late at that time to get instructions from the Department, for we were at the river." [40]

These fiscal inquiries by the War Department coincided with public charges of fraud in the subsistence process. On June 4, 1838, Austin J. Raines of Fort Smith wrote to Commissioner Carey A. Harris, charging the firm of Glasgow & Harrison with not only fraud but bribery. His charges related to Creek subsistence in 1836, but, he said, "The Chickasaws and the balance of the Creeks are fed by the same contractors, or a part of them, say, James Harrison, and your old friend Samuel Mackey—Governor Conway having sold out his interest to Mackey. Can't doubt but that the same course is pursued as stated to you in the other contracts." Raines referred to the practice of hiring unscrupulous commissaries who were given to bribery and fraud regarding ration issues. He sought an investigation, especially in light of the fact that Glasgow & Harrison had just received major contracts to feed the tribes. [41]

Raines claimed to have traded for fifteen years from St. Louis to the Rocky Mountains, Santa Fe, and Mexico. He had served as consul to Monterrey, Northern California, and Texas and claimed he had been backed by more than thirty members of Congress for rank of lieutenant colonel of the Second Regiment of the Dragoons. He claimed, as well, to have written, at the request of the Secretary of War Lewis Cass, a report on the Indians occupying the prairies and Rocky Mountains. [42] Raines now harkened back to some of the matters addressed in Cass's report.

Raines raised the specter of Indian war, an issue that had resounded loudly on the Arkansas frontier. For months, Arkansans had been requesting, as backlash to Indian removal, the establishment of more forts and the increase of troops on their western border. The fraud perpetrated on the Indians regarding rations might just be the thing to set off a war. "Why should these people remain quiet on your border? Have they done so when they were surrounded by a white population?" he asked. "No; they have shown their teeth, and some of them have *bit* badly. Will they not in a few years be better able to war, and present a stronger front than they have ever been? Have they not a country of a thousand miles in extent to the Rocky Mountains, where they can retreat, if they are hard *pushed*? Can you chastise them in this vast region, if they were driven to extremities? No, sir, never." [43]

Though Raines claimed knowledge of fraud only among the Creeks and Cherokees, officials began to take note of the Chickasaws' condition. Upshaw was back in Mississippi recruiting another group for removal when he received the letter from William Guy, written in the middle of May 1838, that he was starving along with the Chickasaws because of neglect by the contractors. Guy's letter confirmed reports that Upshaw received from Colonel Benjamin Clements and Major Felix Lewis who had been west and arrived back in Mississippi. As Guy said, the rations were available; the contractors were simply not delivering them. [44]

Late in the summer of 1838, suspecting that Commissioner Harris had not forwarded his letter to Secretary of War Joel R. Poinsett, Raines wrote a second letter to the secretary himself. He renewed his charges against Glasgow & Harrison, asking Poinsett to authorize an investigation. General Matthew Arbuckle, William Armstrong, and Captain B. L. E. Bonneville, already stationed on the Arkansas frontier, could do justice to all, he said. If no investigation was forthcoming, he threatened to take the matter to Congress. [45] Harris allowed his friend J. S. Conway of Arkansas to read Raines' letter. Conway dismissed Raines as "a man without character," who had been discharged as an agent for the company because he was a scamp and a "discredit to the company." There was nothing to Raines' charges, Conway claimed. However, he added, "Should you receive such charges from a respectable source, the matter should without doubt be examined into." [46] And there the matter apparently rested for the time being.

In early September, head men as well as the Chickasaw Commissioners Ishtehotopa (the minko), George Colbert, Isaac Alberson, and James Colbert (in the place of Levi Colbert, who had died) petitioned Commissioner Harris to extend the period of rationing for an additional seven months, beginning January 1, 1839. Citing severe illnesses, a general drought that persisted in the Indian country, and the arrival of many people too late to make a crop, they argued that the additional rations would carry the Chickasaws through until the harvest of 1839. Because they had received beef in their first year, they asked for "about an equal provision of pork and stock hogs for the seven months meat ration." [47]

Because the Chickasaws' cash fund was depleted and their remaining money was invested and earning little interest, securing the cash would be a long process. Wheels were normally slow to turn, but they were probably inhibited this time by the fact that Harris shortly thereafter suddenly resigned under a cloud of suspicion regarding his fiscal policy in Indian removal and amid rumors that he was speculating in Chickasaw lands in Mississippi. [48] Harris was replaced immediately by T. Hartley Crawford, who managed affairs much differently than Harris had.

What the Chickasaw leaders had requested would be costly to the nation. On January 1, 1839, subsistence for an estimated 4,600 Chickasaws would cease. Crawford predicted that the cost of continuing the rations for seven months would cost $155,240. Because the Chickasaw cash fund was depleted, he raised the options of selling some of the Chickasaw invested stock or borrowing against future interest. Sale of the bonds required approval by the president and the Senate. Following Secretary Poinsett's recommendation, the president and Senate approved the sale, however not until early 1839. [49]

Charges of fraud against Glasgow & Harrison had forced Collins and Armstrong more and more to defend their decisions to let contracts to that firm. In September 1838, for example, Collins had awarded them the contract to feed the indigent Indians of Indian Territory. He originally had received eight bids: two from Little Rock, including Glasgow & Harrison; three from elsewhere in Arkansas; one from Fort Gibson; and two from Missouri. Collins rejected them all

(189)

because they were too high. Three days later, he awarded the contract to Glasgow & Harrison at fourteen cents and seven mills. Collins rationalized his action as follows. First, he argued, there was a scarcity of goods. There would soon be about 30,000 Indians on the frontier who required subsistence: 6,000 indigent Indians: 16,000 Cherokees, 2,000 Seminoles, and 6,000 Chickasaws. The demand resulted in high-priced goods that had to be hauled long distances. Demands for livestock had created a regional scarcity and high prices, some cattle recently reaching five to six cents a pound. Belief by local residents that a large military presence would be necessary to patrol the frontier caused them to hold back goods, waiting for higher prices. Then the lingering drought had reduced production. Second, supplying the rations would be costly to the contractors. Glasgow & Harrison looked to Illinois and Indiana for corn supplies, as they had done in the previous spring, purchasing 10,000 bushels, none of which had reached the Indian Territory because of the low water and lack of keel boats between Little Rock and Van Buren. Because the Indians were scattered, they would have to supply more depots and hire more employees. Their expenses were increased because they used fifty men. Finally, Collins said he was lucky to find someone who was willing to take a contract under such circumstances.[50]

(190) A few days later, Collins awarded a contract to subsist 8,000 Cherokees for three months. All bidders were Arkansans except Glasgow & Harrison, who won the low bid. When he sent the contracts to Commissioner Harris, he appealed for permission for the contractors to substitute livestock on the hoof for the standard butchered meat ration. Officials on the scene in Indian Territory knew better than the government in Washington what was best for the people, he claimed. "Experience proves," he wrote, "that, where these poor and reckless creatures are fed with bread and meat rations at stated periods, they are too prone to look forward to the day of issue, without making any efforts to accumulate the means of depending on their own resources; whereas, if supplied with a cow or a sow, and taught the advantages of having the milk of the former, and the increase of both, and urged meantime to subsist each one of his family on the corn part of his ration, and, by means of his hoe and gun, they are more likely soon to

be independent, and able to provide for themselves."[51] Though Collins was expressing a philosophy that might have appealed to a society that considered itself superior to the tribes, the fact was, as events would prove, meat on the hoof was much more lucrative to the contractors than butchered meat.

Collins' appeal in Glasgow & Harrison's behalf might have worked with Harris, but Crawford was less receptive to Glasgow & Harrison's favored status. In early November, the firm asked the government to extend their three-month contract to the entire year. Crawford informed them that they must go through channels and directed Collins to stay within government regulations. Crawford also rejected outright Collins' appeal that meat be issued on the hoof, saying the purpose for rations was to feed people, not to provide them livestock for future use.[52]

Rumors were also afloat that Collins was in collusion with Glasgow & Harrison. A company had formed in Columbus, Georgia, purposefully to bid on subsistence contracts. Though their agent reached Little Rock too late to bid on the three-month Cherokee contract, they determined to remain in the bidding for the remaining nine months. What disturbed them was Collins' discretion in such contracts. An official of the company wrote to Crawford, "If the letting of this contract be left to the discretion of Captain Collins, it is obvious that he may, at his option, (or mere caprice,) give it to Glasgow & Harrison at their own price, or at least at a much larger sum than others would be willing to take it at."[53] One should note, however, that there may have been more than just sour grapes at work here. J. C. Watson, one of the officers of the company, was surrounded by questions about his actions arising out of slave claims he had made against the Seminoles, as well as his speculation in Creek lands.

Undaunted, Glasgow & Harrison continued to press the War Department for a monopoly on subsistence of the Indians. Whether or not it was with the knowledge of Collins and Armstrong, in early December Glasgow & Harrison once more asked the government to extend their contract to cover the entire period of Chickasaw and Cherokee subsistence. This time, Crawford tersely told them that such an agreement would violate federal law that required advertised bids and that they must take their "chances with the bidders." With the contract in place, Collins attempted to make it more lucrative for Glasgow & Harrison by requesting that a supply depot be established at Fort Towson rather than on the Boggy because it would be harder and more costly to supply at Boggy. And he suggested that additional depots might be established at Pickens and on the Canadian, both an easier hauling distance from Fort Coffee. These blatant requests for favoritism in behalf of Glasgow & Harrison may have motivated Crawford to look critically at the new contract Collins made with the firm to subsist the Chickasaws for an additional seven months. One provision in the contract allowed Glasgow & Harrison the option of substituting three-quarters pound of fresh pork for one pound of fresh beef. Crawford would not approve that provision because it would make a difference in costs and told Collins he would approve no provisions that departed from government standards. He sent Armstrong a copy of his letter to Collins, telling him that he should consider the instructions to Collins his instructions as well.[54]

Without question, Crawford was attempting to bring under control the apparent license that Carey A. Harris had allowed his underlings in the field. In late December 1838, the Chickasaws renewed their request for seven months' additional rations, saying that some of their people were destitute of even necessary items of clothing. The request was followed shortly by another, asking that those who had settled near Fort Towson be given issues of corn rations for their horses. When Crawford received the second and third requests to sell stock, he realized that the Chickasaws had not been informed that their earlier request had been granted. In addition to those requests, Armstrong and Collins asked for an extension of the rations for those whose year was coming to an end. At Doaksville, a prevalence of smallpox and fevers the previous season had reduced the Chickasaws' ability to make a crop. On the Blue and Boggy, there were no supplies. In an attempt to discourage other such requests, Crawford instructed Armstrong to stress to the Chickasaw leaders the long-range advantage of protecting the national fund, which promised to produce considerable interest income during the next year. And he upbraided Upshaw for writing letters to him that were so vague that they were of no use.[55]

At the time Crawford was attempting to bring Chickasaw subsistence under control, thirteen Cherokee contingents arrived in the West. Immediately, the Cherokees began to file complaints against Glasgow & Harrison, who supplied them under the three-month contract.[56] Like the Cherokees, the Chickasaws continued to complain as well. Their complaints in the spring of 1838 had focused on the lack of rations, the quality, and the short measures of corn. Then there had begun a growing complaint about the mode of issuing beef on the hoof, which Crawford was attempting to prevent. The Chickasaws estimated that, on average, they had been cheated out of a third of the poundage due them. Alfred Hume, who attended an issue in May 1839, believed the cheating was deliberate. The issue took place at William Guy's, the issuing depot on the Boggy. The issue began with Guy's listing each Chickasaw captain's name and the amount of beef his company was to receive. A man named Turner, an agent for Glasgow & Harrison, was assistant agent. Turner deducted from 150 to 300 pounds for every 2,000 due a captain. Hume, who claimed to be a disinterested party who was not a permanent resident of the Chickasaw Nation, learned that the deduction was a commission for the issuing agent, for whom no provisions had been made. At this same issue, a herd of cattle arrived and were to be issued on the hoof. Guy was called away and asked Hume to assist Turner. The first captain to receive an issue was Topulke, who was due about 3,300 pounds. "Mr. Turner turned out five small cattle, and asked me what I thought they would weigh," Hume said, "and I said twelve or fourteen hundred pounds. He said he thought they would weigh the full amount due the captain, and told the captain to take them. I then told Mr. Turner that I would bet him the amount of the cattle they would not weigh fifteen hundred; that the cattle might be killed and weighed. He made some answer, I don't remember what, and the subject was dismissed. The captain received the five cattle for the amount he was entitled to."[57]

Guy claimed that as commissary he did not at first trust his own estimates of cattle weights on the hoof. He called on John Penn to assist him, but Penn got into an argument with Turner and said he would have nothing else to do with it. Guy knew that the agents overestimated the weights, although he tried, he said, to have the issues made prop-

(193)

erly, and he often had controversies with the contractors' agents over the matter. Many of the Chickasaws knew they were receiving short rations, he said, for they were just as capable of estimating weights as the agents were. Guy felt more confident about the corn ration, for he had a reliable measure that he used in making the issues. Toward the end of the extra seven months of issue, Glasgow & Harrison's agent left Boggy before the issue was completed, but he did not leave enough cattle to complete the issue, according to Guy. If they had been issued immediately, the deficiency might have been about 3,000 pounds, but some were lost, stolen, or driven off. The Chickasaws were slow in coming in for their rations and some never came at all. When he left the Boggy, the contractor's agent provided a list of Chickasaw captains who were due rations of corn as well, and although he claimed to have left sufficient supplies to make the issue, they were not secured. Some of them were stolen, and some Chickasaws never received a corn ration that was due them.[58]

Elsewhere, Glasgow & Harrison failures seemed common. Slone Love, for example, left Fort Coffee in January 1838 and settled near Fort Towson, and for the next year served as interpreter at the issuing depot, where issues were made by David Folsom, a Choctaw. However, when the rations were extended for seven months under Glasgow & Harrison, pork and beef were issued on the hoof, and estimates created great difficulty and dissatisfaction. Near the end of the period, Glasgow & Harrison turned the issues over to Joel Nail, a Choctaw, and as a result, many Chickasaws did not know whom to apply to for rations and therefore did not receive any.[59]

Such failures were not as critical as they had been the year before. By the time the Chickasaw commissioners asked to extend the ration period, some Chickasaws in the Blue settlement were on their way to recovery. Richard McClure and his family, for example, had raised a corn crop, had livestock, and believed he did not need the rations that were due him. Thus he sold them back to Glasgow & Harrison at four cents per pound for the beef and $1.87 ½ a bushel for the corn.[60]

When the Cherokee complained in the spring of 1839, Crawford finally began to take closer notice of Glasgow & Harrison. He pointed to a number of troublesome matters regarding the firm and made it clear where the War Department stood. What he told Armstrong regarded not only the Cherokees, but the Chickasaws and Seminoles as well. He directed Armstrong to guard against the contractor's constant requests to increase the amount of rations or to substitute one ration item for another and to maintain at all times the government ration standards in both amount and quality. Any substitutions should be carefully considered. Armstrong had recently asked for and received $100,000 on behalf of the firm, who had complained to him about a lack of cash flow. To Crawford, this appeared to be an advance, and he directed Armstrong to pay them only what their contract called for. The Cherokee complaint, Crawford said to Armstrong, "makes it my duty to require a particular and detailed report on the subject, setting forth your views and opinions on the whole subject of rations in the Indian country." He was particularly interested in what funds had been spent, for he had not had an account from Collins in nearly a year.[61] This appeared to be the first feeble and failed effort to investigate fraud in Indian Territory, and it was one of the first indications of the short accounts that would ultimately bring Collins down.

Crawford's close scrutiny of affairs in Indian Territory was partly fueled, no doubt, by the appearance of Raines on the scene once more. In May of 1839, he returned to Fort Smith from Texas, where he had been for eight months, and learned that no investigation of his charges against Glasgow & Harrison had started and that now, he alleged, the contractors were "playing the same game on the Cherokees" that they had played on the Creeks. In a letter to Crawford, he claimed to have documented evidence of fraud that government officials were not privy to and once more threatened to take the matter to Congress if the War Department did not act.[62] On their part, Glasgow & Harrison claimed that issues had gone off without difficulty to the Chickasaws, Creeks, Seminoles, Osages, and Quapaws. They blamed the Cherokee problem on pre-removal promises made to the Cherokees, whom they called "an unreasonable and complaining people."[63]

Their statement regarding the Chickasaws was clearly untrue. There had been great difficulties, but by the spring of 1839, complaints had diminished in the Chickasaw country. Distance, a lack of commercialism on the frontier, and the economic stress of starting over had

(195)

resulted in trying times for the Chickasaws. But recovery had begun. Unfortunately the business of Chickasaw rations from 1837 onward had been little short of a fiasco. The result was depletion of the Chickasaw fund on deposit in the U. S. Treasury and the sell-off of a part of the fund invested in state banks. Much of the Chickasaw loss was the result of waste and fraud. The final period for subsistence was scheduled to end during the summer of 1839. As the end of subsistence approached, it appeared that those most deeply involved in creating the loss were secure in their arrangements with Armstrong and Collins. However, Austin J. Raines had made some serious accusations that the War Department could not ignore much longer.

NOTES

1. William Armstrong to C. A. Harris, December 7, 1837 (Chickasaw Emigration A294), National Archives Microfilm Microcopy M234, Letters Received by the Office of Indian Affairs, 1824–81, Roll 143, hereafter cited as M234, followed by the roll number.

2. Armstrong to Harris, January 1 and January 19, 1838, with enclosures (Chickasaw Emigration A305 and A316), M234-R143; Abstract of Disbursement for Contingencies up to 30 Day of June 1839 (C1039), M234-R137.

3. Armstrong to Harris, December 7, 1837 (Chickasaw Emigration A294), M234-R143.

4. Articles of Agreement, December 8, 1837, 27 Congress, 3rd Session, *House Report 271*, 73–74, hereafter cited as *Report 271*.

5. Upshaw to Harris, January 2, 1838 (Chickasaw Emigration U31), M234-R143.

6. Statement of Richard McClure, February 16, 1842, *Report 271*, 117–18.

7. Statement of Slone Love, February 20, 1842, *Report 271*, 120.

8. Armstrong to Harris, January 19, 1838, with enclosures (Chickasaw Emigration A316), M234-R143.

9. *Ibid*.

10. Extracts from contracts, September 7 and December 1, 1837, *Report 271*, 85; Armstrong to Harris, January 19, 1838 (Chickasaw Emigration A316), M234-R143.

11. Extracts from contracts, January 1, 1838, *Report 271*, 86. Doak & Tim renewed their one-year contract on January 1, 1839 to supply all new emigrants who might arrive at Doaksville.

12. James Harrison to Collins, January 5, 1838, *Report 271*, 158; Armstrong to Harris, January 17, 1838 (Chickasaw Emigration A315), M34-R143.

13. *Arkansas Gazette*, January 17, March 7 and 9, 1837, and June 13, 1838.

14. Articles of Agreement, February 1, 1838, and Receipt, March 1, 1838, *Report 271*, 71–76.

15. Ethan Allen Hitchcock, *A Traveler in Indian Territory: The Journal of Ethan Allen Hitchcock*, Grant Foreman, ed. (Cedar Rapids, IA: The Torch Press, 1930), 227–28.

16. *Ibid.*, 228.

17. *Ibid.*, 95.

18. Statement of Richard McClure, February 16, 1842, *Report 271*, 117–18.

19. *Ibid.*

20. Armstrong to Harris, February 16, 1838 (Chickasaw Emigration A331), M234-R143.

21. Kingsbury to Harris, April 20, 1838 (Chickasaw Emigration K93), M234-R143.

22. *Ibid.*

23. Statement of R. J. Humphreys, February 20, 1842, and Statement of Richard McClure, February 16, 1842, *Report 271*, 120 and 118, respectively.

24. Statement of William R. Guy, February 21, 1842, *Report 271*, 121.

25. A. M. M. Upshaw to Harris, June 7, 1838, *Report 271*, 122.

26. Statement of R. B. Crockett, February 11, 1842, *Report 271*, 115.

27. *Ibid.*, 115–16.

28. *Ibid.*, 115.

29. Kingsbury to Harris, April 20, 1838, and May 18, 1838 (Chickasaw Emigration K93 and K101), M234-R143.

30. Armstrong to Harris, April 30, 1838 (Chickasaw Emigration A367) M234-R143.

31. Kingsbury to Harris, May 18, 1838 (Chickasaw Emigration K101), M234-R143.

32. Statement of R. J. Humphreys, February 20, 1842, *Report 271*, 120.

33. Statement of Richard McClure, February 16, 1842, *Report 271*, 118.

34. Hitchcock, *A Traveler*, 178.

35. Statement of Robert B. Crockett, February 11, 1842, *Report, 271*, 116.

36. See National Archives Record Group 217, Records of the U. S. Department of the Treasury, Accounting Officers of the Department of the Treasury, E524, Chickasaw Payments, 1833–66, Box 2, File 12. Hitchcock, *A Traveler*, 179. Johnson's Chickasaw wife, Rebekah Courtney, was the daughter of Peter Courtney and Sallie Wolf, who later married

(197)

Tarntubby (or Tontubby). Rebekah bore Johnson two children in 1841 and 1843 and died about 1844. Johnson wanted to take the children back East, but the grandmother threatened Johnson with death if he did so. Leaving the children, he went to the East, remarried, built a new life for himself as a wholesale whiskey dealer, and did not return to the West to see his children for over three decades. His story is told in Neil R. Johnson, *The Chickasaw Rancher*, Revised ed., C. Neil Kingsley, ed. (Boulder, CO: University of Colorado Press, 2001).

37. Statement of McClure, February 16, 1842, *Report 271*, 118–19.

38. J. A. Phillips to Harris, May 4, 1838 (Chickasaw Emigration P305), M234-R143.

39. Upshaw to Harris, August 1, 1838 (Chickasaw Emigration U54), M234-R143.

40. *Ibid.*

41. A. J. Raines to C. A. Harris, June 4, 1838, *Report 271*, 124–29.

42. Raines to T. Hartley Crawford, May 8, 1839, *Report 271*, 131; Jonathan Elliot, *The Diplomatic Code, Embracing a Collection of Treaties and Conventions between the United States and Foreign Powers: From 1778 to 1834, with an abstract of Important Judicial Decisions, on Points Connected with Our Foreign Relations.* 2 vols. Washington, D. C.: Jonathan Elliot Jr., 1834), I: 24.

43. Raines to Harris, June 4, 1838, *Report 271*, 128.

44. Upshaw to Harris, June 7, 1838 (Chickasaw Emigration U50), M234-R143.

45. Raines to J. R. Poinsett, July 27, 1838, *Report 271*, 130.

46. J. S. Conway to Harris, July 14, 1838, *Report 271*, 129.

47. Armstrong to Harris, September 19, 1838, with enclosure (Chickasaw Emigration A405), M234-R143.

48. For the current state of the Chickasaw fund, see National Archives Record Group 75, Records of the Office of Indian Affairs, Records of the Commissary General of Subsistence, Entry 253, Chickasaw Removal Records, Chickasaw Volume 2, 27–29.

49. Crawford to Poinsett, December 24, 1838, Poinsett to President, December 26, 1838, Crawford to Armstrong, January 22, 1839, and Crawford to Armstrong, March 2, 1839, Chickasaw Volume 2, 13–14, 20–21, 35.

50. Collins to Harris, September 18, 1838, *Report 271*, 158–60. The drought Collins referred to was widespread had created difficulties for the Cherokee removal.

51. Collins to Harris, October 8, 1838, *Report 271*, 160–61.

52. Crawford to Collins, November 12 and 26, 1838, *Report 271*, 162–63.

53. A. Iverson to Crawford, November 7, 1838, *Report 271*, 161–62.

54. Crawford to Glasgow & Harrison, January 30, 1839, Crawford to Collins, March 22, 1839, and Crawford to Armstrong, March 29, 1839, Chickasaw Volume 2, 33–34, 42–44; Extract from a contract, March 1, 1839, *Report 271*, 87.

55. Crawford to Armstrong, March 29, 1839, and Crawford to Upshaw, April 6, 1839, Chickasaw Vol. 2, 44–45, 48.

56. See, e. g., Thomas Freman [*sic*], et al. to Matthew Arbuckle, April 16, 1839; John Ross et al. to Arbuckle, April 19, 1839, George Still, et al. to Arbuckle, April 19, 1839; and Ross to Arbuckle, April 23, 1839, *Report 271*, 148–52.

57. Statement of Alfred Hume, February 17, 1842, *Report 271*, 119.

58. Statement of William R. Guy, February 21, 1842, and List of Chickasaw Captains and Statement of A. P. Sheldon, February 21, 1842, *Report 271*, 122–24.

59. Statement of Slone Love, February 20, 1842, *Report 271*, 121–22.

60. Statement of McClure, February 16, 1842, *Report 271*, 119.

61. Crawford to Armstrong, June 12, 1839, *Report 271*, 152–53.

62. Raines to Crawford, May 8, 1939, *Report 271*, 131.

63. Glasgow & Harrison to Crawford, April 25, 1839, *Report 271*, 166.

INVESTIGATIONS OF FRAUD

A S THE SUMMER OF 1839 APPROACHED and Chickasaw economic recovery and self-subsistence were under way, there was growing suspicion in official circles regarding the actions of Glasgow & Harrison, who had a near monopoly on contracts to supply rations for not only the Chickasaws, but other tribes as well. In addition, the possible failures of William Armstrong, the acting superintendent for the Western District, and R. D. C. Collins, disbursing agent for Indian removal at Little Rock, had concerned Commissioner T. Hartley Crawford. Only weeks after he had replaced Carey A. Harris as commissioner, Crawford began to believe that the officials in Arkansas and Indian Territory had been lax in following government regulations regarding contracts, and he exerted great effort during the early months of 1839 to bring officials and contractors into compliance. Although accusations of fraud had been renewed by Austin J. Raines of Fort Smith, the government had not acted. It would, in fact, be months before an investigation of the charges started and years before it was completed. The War Department finally sent Major Ethan Allen Hitchcock to the Indian Territory to investigate the rumors of fraud. What Hitchcock discovered was not only evidence of widespread fraud on the part of contractors and merchants, but evidence that involved major political figures. His report caused such a reaction in Washington that it brought the legislative and executive branches of government to the brink of a constitutional crisis. Unfortunately, the affair produced no favorable results for either the Chickasaws or the other tribes.

Crawford had not pressed Raines' charges, perhaps because of the strong support Armstrong continued to give Glasgow & Harrison. Armstrong said to the partners, "The contracts you have are so very large, and, as far as my knowledge extends, been so faithfully complied with, that I would cheerfully give you any aid or assistance I could to advance you in your engagements."[1] Although he had orders not to allow substitution of one ration for another, he continued to push Glasgow & Harrison's requests to do so. In early September 1839, he finally reported on the complaints about rations as Crawford had requested three months earlier. Armstrong's report was silent on Raines' charges, but Crawford could no longer ignore them. The Chickasaw seven months' extension had closed at the end of July, and other ration issues for other tribes would also soon end. Thus he directed Armstrong to investigate Raines' complaints, showed Raines' letters to Glasgow & Harrison, and gave Armstrong authority to call both Raines and the contractors to appear before him to give statements. "The Department will then see the whole ground," Crawford said.[2]

While Armstrong supposedly followed Crawford's orders, a Missouri resident, through his congressional representative, accused not only Glasgow & Harrison with fraud, but also R. D. C. Collins, whose accounts as disbursing agent for Indian Removal had come under scrutiny. Collins, he alleged, ignored bids lower than those submitted by the firm in return for one-sixth of the estimated $500,000 that the contractors expected to make from subsisting the Indians. Although the bid figures cited in the Missourian's letter varied greatly from those submitted by Collins, Crawford could hardly ignore a letter referred to him by a member of Congress and directed Joshua Pilcher, superintendent of Indian affairs at St. Louis, to investigate the charges.[3] Crawford wanted a thorough investigation, not only of the specific charges, but those made by Raines and new ones from others, alleging that the contractors had issued receipts rather than rations and that the ration receipts were being used as scrip in Indian Territory. "These charges are of the gravest character," he said, "and require the most rigid investigation which can be made, directed by a determination to expose fraud if it shall be found to exist." Pilcher was to authorized to call all parties concerned before him to respond to the allegations.[4]

Meanwhile, Armstrong's "investigation" of Raines' charges provided little. James Glasgow wrote his own defense and garnered letters of support from friends. They branded Raines a liar, swindler, gambler, embezzler, and all-around good-for-nothing, and Glasgow sent the documents to John Miller in the House of Representatives. Raines, who had only recently returned to the region from a trading expedition to the Southwest, visited Armstrong. When the superintendent informed him of Glasgow & Harrison's personal campaign against him, he attempted to blunt the criticism. However, within a month, he suddenly withdrew his charges, alleging that the government delays in investigating made it difficult now to collect evidence. He prepared to leave for Mexico a few days later and urged the government to pay all the accounts of Glasgow & Harrison.[5] This was an abrupt turnaround in affairs.

Armstrong had apparently brokered a deal to settle the affair. Raines claimed that he withdrew from the fray because Glasgow & Harrison had paid him what the firm owed him for his part of the Chickasaw rations contract. Armstrong's orders to investigate his complaints had frightened the firm, which offered to compromise with him. They were so frightened, he said, that they let him determine the final figure. He could have asked for much more but settled, he claimed, for what they owed him; if he had taken more, he could have been accused of taking a bribe. The settlement was "under the eye and sanction of Capt. William Armstrong." Raines left his evidence with Armstrong, but left other evidence with the War Department to use in an investigation if the government chose to make one.[6] Raines justified his actions by asking what else he could have done "against such a combination of influence." He had tried to get the contractors to pay what they owed him. Failing that, he had tried to get an investigation started. Finding the government unresponsive, what more could he do? "Where were my means of continuing the contest against these modern Shylocks with their scions of employees and not only with them but all the power of a corrupt administration to back them?" With few exceptions, government officials, Indian agents, and others "were banded to prevent inquiry into abuses." Without help and encouragement from the War Department, he had retreated.[7]

Raines' withdrawal was what Armstrong wanted. He immediately dropped his investigation. Publicly, he blamed the entire affair on Raines' bitterness against James Harrison. Although Raines claimed that he had left his papers with Armstrong, Armstrong claimed that he had returned all of Raines' letters and kept no copies of them, simply

(203)

because Raines wanted them. No matter which of the two was lying, the letters were gone, effectively destroying what evidence they might contain. No loss, said Armstrong, because they were, after all, "merely repetitions of abuse of James Harrison," a statement that was hardly true if the letters he held compared to those Raines had sent to the War Department. While vilifying Raines, Armstrong went to lengths to exonerate Glasgow & Harrison and defend the company's contracts: "The contracts with Glasgow & Harrison have been very great for subsisting the different Indian tribes. In no one instance, to my knowledge, have they failed to meet their engagements. For this they deserve great credit. A failure would not only have been an inconvenience and expense to the Government, but would have created great dissatisfaction with the Indians."[8] It is not likely that Armstrong was oblivious to what had been transpiring regarding the firm's actions in Indian Territory; he was simply lying. He knew well that they had failed in a number of ways, as the Chickasaws' experience had demonstrated, and if what Raines said was true, Armstrong may have been privy to their action.

Pilcher, who had begun his investigation in Missouri, followed Armstrong's lead, doing his share of white-washing. Responses to his questions, in his view, exonerated Collins. At any hint of criticism of Collins, Pilcher challenged the veracity of the accuser. His report was biased, defending his fellow army officer and bureaucrat and attacking evidence against him that affidavit makers presented. By the time Pilcher reached Arkansas in late March, Raines, Glasgow, and Harrison were gone. The reason Armstrong gave him was that Raines had been bought off by Glasgow & Harrison. Pilcher reported that Armstrong could tell Crawford anything "deserving official notice" on the matter and left it at that. It was later revealed that Arnold Harris, who afterwards became sutler at Fort Gibson, had been authorized by Glasgow & Harrison to arrange the compromise with Raines so that the company could remove any obstacles to getting paid by the government. Although they instructed Harris to offer as much as $20,000, Raines settled for $13,000. With Raines' accusations out of the way, Pilcher decided not to investigate the misuse of ration receipts because, he said, there was no proper officer at Fort Gibson to interview and in his "own deliberate judgement" the contractors were within their rights. So ended Pilcher's investigation, despite the fact that General Matthew Arbuckle, commander at Fort Gibson, was by then convinced that Harrison had ordered short rations in the Creek issues. Arbuckle was clearly disappointed in Harrison, whom he had earlier defended, but the validity of Raines' charge did not change his opinion that Raines was a scoundrel.[9]

While some instances of potential fraud had come under federal scrutiny, other ways opportunists had raided the Chickasaw fund continued without remedy. A good example was the action of the former Chickasaw agent, Benjamin Reynolds. Shortly after their arrival in the West, many Chickasaws applied to Armstrong for funds they had left with Reynolds in Mississippi for safekeeping. Some were so-called "incompetents," those that the Chickasaw commission had deemed unable to do their own business and therefore needed to have the money they received from the sale of their allotments protected from merchants and others who might prey on them. Most, however, were the so-called "competent" Chickasaws who had not wanted to risk taking large amounts of cash west with them and who had been led to believe that they would receive the money upon their arrival. The arrangement between them and Reynolds was unfortunately private. In the West, receipts from Reynolds were common among the Chickasaws. Using the receipts as collateral, they went into debt to the Choctaws and others, believing they would be able to retrieve their money, thus allowing them to pay their creditors. Not only did they need money desperately, but their money was drawing no interest. Most were unwilling or unable to return to Mississippi or Alabama to try to collect it in person. In October 1838 the Chickasaws in council asked for the funds that Reynolds held. Nothing was done to retrieve the funds as long as C. A. Harris was commissioner. However, shortly after T. Hartley Crawford assumed office in 1839, he sought to intervene. He was diplomatic with Reynolds at first. He knew that the Chickasaws had repeatedly asked for their money, he told Reynolds, but perhaps Reynolds was having difficulty in remitting it. The Chickasaws should not have to bear the expense of a trip to Mississippi to collect it, so Crawford offered the services of United States authorities to help out both Reynolds and the

(205)

Chickasaws. He asked Reynolds for a list of people and the amounts Reynolds had on deposit for each so that Crawford could arrange payment through the land offices in Pontotoc and Little Rock.[10]

By that time, Reynolds had stopped communicating with Washington. In July 1838, he had been asked when he expected to wind up agency affairs in the east and whether he intended to go west as agent. He did not respond. In late January 1839, Crawford asked Reynolds to remit any funds he held and were due "incompetent" Chickasaws so they could be invested. At the same time, the secretary of war terminated W. H. Carroll, the approving agent for contracts for Chickasaw lands, and asked Reynolds for all deeds approved after January 7, but again Reynolds sent no response. On March 3, Reynolds' appointment expired, and Upshaw became Chickasaw agent in his place. Crawford asked Reynolds to turn all public property, records, and the "competent" Chickasaw money over to Upshaw. Crawford directed Upshaw to talk to Reynolds, but he found dealing with Upshaw little better. Upshaw met with Reynolds on March 21, 1839, and Reynolds began preparing his books for transfer. He supposedly finished the books, but Upshaw did not indicate what happened to them. As late as the summer of 1841, Crawford still had not heard from Reynolds or from Upshaw regarding the books, and he instructed William Armstrong to find out how much Reynolds owed the Chickasaws and go to Alabama to see him if necessary. Reynolds died, and the records were passed on to his executor, A. Barton, who also died. In 1849, Commissioner of Indian Affairs Orlando Browning made an appeal to Barton's executor to turn the books over because they meant a great deal to the Chickasaws.[11] Through the years, Reynolds and his executors apparently had private use of the Chickasaws' money.

Chickasaw calls for their money reflected the state of affairs in the West. By the end of 1838, the Chickasaws had no cash flow because their funds had been invested. Sale of Chickasaw reserves in Mississippi and Alabama had produced nearly four million dollars. Sale of other lands had brought more than two and a half million for a total of more than six and three-quarters million dollars. Of that, $115,000 had been invested in Arkansas State Bank stocks for the orphans, over $360,000 elsewhere for the "incompetent" Chickasaws, and more

(206)

than $2 million for the Chickasaw Nation from the sales of un-allotted lands. Out of the latter funds, the 5,508 Chickasaws who had removed had been subsisted, but the Chickasaws owed a large debt—they had not yet paid the Choctaws for the Chickasaw District.[12]

The handling of these funds had opened the door to fraud. Carey A. Harris had been in charge of investing the orphan and "incompetent" funds, while the Treasury Department oversaw the Chickasaw National funds. On January 11, 1837, Benjamin F. Butler, interim secretary of war, had given Harris authority to invest orphan funds. On May 4, Harris authorized Jacob Brown, former disbursing agent for removal at Little Rock, now president of the Bank of Arkansas, to sell at par to the War Department $300,000 in Arkansas bank bonds for fifty years. In February 1837 and January 1838, $115,000 was invested. From the beginning of his administration, Secretary Joel Poinsett believed the arrangement was questionable. On November 3, 1838, shortly after Harris's resignation, he withdrew investment power from the commissioner's office and forbade all similar arrangements in the future, and Crawford began depositing Chickasaw orphan and "incompetent" interest in the U. S. Treasury, where it should have been from the start. As soon as Crawford had taken office, the Arkansas bank's president, William Field, had begun to press for the remainder of the promised $300,000 of Chickasaw funds. In spite of Poinsett's orders, investments of an additional $31,000 in March and August 1839 brought the total investment in Arkansas to $146, 000. Despite Field's appeal for more funds, none was forthcoming.[13] Late that year, Poinsett asked Crawford to look into the arrangement. Crawford wrote, "The agreement being regarded as a bad one for the Indian, of whose interest the Department is the guardian, there was felt a strong desire to get rid of it, but the exercise of the authority delegated to Mr. Harris by Mr. Butler, then for the first time made known to you, was considered a pledging of the faith of the Department."[14] The Chickasaws would be decades in recovering their money, much of which went into the pockets of Harris, Collins, and possibly other officials, as subsequent events revealed.

The investigation into fraudulent dealings in rations languished. Following Pilcher's report, there was no official action for a number

(207)

of months. Despite the settlement with Raines and despite Pilcher's report that all was well in Indian country, the War Department finally put some credence in Raines' claims. The decision to act may have been simply the result of an opportunity seized by John Bell during a period of contention in Whig administrations. Five men served as secretary of war and an additional one as acting secretary during the administration of Whig President John Tyler, which spanned 1841 to 1845. The instability of the office resulted, among other things, in a growing conflict between the Congress and the Executive branch regarding Indian affairs. In 1840, the House Committee on Indian Affairs had produced a scathing indictment of the War Department's handling of Cherokee affairs after the killing of the Ridges and Boudinot. When the report failed to emerge from committee because of a five-to-four vote, member John Bell of Tennessee, formerly Speaker of the House, leaked it to the *National Intelligencer*. This political conflict followed allegations of fraud and conspiracy that had clouded Indian affairs during the last half of the Van Buren presidency, from 1837 to 1841. During his brief administration in 1841, Whig William H. Harrison appointed Bell his secretary of war. When Harrison died, his cabinet soon resigned because of Tyler's refusal to sign Whig bills. During his short tenure, Bell appointed Hitchcock to investigate the ration system for removed tribes.

(208)

Accusations had persisted that not only had Glasgow & Harrison committed fraud, but Collins was in collusion with them. Although the accusers clearly exaggerated the extent of the contractors' failures, they alleged corroboration of their accusations by people high up in the government. With the accusations hitting closer to home, there was apparently growing interest among officials. In his report in the late spring of 1841, Secretary of War John Bell alleged wrongdoing by certain unnamed contractors and others involved in subsistence of the Indians in the Southwest. These accusations drew fire from James Glasgow, who asserted the honesty of his firm, even though it had not been named by the Secretary. Nevertheless, the secretary issued instructions for a thorough investigation by Major Ethan A. Hitchcock. After a stop in Little Rock, special investigator Hitchcock arrived in Indian Territory about the first of December and remained nearly two months.

Unfortunately Raines had died in mid-November on his way to Little Rock.[15] Although Hitchcock had lost one of the significant players in the affair, he persisted.

Once in the Indian Territory, Hitchcock found that the figures he had at his disposal did not add up. For example, although the contract had called for Glasgow & Harrison to be paid twelve and a half cents per ration, records indicated they had been paid $704,000, presumably for issues to the Chickasaws. Because there were fewer than 6,000 Chickasaws, each ration would have cost more than thirty cents.[16] On his way from Doaksville to Fort Towson in early March 1842, Hitchcock did some calculations: "Take the Creeks at whatever number received rations say 12,000 or 14,000 or whatever the number was, and see what their rations cost at the contract price. Then see what, in proportion it would have cost to ration the Chickasaws, 4, 5, or 6,000." Then if one accepted that the million rations had been bought in 1837 at Chickasaw request—which Hitchcock did not believe—the cost could not have been more than $200,000, although more than twice that had been charged to them. If the Creek rate had been unreasonable as much as one-third more than it should have been, "a corresponding advance must be made upon the charged expenses of the Chickasaws." The extra seven months' rations would "ease off the ground of complaint to some extent, but not much if the whole arrangement was a mere trick to get rid of the public rations bought by and spoiling on the hands of Government agents."[17]

Hitchcock figured it still another way, but to him it always came out the same. He concluded that the Chickasaw leaders did not intend for the government to buy rations for all Chickasaws in 1837 but for the superintendent of removal to buy rations only for those who were ready to remove at that time. "Instead of charging the Chickasaws with 1,300,000 rations costing possibly 130,000 in rations [given to the traders to prevent their spoiling] besides what has been paid in money to the contractors Harrison and Glasgow." The Chickasaws had been grossly overcharged. The government could not claim that Chickasaw failure to emigrate had been at fault, for they had specifically asked that the superintendent of their removal should purchase their provisions. Even if the argument that the Chickasaws were at fault were sound,

(209)

there was a huge amount of expenditure that could not be explained or justified. He concluded, "The truth is and may as well be stated, the rations were not purchased for the Chickasaws, but for general issue to emigrant Indians; and when it was ascertained that they were likely to spoil on the hands of the Government agents a mode of getting rid of them was adopted resulting in an enormous wrong upon the Chickasaws." Then, after all, with all the rations on hand, the Chickasaws on the Blue and Boggy had gone months without rations.[18]

Long before he left Indian Territory, Hitchcock had created a priority list of topics he needed to report on besides the rations fraud. At the top of the list were Simeon Buckner and the Chickasaw "incompetent" funds. He also wanted to recommend dismissing Upshaw as Chickasaw agent but wanted to let Upshaw save face by saying that he had lost the confidence of the Chickasaw leaders. There were also charges that Upshaw was using the Chickasaw blacksmith for his own purposes. Luther Chase, not of sterling character but a major informant for Hitchcock, claimed that Upshaw was in partnership with Simeon Buckner. Chase alleged that Arkansas Governor Archibald Yell owned one-third of Buckner's steamboat *Indian* and gave up his partnership to Upshaw through a deal brokered by Buckner, who argued that the Chickasaws would not ride in the boat if he, Buckner, owned it, but would if Upshaw did. And Hitchcock had other suspicions as well. In March 1842, he reported from Fort Smith to the Secretary on the "incompetent" fund and on Buckner. He also sent a long letter to William Armstrong. He wrote to himself: "This last is a very serious paper and will form a kind of crisis in my examinations into provision frauds."[19]

By the time he wrote Armstrong, he had taken a large number of depositions that indicated not only failures on the part of Glasgow & Harrison, but potential failures on the part of governmental officials. He found the accounting system inadequate to explain how funds had been expended. But his interest in Armstrong's action or inaction went beyond fiscal matters. Thus to Armstrong he posed a number of questions. What had Armstrong done to prevent failure of the contractors to issue back rations? Why had no "correcting power" stopped the issue of ration tickets, short rations, or overestimation of weight in live animals? According to records, $746, 279.92 had been paid for rations out of the Chickasaw fund, $701, 989.49 of which was listed as having been issued, but there was no evidence of its disposition in the Chickasaw country. What became of it? Under one contract, Lorenzo M. Clark received $32,674 worth of Chickasaw provisions from the government, but only $5,476.78 in repayment could be accounted for. What had been done to collect the Chickasaws' remaining funds? Hitchcock questioned the arrangements with Glasgow & Harrison. If that firm had adequately supplied the Potawatomis on the Missouri River, why had they failed to supply the Chickasaws in Indian Territory? Why had Armstrong failed to investigate charges by A. J. Raines? If other people knew that Arnold Harris had arranged a settlement with Raines for Glasgow & Harrison, had Armstrong not heard about it and therefore realized the need to investigate the possibility of fraud?[20]

In response, Armstrong presented himself as having no knowledge of wrongdoing and lacking authority to do anything about if he had. That he had authority is unquestionable. Because Upshaw overestimated his ability to get large numbers of Chickasaws to remove, Commissioner Harris became afraid that their arrival in the West might cause "emergencies to be provided for without admitting the time necessary to consult" his office. Thus he authorized Armstrong to "act in any exigency which may arise," and be governed by his "own sound discretion as to the present disposition of those Indians, and the mode of subsisting them." [21] His instructions to Armstrong were explicit.

(211)

Yet Armstrong also denied any role in making contracts and laid responsibility on Collins, who had died in 1841. The military officials stationed in the Territory oversaw the rations to Creeks, Seminoles, and Cherokees at Fort Gibson, and were not obligated to report to him, Armstrong said, except for the Chickasaws. Their affairs were overseen by G. P. Kingsbury, who by 1842 was also deceased. It was not until rationing was nearly over in 1839 that the process was turned over to civilian agents, and Armstrong assumed a role; he was only fulfilling the government's contractual responsibility in presenting and paying the accounts of Glasgow & Harrison. Armstrong denied knowledge that any ration tickets were issued to the Chickasaws as substitutes for rations. Perhaps they had, however, been issued to the Creeks and Cherokees, but he "never countenanced the exchange, except in extreme cases." If short rations had been issued or weight of livestock overestimated, the issuing commissaries were to blame because he had never witnessed an issue. He disavowed any knowledge of how the original Chickasaw rations had been obtained or who had done it. The first he knew of the rations was their arrival. He had been charged only with helping to dispose of them to prevent as much loss by spoilage as possible. Armstrong also dismissed the Raines affair: "Raines is dead, and I have no disposition to say any thing about the reports he may have made." He did the same regarding Collins' role in the contracts: "As he is dead, it is at least an act of justice to say that no censure is attached to him. . . ." Finally, he denied any knowledge of Glasgow & Harrison, but avowed that they had "always fulfilled their contracts."[22] Thus Armstrong flatly denied any blame for anything. That Armstrong was openly lying about some of these matters is unquestionable. He was evasive about others, and he was hiding behind the recent deaths of Raines, Kingsbury, and Collins.

Hitchcock knew Armstrong was lying, and he believed him corrupt. He had obtained some damaging information about Armstrong. Thomas C. Wilson told Hitchcock "that Captain Armstrong came to this country $20,000 in debt; that he has paid his debts and is now worth $40,000. This in a few years on a salary of $1500, while supporting an expensive family. That, to be sure, he has a corn field at the Agency and can sell corn at fifty cents a bushel, but that would not support his family." Luther Chase alleged that Armstrong had openly laughed about the fact that Buckner's *DeKalb* had charged for hauling 80 tons of Chickasaw property but had actually hauled a load that was later carried by a four-mule team in four wagon loads. Although Chase would talk about this matter, he refused to tell Hitchcock about reports of Raines' having been bribed to suppress a letter from Harrison to him. And there was a closer tie than Armstrong admitted between Arnold Harris, who had handled the Glasgow & Harrison bribe with Raines. Harris, who was married to Armstrong's niece, was the sutler at Fort Gibson, and owed $30,000-$40,000. Hitchcock interviewed a New Orleans merchant named Labette, who was on a collecting tour. He had come to collect for $8,000 in goods he had sold to Harris, who had also cost Labette money in an insurance fraud on goods shipped from New

York. Armstrong, without question, was deeply involved in loose and fast dealings involving federal and Indian money. Labette simply cut his losses and took a draft on the Army paymaster, Col. Wharton Rector, in favor of William Armstrong for $4,100.[23] When Hitchcock left the Indian Territory for Washington, he had no way of knowing that he would be returning to a hostile political atmosphere. Chase's hesitancy to discuss Armstrong suggests that he perhaps understood better than Hitchcock the political influences that sustained Armstrong.

While Hitchcock was still in Indian Territory, the House Committee on Public Expenditures had begun its own investigation of improprieties in the Chickasaw removal. The committee published two reports shortly before Hitchcock filed his. Their focus was on the claims of Simeon Buckner and the actions of former Commissioner Carey A. Harris. In 1839, Buckner had billed the Chickasaw funds over $108,000 in passenger, baggage, and demurrage fees. While the house committee questioned the paucity of evidence submitted for payment, other claims had been paid with as little, so they could do little more than suggest that some "higher evidence" should be required than "the conscience of an Indian conductor or steamboat clerk." Although the congressmen were correct in questioning the accuracy of Buckner's numbers, their suspicion was somewhat misplaced concerning the amount of baggage. Buckner's bill was for over $54,000, the largest item in his claim. They had difficulty comprehending a bill for 1,064 tons because of their standard of judgment. Regulations regarding removal of the other tribes had allowed each person only thirty pounds of baggage. In addition, the congressmen's incredulity was intensified by their lack of knowledge of Chickasaw society, specifically property ownership, which they judged by their concept of a nomadic tribe: "With the knowledge that the stock of the Indians had been driven across by land, we are at a loss to conceive what items of Indian property could have constituted this large total of baggage. They must have carried an unusual amount of *paints and blankets*. The regulations of the department, in other cases, have assumed that 30 pounds per capita was a fair average for a race whose traveling equipments are usually a gun, a box of paint, and a blanket, and perhaps a bow and arrows; especially is the overage full, when applied to a large body composed

(213)

of warriors, squaws and children. Thirty pounds per capita would have given to these 3,001 Indians 45 tons of baggage, instead of 1,064 tons with which they were charged."[24]

The congressmen also challenged the demurrage charges of over $14,000. They calculated hypothetically that the government could have bought four steamboats for $20,000 each, and, including boat personnel, could have removed the Chickasaws for an estimated $92,000, over $16,000 less than Buckner had charged, and still had the boats at the end of removal. The government could have done it for less if it had hired four boats at $200 per day. The only way the congressmen could explain Buckner's figures was to say "that in this case there has been an unpardonable neglect of all prudence and economy in the disbursement of the public money, and such as well merits the severest censure."[25]

What the congressmen found even more astounding was that on July 2, 1840, Buckner had been paid an additional $37,749. This claim grew out of the decision of a large number of Chickasaws in November 1837 to go by land from Memphis rather than take Buckner's boats. Buckner openly admitted that no more than 3,001 Chickasaws took his boats, but he claimed payment for the others because they *should* have taken his boats. To the congressmen, there was no basis for the claim, and they suspected that Buckner had exaggerated his expenses regarding the use of his boats. Ample testimony indicated that the number of boats he put into use was unnecessary. It appeared that he carried far fewer Chickasaws and less baggage per load than the boats could have taken in order to inflate his expenses. Finally, they questioned why Buckner had waited two years to make the claim rather than filing it when he had been paid for his services. The committee concluded that Buckner's claim was so flimsy that it had been the political influence of Vice President Richard M. Johnson that had caused the Treasury Department to pay.[26] Johnson, a career politician, had spent thirty years in the U. S. House and Senate. A staunch Jackson supporter, he was the Democratic nominee with Martin Van Buren in 1836 but did not receive enough electoral college votes to win election. The decision went to the Senate, which elected him vice president. In general, he was a man who had many friends in high places.

Buckner did not deny Johnson's role in his claim. In obtaining the payment, Buckner admitted, he "had no agent but the good will and assistance of Col. R. M. Johnson, who aided in the proper presentation of the papers. Col. Johnson introduced him, and attended him almost daily, until the requisition was obtained." Before it was obtained, Johnson had tried to sell Buckner his Arkansas plantation and slaves, but Buckner had refused. On the day they were leaving the War Department, where the requisition had been issued, Buckner asked Johnson what he could do to repay him for his help. Johnson asked for a loan. The requisition was paid in two parts, $18,749 to Buckner and $18,000 to Johnson. On the day the requisition was paid, at Johnson's request, he gave Buckner an interest-free note for his half. Was this a payoff? Buckner received no money in payment for the $18,000, but in April 1841, Johnson gave Buckner an undivided one-half interest in his 400 acres and buildings at White Sulphur Springs, Kentucky, which Johnson leased for Buckner.[27]

A month after exposing Buckner and Johnson's actions, the same House committee published its findings on the actions of C. A. Harris, who had suddenly resigned as commissioner of Indian affairs on October 19, 1838. The resignation resulted from bad feelings between Harris and David Kurtz, chief clerk of the Office of Indian Affairs, who had criticized Harris's fiscal procedures. When Harris was away from the office one day, he ordered his wife to open the correspondence before passing the official correspondence on to Kurtz. Among the letters he received was one from Thomas J. Porter of Mississippi, urging Harris to use his influence to help Porter acquire some Chickasaw land he had bid on, intimating that Harris had an interest in it. Mrs. Harris was apparently unaware that the letter was not official correspondence. Kurtz took it to Secretary Joel R. Poinsett, who apparently believed the letter raised suspicion and passed it on to President Martin Van Buren. The president asked Harris to explain himself, and dissatisfied with the response, asked for more information. Harris resigned rather than respond. By the time the House began its investigation in the spring of 1842, the papers related to the case had disappeared. It appears that they had remained separated from the other official correspondence in the War Department as long as Poinsett was secretary. Shortly before

(215)

he left office, the papers were delivered to him, never to be seen again. He later said that he had no knowledge of them. Still, the congressmen viewed these events with suspicion.[28]

While these suspicions of corruption were based on circumstantial evidence, charges of fiscal malfeasance were more factually based. The congressmen concluded, "The public mind is undoubtedly impressed with the conviction that there has been an improper use made of the funds appropriated for the Indian bureau, or that a laxity in the disbursement of those funds has prevailed, which opened a wide door for individual favoritism, at the expense of the Government or of the Indians." For example, in April 1837, Harris had purchased $200,000 worth of rations on the open market in New Orleans rather than submitting the purchase for bidding as the law clearly required. While Harris's motive may have been sound, he could have bought the rations much more cheaply at St. Louis, Louisville, or Cincinnati, as the purchase of Chickasaw rations had illustrated. The Treasury Department calculated a loss of nearly $67,000, but the congressmen believed that figure was extremely conservative. They also believed that the Chickasaw fund had been systematically raided. They cited as an example the loss of over $31,000 to Lorenzo Clark and his partner David Thompson, who defaulted on their subsistence contract with the government over four years earlier.[29]

(216)

In the wake of these investigations, Hitchcock knew that his report would be controversial, not simply because of the accusations that had been leveled at those involved in removal, but because it pointed fingers at others. He wrote his mother shortly before he filed his report: "One thing is pretty certain—I shall arouse some violent hostility, but that I cannot help, as I must tell the truth as to my discoveries of fraud in the Indian Country."[30] This came after three weeks of hostility directed toward him. When he arrived in Washington on April 5, he was "well received" by Secretary John Spencer, Commissioner Crawford, and Winfield Scott, General of the Army. But Hitchcock crossed a line when he told Spencer that Armstrong was corrupt and should be removed, and when he condemned Glasgow & Harrison. He soon became convinced that a cover up of Armstrong and others was afoot in the executive branch. When he applied for information, he caught the second auditor in a "deceptive" and "virtually a false report" about the Chickasaw rations in an effort, he believed, to "screen" Armstrong. Then the chief clerk of the War Department intimated that former Secretary John Bell would be in danger if Hitchcock's report accused Armstrong because Bell had ordered the investigation. Hitchcock said of the clerk, "He enlarged on the influence and power of the family in Tennessee. The next day, he twice renewed the same theme and expressed again the very same words. He was emboldened to recur to it because I did not insult him when he dared to address me at first." Hitchcock chose to keep his indignation in check and simply say that he could not help it if Bell and Armstrong came into conflict. Spencer, who stayed at the same boarding house as Hitchcock, began to avoid him. Commissioner Crawford, who had worked hard to bring fiscal and other matters in the commissioner's office under control, began to make excuses for Armstrong and to generalize that Indians could be made to testify to anything. Hitchcock, however, outraged at what he had discovered in the Indian country, said, "I shall make my report without regard to anything or anybody but the facts."[31]

Hitchcock had underestimated the close ties of the Armstrong family to Andrew Jackson, who still wielded considerable power. Jackson's regard for the family came primarily through his love of Robert, William's brother, who had served under him in several military campaigns. In 1843, Jackson named his grandson after Robert: "thinking as I was of Emuckfau heights, Enotochopco, and Talladega, we named the son Robert Armstrong—remembering when he fell desperately wounded, he cryed [*sic*] out, some may fall, but my brave fellows, save the cannon. Therefore the name, that if the child live, he may perchance aid in saving the Republic, and perpetuating our glorious union." His high regard for Armstrong led Jackson to will his case of pistols and sword "worn by me throughout my military career," to Armstrong. His feeling for Robert Armstrong spilled over onto his brothers Francis and William. It had been loyalty to Jackson that had gained Francis his position as Choctaw Agent West and superintendent of Indian affairs for the West. When Francis died, William took his place. Jackson's devotion to the Armstrong family would remain strong well after Hitchcock's investigation and report. In the fall of 1843, Jackson sent one of his

(217)

favorite mares, Talladega, to the West with his friend: "my friend Major Wm. Armstrong and Govr. Butler of So. Carolina has taken her and a two year old filly to arkansa [*sic*], with a two year old stud by Merman, half brother to Talladega." [32] Apparently as a result of his closeness to power, Armstrong had enriched himself on a meager salary in a short time. When Hitchcock arrived at Little Rock on November 12, 1841, he learned that "one Indian agent came here so poor that a man with a $400 claim against him was glad to settle for $100. Now he owns a considerable number of negroes and has offered $17,500 for a plantation." [33] His description fit Armstrong.

Hitchcock's report, filed on April 28, 1842, was an indictment of the subsistence process and, potentially, government officials and contractors. Specifically, he concluded that Commissioner C. A. Harris had ordered Searight to obtain a million rations with Chickasaw funds before he received application for subsistence from the Chickasaw leaders. Any loss should not have fallen, therefore, to the Chickasaws. The superintendent of Chickasaw removal, who had more specific numbers than anyone concerning those likely to remove, had no power relating to subsistence. When it became obvious that most Chickasaws would not remove in 1837, efforts by Armstrong and others to save the massive supplies from wasting through rot, in fact, resulted in losses, a prime example being the contract with Lorenzo Clark, who still owed the government over $27,000. [34] But that was loss by out and out defaulting, not the low dealing and other methods used elsewhere in the subsistence process.

Hitchcock also condemned official action regarding Glasgow & Harrison. He found totally unacceptable Armstrong's and others' attempts to explain the high prices of the contracts. The allowance for transportation was unreasonable. Glasgow & Harrison were not supposed to issue the old rations to the Indians but were to substitute new ones; thus to Hitchcock, transportation of the old goods was not a factor. The key factor was the price of each standard government ration. Why, he asked, could Glasgow & Harrison obtain contracts for over twelve cents when contracts for rations elsewhere in the West were being made at the same time for nearly half that? Hitchcock came close to calling Armstrong a liar regarding his role in the contracts. They had not been faithfully fulfilled, and Hitchcock presented a long list of abuses. "It is certain," he wrote, "that no man can travel through the Indian country and leave it without being painfully convinced that the Indians were deeply and unmercifully wronged." And it was clear that Armstrong had been a key person in that wrong.[35]

Hitchcock's report forced the executive branch of government to draw constitutional lines in order to protect political friends. In the wake of the Buckner investigation and Hitchcock's return, the House wanted to expand its investigation to accusations of fraud in Cherokee subsistence, which in its course shed light on attrition of the Chickasaw fund.[36] On May 18, 1842, the House formally asked Spencer for any reports relating to fraud among the Cherokees—presumably the Hitchcock report—which the executive branch wished to keep from the public.[37] Two days later Hitchcock talked to Spencer about it: "He says he will not furnish the report. There may be a squabble. Even impeachment is threatened."[38] On June 1, the House empowered the Indian Committee to call "for persons and papers on the subject of fraud," investigated by Hitchcock in the West. Again Spencer refused, saying that Hitchcock's report was *ex parte* and to publish it would be unjust to those implicated. On June 4, Hitchcock wrote, "He says this evening that it has now become a question of principle, and the House shall not have the report without his heart's blood. I hope his motive for withholding is good, but politicians are slippery bipeds. He knows, as well as any man can, that I conducted the investigation with perfect fairness. I am sure there is no appearance of partiality or bias of any sort." The House, meanwhile, entered a period of "violent" debate on the issue.[39]

By the middle of June, it was clear that the War Department would rather have Hitchcock "out of the way." Spencer was afraid the House would call Hitchcock to testify. Hitchcock promised the secretary that the House would not get the report from him. Still, Hitchcock suspected, Spencer would rather have had him out of the way. Mrs. Spencer urged her husband to appoint him as Inspector General of the Army, apparently as a means to mollify him. Crawford tried to bring him into his office because of his familiarity with Indian affairs, and General Scott severely challenged Hitchcock's integrity in a letter to

(219)

Spencer and declared that he would send Hitchcock to his regiment in Florida as soon as the War Department released him from his special assignment. When Hitchcock broached the subject to Spencer at their boarding house, the result was an angry confrontation in which, to Hitchcock's surprise, Spencer asserted that Hitchcock was under his exclusive control and no one else's. By the end of July, Hitchcock and Spencer had repaired their relationship, and a few days later, Spencer wrote a letter, testifying to Hitchcock's good work and character.[40] The change likely occurred in the secretary because he had received a ruling from the Treasury Department that criminal charges of fraud could be avoided.

In the wake of the congressional request for Hitchcock's report, Spencer had sent it to the solicitor of the treasury with strict orders to keep it confidential and with questions he wanted Solicitor C. B. Penrose to answer. Were the contractors responsible for not delivering goods according to contract or for committing fraud? If so, was there evidence enough to justify a suit? Were there others who were liable to the government? If there appeared to be misconduct that could be prosecuted, he directed Penrose to take action. Finally, and separately, he asked Penrose's opinion of Armstrong's conduct regarding the contracts. Penrose concluded that the contract with Glasgow & Harrison was "improvident" and that they failed to meet their agreement because of inferior rations, which were issued irregularly and fraudulently. He also concluded that they were guilty of issuing ration tickets, which they bought back at discounted value, causing a loss to the Indians. Most of this, he concluded, was a result of the contractors' having left the matter of issue to underlings, not as a result of conspiracy and thus ruled out criminal proceedings. The people involved were scattered, and some had refused to talk to Hitchcock because of "delicacy" of the subject or "unsettled accounts" they had with Glasgow & Harrison. The contractors had already been paid. It might be possible to re-examine their accounts, but the effort and expense necessary to garner evidence and pursue the case would not be feasible. Penrose faulted the government agents for not overseeing execution of the contracts more closely. The only case worth pursuing was that of Lorenzo N. Clark, who had failed to fulfill his contract of December 8, 1837.[41]

Crawford had tried unsuccessfully to collect Clark's debt for some time. In the summer of 1840, he had pressed Armstrong to collect it. By that time, Collins had left the War Department service, and Crawford directed Armstrong to see him, get Clark's note and other pertinent evidence of what Clark owed, and collect the debt. Because Clark had made his contract as a subcontractor with Glasgow & Harrison, Armstrong suggested that the amount due be charged to what the government owed Glasgow & Harrison. It had appeared for a while that settlement of the debt was on its way in early 1841, Crawford even giving Armstrong permission to grant Clark "a little indulgence," but Crawford found a huge discrepancy between what stores Armstrong claimed Clark had received and what Collins had reported.[42] Thus the debt remained uncollected when Hitchcock filed his report in the spring of 1842. It is remarkable that no one made mention of Clark's connection to Glasgow & Harrison during Hitchcock's investigation.

In clarification of his findings, Penrose argued that Glasgow & Harrison had clearly failed to meet their contracts, but the government had been party to those documents and failed its obligation. "It is apparent," he said, "that the Indians were wronged, and that the government officers did not guard their interests. The question is: Is it prudent to commence legal proceedings with proof not more specific as to time, quantities, and sums? So far as it is specific, the amount disclosed is inconsiderable, compared with the vast outlay."[43] A little thievery, then, (*221*) could be condoned if it meant hiding the role of government officials involved in it. Although the Whigs held the White House, it was evident that the personal relationship between the one man who could clarify the matter, William Armstrong, and former President Andrew Jackson was too strong to overcome.

As the House had continued to debate Spencer's refusal to deliver the report, it was rumored that those implicated in it would make "a desperate assault" on Hitchcock. He wrote, "Since the General's assault, I have felt almost unequal to keep up under the combined attack of the General-in-Chief and the friends of exposed rogues. I feel very much the want of an independent fortune that would enable me to defy the General himself and retire from the army. This is the greatest trial I have ever had. If I should tell the truth I should be the first arrested and then court-marshaled for disrespect to the General-in-Chief." He began to wish that his report might never be published. "Though I think it perfectly fair it will bring upon me, if published, the most bitter and virulent attack from the rascals I have exposed in that report." Hitchcock left Washington in late August with his report in the middle of the constitutional debate between two branches of government.[44]

On August 13, the House had renewed its request for Hitchcock's findings. It was ignored by the president. It may have been executive privilege, but his explanation to the House later suggested that the implication of War Department officials—Poinsett, Harris, Armstrong, and Collins particularly—might have been embarrassing. In January 1843 Congress renewed the request. President John Tyler, in response, argued that the request was a challenge to executive authority, but fear that continued silence might be construed as giving validity to the charges, he decided to comply. He argued, however, the futility of investigating fraud because so many of those involved in subsistence were dead or no longer in the Southwest, the cost would be prohibitive, and prosecution would be ineffectual.[45] Nevertheless, the House Committee on Indian Affairs reported in February 1843, including in their lengthy report the results of Hitchcock's investigation.

In response to the congressional investigation, James Harrison defended the Glasgow & Harrison firm. He branded Raines, whose accusations had started the whole affair, as a disgruntled former employee, who was a profligate, an embezzler, and a gambler, and argued that Harrison's order for short rations was to recoup goods that had formerly been issued in excess by mistake. As for the payoff to Raines, it derived, Harrison argued, from a verbal promise made by Thomas Tunstall, a former partner, before he left the firm, and Glasgow & Harrison felt obligated to pay it after Raines threatened to prevent Glasgow & Harrison from collecting their accounts with the government if he did not get paid. Harrison denied any knowledge of either the alleged issuing agent or the Chickasaws who charged that they received short rations at the Boggy Depot. Although he admitted that short rations might have been issued, he personally had not been within a hundred miles of Boggy. As with this charge, he denied any wrongdoing charged in other testimony and defended the practice of issuing ration tickets as something the Indians desired. He admitted the irregular issues to the Chickasaws and other tribes early in the contracts because of the distance, the weather, and conditions of the roads. And the Chickasaws did receive poor cattle but only in the early spring when there was no range. But damaged corn and flour? Harrison denied that any such items were issued, claiming that the company had not issued any of the stored goods that the government had turned over to them. Harrison made his statement from memory, offering no documentation, but he supplied a sheaf of letters from individuals who attacked Raines' character.[46]

The president had managed to stall long enough that everyone in the executive branch, particularly the War Department, escaped exposure and prosecution. Armstrong had managed to hide his favoritism to Glasgow & Harrison. Richard Johnson had managed to secure his share of the money Simeon Buckner obtained for services he had not rendered the Chickasaws. Hitchcock's findings went without investigation. But it was clear that a number of War Department officials as well as others were tainted, among them Collins, whom Armstrong had shielded from censure after his death.

Hitchcock had suspected Collins of fraud, but he was deceased by the time Hitchcock arrived in the West. Collins had been in Arkansas a number of years, overseeing the laying out of roads, before he replaced Captain Jacob Brown on February 8, 1837, as principal disbursing agent for Indian removal west of the Mississippi.[47] His actions, following in the footsteps of his predecessor, laid the groundwork for additional fraud but fell outside Hitchcock's investigation because it had to do with the establishment of Arkansas banks.

It was in the waning years of a banking frenzy that had swept the country that Arkansas became a state and established its first banks. In 1830, for example, in the Mississippi Valley and west of Pittsburgh, south of Canada to the Gulf, only thirty banks existed. As an early historian of Arkansas banking said, "While a banking mania seized the people about the year 1834, continuing through 1835 and 1836, still the desire and apparent necessity of banks in Arkansas, and more particularly banks of issue, were keenly felt." Indian removal had, without question, fed the desire because of Arkansas's remoteness from banking

(223)

centers. Although there were only 47,000 whites in the territory, there was "an urgent desire," the historian suggests, to admit Arkansas to the Union in 1836 so as "to obtain from such State Government proper authority to create such banks." Thus the first state legislature created the State Bank and the Real Estate Bank of Arkansas. He goes on to say that the directors of the banks were "wholly unworthy of the trust they assumed" and "undeserving of confidence or respect." He adds, "No enemy could have so seriously injured the State of Arkansas, even by the most studied and assiduous efforts, as did the men who were entrusted with the management of these banks. The actual loss was infinitesimal in comparison with the indirect loss caused by the destruction of confidence."[48] Among those men were Jacob Brown, R. D. C. Collins, Carey A. Harris, and others identified with Chickasaw removal.

Jacob Brown paved the way for Collins' actions. For several months before leaving his job as disbursing agent for removal, Brown served as president of the Arkansas State Bank as well. It had been established by an act of the Arkansas General Assembly in November 1836, with an expected capital of $1 million to be raised primarily from the sale of bonds. Instead of the expected capital, the sale of bonds fell far short. In time the bank would base much of its capital on non-specie notes drawn on non-specie paying banks in Ohio, Kentucky, Louisiana, and Mississippi.[49] Shortly after Brown left the office of disbursing agent, he went to Washington where he obtained a verbal promise of $300,000 of Chickasaw orphan funds to be invested in Arkansas State Bank bonds.[50] According to the agreement, the State Bank would sell to the War Department, at par, $300,000 in Arkansas State bonds with fifty years maturity at an annual yield of 5 percent. The money was to be derived from the land sales for Chickasaw orphans in Mississippi. On the day this agreement was made, Harris ordered the transfer of $100,000 from the Agricultural Bank of Natchez and its branch at Pontotoc to Brown and promised to transfer the remaining $200,000 shortly thereafter.[51] On the day following the agreement, Harris ordered the sale of the remaining Chickasaw orphan lands. However, delivery of the funds was delayed until the summer of 1837, when the first installment went to Little Rock.[52]

Onset of the nationwide Panic of 1837 undermined the banking plans. Chickasaw land sales dropped, and the remaining expected funds did not materialize. It was not until late November 1837 that Harris had Chickasaw orphan funds available to purchase more Arkansas bonds, but only fifteen. The bonds were delivered in January 1838.[53] Thus $115,000 of Chickasaw money had now been invested in the bank. Meanwhile, Brown had resigned from the bank amid charges that he had a conflict of interest, not having resigned his Army commission when he became president of the bank.[54] Never solvent, the bank was a failure from the start and became a casualty of the Panic of 1837. In August 1837, the bank began discounting notes and issuing post-dated notes. As a non-specie paying bank, it could obtain no credit and loaned out and discounted more than it took in.[55] As the bank grew weaker, president William Field appealed for the remainder of the $300,000 Harris had promised. However, by then Harris had resigned under a cloud of suspicion. When in September 1840 Field renewed his request, Commissioner T. Hartley Crawford, Harris's successor, reported to Secretary Poinsett, "It appears that the stock has depreciated much in value since the engagement was made and it remains for you to decide."[56] The bank ultimately received only little more than a third of what Carey Harris had promised. The additional money was set apart to establish bank branches in the towns of Fayetteville and Batesville. As Arkansas bankers later said, the policies adopted by the bank were never based on good banking practices but were made for the convenience of the directors who used the funds to further their own enterprises. As a result, in the summer of 1843, the bank went into receivership. Among those affiliated with the bank and were therefore apparently beneficiaries of its funds were John Wilson, speaker of the Arkansas House; Sam C. Roane, president of the Arkansas Senate; and James S. Conway, governor and a founding member of Glasgow & Harrison.[57]

Even more blatant favoritism toward bank officials and stockholders characterized the Real Estate Bank of Arkansas, which was basically an appendage of the State Bank. William Field was named the first director of the State Bank and manager of the Real Estate Bank in early November 1836.[58] As it was established by the Legislature of Arkansas in 1836, the Real Estate Bank capital was based on $2 million in bonds of the State of Arkansas. The state held mortgages on real estate securing $2.25 million of stock. The bonds could be disposed of only at par value and were to bear 5% interest. But banks stopped paying specie in May 1837, and the nation went into a panic. Yet in November 1837, the legislature raised the interest paid on Arkansas bonds to 6 percent. In May 1838, New York and New England banks began paying specie again, and the bond market rallied. The Real Estate Bank sold $500,000 to the U. S. Treasury, $1 million to North American Trust and Banking Company in New York, and $30,000 to Richard M. Johnson of Kentucky, the future partner of Simeon Buckner. The Real Estate Bank opened for regular business on December 12, 1838, paying out specie on discounted notes, and in less than a month it had loaned out more than half a million dollars. On November 2, 1839, the bank ceased paying specie and became a bank of issue for paper money. In its operation, it favored stockholders over non-stockholders, so that at one time stockholders owed the bank $1,499,672.10 and non-stockholders owed $423,571.56, of which $177,542.25 in loans had been endorsed by stockholders. Among the original trustees who were indebted to the bank were C. A. Harris, John Drennen, and L. N. Clark, all of whom had been involved in the business of Chickasaw removal.[59]

A prominent figure in the operation of the Real Estate Bank was R. D. C. Collins, disbursing agent for Indian removal west of the Mississippi. Collins apparently had no objections to wearing two hats. By early March 1837, he had replaced Jacob Brown as disbursing agent at Little Rock, and in November following that, he became cashier of the bank.[60] From that point on, Collins clearly used his public position to support his private affairs. Rumors floated that he was in league with Glasgow & Harrison. It had been such rumors, in fact, that had led to Pilcher's and Hitchcock's investigations. Collins certainly seemed anxious to process the claim of Glasgow & Harrison in the summer and fall of 1838. He simply asked Harris for money to pay them without submitting an estimate of funds as the regulations required. Crawford, a few days after assuming office, complied somewhat reluctantly with a request for $150,000.[61]

Crawford's concern about Collins' lax record keeping was well founded because Collins became deeply involved in real estate ventures

in Arkansas. In the summer of 1838, he was among a group of speculators who laid out a town on the north bank of the Arkansas River
"immediately opposite the State House." It was called D'Cantillon after Collins' middle name. Simeon Buckner was also affiliated with the
scheme. A plat was put on display at the Arkansas State Bank, where
buyers selected lots.[62] Buckner, who at the time was pushing his questionable claims against the Chickasaw fund, had resettled in Arkansas.
In January 1838, he put the steamboat *Itasca*, and the *Fox*, which he
captained himself on a regular round trip each week from Little Rock
to Memphis. The *DeKalb* plied between Little Rock and New Orleans.
Buckner, as well as William Field and others associated with the Arkansas State Bank and Real Estate Bank, were also founders of the Little
Rock Manufacturing and Mining Company, chartered in April 1838.[63]
Collins' career in the bank continued to grow. In the summer of 1839,
he was elected to the board of the main bank at Little Rock and became
president of the bank that fall. In July of 1840, William E. Woodruff
replaced Collins as president. One of the directors at that time was
Simeon Buckner. By that time, Collins was apparently drinking heavily.
He had been relieved of his duty in the Army in early 1841 and died that
summer.[64]

Collins' decline as a guardian of federal funds had been precipi-
tous. At first he had been almost zealous in his concern. Jacob Brown
had selected Collins as his replacement and enthusiastically endorsed
him, but to his dismay, Collins had been on the job only a few months
when he accused Brown of being responsible for the spoilage of rations
at Fort Gibson that had been bought for a Creek and Seminole removal
that had failed to occur and for the spoilage of Chickasaw rations stored
at Fort Coffee. By the time he made these accusations, he had become
an advocate for Glasgow & Harrison. With the assistance of William
Armstrong, he made contract after contract with the firm until it had
a monopoly for supplying rations to nearly all of the removed tribes
and had received the major part of the spoiling Chickasaw, Creek, and
Seminole rations. Collins' record keeping became unreliable. He asked
Harris for money to "meet expenses" without explanation. If asked for
justification of requests, Collins reported that receipts had not been
received, claims for Chickasaw removal had not been turned in, or it

was impossible to determine at any given time exactly what was owed the contractors. Nevertheless, Harris continued to send large sums of money to Collins.[65]

When Collins died, the language of the report was guarded. It said, for instance, "His brother officers who served with him, will bear testimony to his correct and officer like conduct while attached to the line." The writer said, "If he ever had an enemy that enemy must have been made one by the conferring of a benefit upon him; for knowingly Capt. Collins never wronged or injured a human being. Charitable to a fault, poverty or distress never appealed to him in vain. Kind and benevolent in every impulse, he never wounded the feelings or even the self-love of any man by a word. If faults he had they were such as recommend him more dearly to those who knew him, as springing from the entire goodness of his heart and thorough devotedness to those whom he thought his friends." [66] Was this a way of saying that Collins was an "easy touch?"

After his death, details of his dealings emerged. Collins had apparently mixed War Department money, primarily Chickasaw funds, with Arkansas Bank funds and made some bad loans as an official of the bank. Luther Chase, one time a cashier of the State Bank branch at Arkansas Post who doubled as a clerk for Collins, said that the first time he settled Collins' account after taking the position as clerk, he found a deficit of about $18,000, which later proved to be in Collins' accounts, not the government's. Chase became alarmed and wanted to quit, but Collins persuaded him to stay for about a year. Even after he left, Chase continued to do accounts for Collins on occasion. Once he found a deficit of some $200,000. When he pressed Collins about it, Collins admitted that he had loaned about half that amount to different people. When Collins began to realize the difficulty he was in, he hinted at committing suicide.[67] Despite Collins' misdoings, Chase said that he "was in the main an honest honorable man of the kindest feelings in the world and that he was ruined by the blackest villainy ever practiced upon an easy nature."[68]

Collins' mishandling of money had been known for months because he was removed from office. By law, Collins was required to settle his accounts at the Treasury Department on the first day of October of each year. To ensure the settlement, he was required to render his accounts at the end of each quarter. By October 1, 1838, he had not rendered accounts for the fourth quarter of 1837 or the first three quarters of 1838. In the eyes of Treasury officials, he was considered a "defaulter." Still, between October 1, 1838, and July 7, 1839, when he was relieved of his office as disbursing agent, he handled an additional $582,290 in Treasury funds. The congressional report on Collins said, "The facts speak for themselves. That a disbursing officer, who on the first of October 1838, became a defaulter with a large balance then in his hands should afterwards have received, in advance from the Treasury, more than half a million dollars, and be suffered to retain his office for nearly one year, are facts of themselves sufficiently startling."[69]

Chase blamed Collins' ruin on Chester Ashley, a prominent local attorney, deeply involved in real estate speculation. Collins had received unexplained amounts of $20,000, $16,000, and $17,000 at various times. Chase believed the first and another of the three sums came from Ashley. Chase alleged that Ashley "goaded" Collins into deals after Washington became suspicious of his actions by scaring Collins with the prospect of prison, urging him to escape to Texas. Once it was established that his accounts were in deficit, Collins drank harder.[70] In March 1842, Hitchcock looked into Collins' affairs. The former administrator of Collins' estate and Chase, the current administrator, refused to let him see Collins' papers, saying that they contained no useful information. However, they gave Hitchcock a list of men who had allegedly received money from Collins. Some could show that they had satisfied their debts, but others claimed Collins owed them money. Hitchcock heard rumors that in Little Rock "no small number of buildings, brick & frame," had been built "with public money committed to Capt. Collins." Yet the people who occupied the buildings claimed that they owed Collins nothing. Upon his return to Washington, Hitchcock urged the secretary of war to give the U. S. district attorney at Little Rock broad powers to investigate Collins' affairs. Charles B. Penrose, solicitor of the Treasury Department, did so in early April 1842.[71] Two years after Collins' death and a year after Hitchcock's report, it was announced that under Collins' tenure as disbursing agent, $215,369.15 of federal money had disappeared from his accounts.[72] Almost $25,000 of this was from the Chickasaw fund and may have been used to help build the town of Little Rock.

Others helped raid Chickasaw funds in other ways. William Woodruff, former Arkansas state treasurer, who had replaced Collins as president of the Real Estate Bank, resigned in November 1840, only four months after taking office. He apparently learned enough about the affairs of the bank to want to distance himself from them, for only a few weeks later his newspaper, the *Arkansas Gazette*, charged that the directors of the bank used their position for their own gain. Salaries of bank officials also came under fire, and rumors of the potential insolvency became public.[73]

Woodruff's place was assumed by none other than Carey A. Harris, the former commissioner of Indian affairs, who had overseen transfer of Chickasaw funds to the Arkansas State Bank. Harris had resigned his office as commissioner under a cloud of suspicion in October 1838 and had gone directly to Little Rock. By early November, he was one of the directors of the Real Estate Bank and served as cashier at a salary of $3,500, by far the highest of any of the other officers. A year later, he was president and in 1841 a director of the central bank in Little Rock. Only two months after Hitchcock filed his report in the spring of 1842, Harris died at his home town of Franklin, Tennessee.[74] Harris, like Armstrong, was too close to Andrew Jackson to make the investigation too detailed. In 1836 he had served as acting secretary of war and in the spring of 1837 had done Jackson's bidding in helping shape a personal attack on former Commissioner of Indian Affairs Elbert A. Herring.

The confidentiality of Secretary John Spencer's request concerning criminal prosecution in 1842 raises questions about the administration's motives in delaying transfer of Hitchcock's papers to the House of Representatives. Were there others, besides Armstrong, that senior officials had concerns about? By the time Hitchcock filed his report, the House had examined Simeon Buckner's claims, the role of Vice President Johnson, and the fiscal policy relating to removal and speculation in Chickasaw lands in Mississippi that had resulted in the sudden resignation of C. A. Harris as commissioner of Indian affairs. These events and the connections of Collins and Harris to Arkansas banking institutions and Harris's having channeled Chickasaw funds to Arkansas made the cloud of suspicion even darker. Both banks contributed to attrition of the Chickasaw fund through Collins' embezzlement and Harris's unwise investment of orphan funds in the Arkansas State Bank.

Nevertheless, everyone escaped retribution. Officers of the firm of Glasgow & Harrison were not prosecuted. The War Department apparently destroyed the records of Harris's questionable actions as commissioner. Collins escaped retribution because he was dead by the time the suspicions about his embezzlement of removal funds were confirmed and because Armstrong shielded him. Armstrong escaped retribution as well. Even though Hitchcock had pointed the finger at him, he was shielded by the executive department for so long, because of their fear of the closeness of him and his brother Robert with Andrew Jackson, that those who could convict him had died—Kingsbury, Collins, Harris, Raines. It may never be known how much their fraud cost the Chickasaw people. The Treasury Department's accounts were never analyzed. No full investigation took place after Hitchcock's became known. That fact did not escape the attention of some in American society. In the early spring of 1844, N. Sayre Harris of the Board of Missions of the Protestant Episcopal Church, visited the Choctaw and Chickasaw nations. On March 26 he wrote in his diary, "Some of these Southern tribes have been much cheated in various ways—for evidence of which see a faithful and fearless report to Government by one of its most accomplished officers, Col. Hitchcock. Why the publication of a portion of this truth telling document was suppressed by Congress, those concerned best know, and why gentlemen implicated in rather questionable transactions in that quarter were retained in their places of honor and profit, is a question that belongs rather to politics than to morals."[75]

(231)

NOTES

1. Armstrong to Glasgow & Harrison, June 22, 1839, 27th Congress, 3rd Session, *House Report 271*, 168, hereafter cited as *Report 271*.

2. Crawford to Armstrong, October 10, 1839, Armstrong to Crawford, June 23, 1839, and Crawford to Armstrong, July 30, 1839, *Report 271*, 168, 170–71.

3. J. Jones to L. F. Linn, November 20, 1839, Crawford to Joshua Pilcher, December 31, 1839, and Extract from Instructions, February 8, 1840, *Report 271*, 171–73.

4. Extract from Instructions, February 8, 1840, *Report 271*, 173–76.

5. John Miller to Crawford, February 14, 1840; William Glasgow to Miller, January 31, 1840; William Tracey to Glasgow, January 24, 1840; John Lee to Glasgow, January 27, 1840; and Armstrong to Raines, January 30, 1840; A. J. Raines to Crawford, January 27, 1840, and February 13 and 22, 1840; Armstrong to Raines, January 30, 1840; Raines to Armstrong, February 22, 1840; Crawford to Raines, February 18, 1840, *Report 271*, 176–78, 134, and 132–36, respectively.

6. Raines to John Bell, October 30, 1841 (Western Superintendency Emigration R669), National Archives Microfilm Publication M234 (Letters Received by the Office of Indian Affairs), Roll 924. Letters Received is hereafter cited as M234, followed by the roll number.

7. *Ibid.*

8. Armstrong to Crawford, February 26, 1840, *Report 271*, 136–37.

9. Joshua Pilcher to Crawford, May 5, 1840, W. W. Lear to E. A. Hitchcock, March 8, 1842, and M. Arbuckle to Crawford, March 10, 1840, *Report 271*, 180–84, 137, 179.

10. Armstrong to Harris, July 18, 1838, September 28, 1838, and October 12, 1838 (A413, A464, and A480), M234-R137; Crawford to Benjamin Reynolds, November 17, 1838, Chickasaw Volume 2, pp. 10–11, National Archives Record Group 75, Records of the Commissary General of Subsistence, Entry 253, Chickasaw Removal Records.

11. Crawford to Reynolds, November 17, 1838, January 26, 1839, January 31, 1839, February 21 and March 6, 1839; and Crawford to Upshaw, March 7, 1839, and April 6, 1839; and Crawford to Armstrong, August 25, 1841, Chickasaw Volume 2, 10, 22, 23, 26–27, 29, 36–37, 48, 123: Upshaw to Crawford, March 20, 1839, and April 5, 1839 (U68 and U70), M234-R137; Orlando Browning to Executor of A. Barton, Deceased, July 16, 1849, Chickasaw Vol. 3, 74.

12. Crawford to Joel R. Poinsett, February 7, 1839, Chickasaw Volume 2, 27.

13. Crawford to Poinsett, October 23, 1838, and January 4, 1840; Crawford to L. Woodbury, April 24, 1839; and Crawford to Field, September 4, and October 16, 1839, Chickasaw Volume 2, 7, 49–50, 68, 102, 129.

14. Crawford to Poinsett, January 4, 1840, Chickasaw Vol. 2, 129.

15. See, e. g., William Gibson to T. Ewing, July 23, 1841, and James Glasgow to John Bell, June 15, 1841, *Report 271*, 193–94. E. A. Hitchcock to J. C. Spencer, November 15, 1841, *Report 271*, 130.

16. Hitchcock to Spencer, December 14, 1841 (Chickasaw Emigration H969-41), M234-R144.

17. Ethan Allen Hitchcock, *A Traveler in Indian Territory*, Grant Foreman, ed., (Cedar Rapids, IA: Torch Press, 1930), 205; hereafter cited as Hitchcock, *A Traveler*.

18. *Ibid.*, 193–94, 206–07.

19. *Ibid.*, 167–68, 204, 222, 227, 228–29.

20. Hitchcock to Armstrong, March 7, 1842, *Report 271*, 137–41.

21. Harris to Armstrong, November 4, 1837, *Report 271*, 63.

22. Armstrong to Hitchcock, March 12, 1842, *Report 271*, 141–45; *Arkansas Gazette*, July 7, 1841.

23. Hitchcock to Crawford, August 3, 1842, *Report 271*, 145–47; Hitchcock, *A Traveler*, 92, 93, 94, 227, 229. See also E. A. Hitchcock Memoir, January 6–28, 1842, William A. Croffut Papers, Library of Congress, Box 5, Folder 1, p. 31.

24. 27th Congress, 2nd Session, *House Report 454*, 2, 3.

25. *Ibid.*, 3.

26. *Ibid.*, 4, 6.

27. *Ibid.*, 6, 7.

28. 27th Congress, 2nd Session, *House Report 604*, Pt. 1, 4–6, 7–10; Pt. 2, 1–3.

29. *Ibid.*, Pt. 1, 1–4, 7.

30. Hitchcock, *A Traveler*, 232.

31. Croffut, *Fifty Years*, pp. 156–57.

32. Jackson to Francis P. Blair, July 14, 1843, John Spencer Bassett, ed., *Correspondence of Andrew Jackson*. 7 Vols., 1926–35. Reprint ed. (New York: Kraus Reprint Co., 1969), VI: 222. See also pp. 224, 243.

33. Quoted from Hitchcock, *A Traveler*, 13.

34. See Hitchcock to J. C. Spencer, April 28, 1842, *Report 271*, 28–43.

35. *Ibid.*

36. Hitchcock, *A Traveler*, 12–13.

37. *House Report 271*, 2.

38. Ethan Allen Hitchcock, *Fifty Years in Camp and Field: Diary of Major-General Ethan Allen Hitchcock, U.S.A.* Ed. W. A. Croffut. (New York: G. P. Putnam's Sons, 1909), 157–58.

39. *Ibid.*, 158.

40. *Ibid.*, 158–61.

41. Spencer to C. B. Penrose, June 3, 1842, and Penrose to Spencer, July 20, 1842, *House Report 271*, 196–97.

42. Crawford to Armstrong, July 13, 1840, and January 7, 1841, Chickasaw Volume 2, 91, 107.

43. Hitchcock, *Fifty Years*, 161–62.

44. Penrose to Spencer, July 30, 1842, *House Report 271*, 197–200; E. A. Hitchcock Memoir, July 1–August 12, 1842, Croffut Papers, Box 5, File 2, p. 2.

45. John Tyler to House of Representatives, January 31, 1843, *House Report 271*, 19–23.

46. James Harrison to James Cooper, February 15, 1843, *House Report 271*, 201–14.

47. *Arkansas Gazette*, March 7, 1837.

48. W. B. Worthen, *Early Banking in Arkansas* (Little Rock: Democrat Printing Co., 1906), 4, 5.

49. *Ibid.*, 41–56.

50. *Arkansas Gazette*, November 18, 1836; April 11, 1837.

51. Harris to Brown, May 4, 1837, Harris to President, Agricultural Bank of Natchez, May 4, 1837, and Harris to James Whitcomb, May 5, 1837, Chickasaw Vol. 1, 156, 157, 158–59.

52. *Arkansas Gazette*, July 11, 1837.

53. Harris to S. Cooper, June 29, 1837, Harris to Brown, November 19, 1837, and Harris to A. H. Sevier, January 16, 1838, Chickasaw Vol. 1, 175, 226, 234.

54. *Arkansas Gazette*, November 8, 1836, and November 21, 1837.

55. Worthen, *Early Banking in Arkansas*, 56.

56. Crawford to Poinsett, October 13, 1840, Chickasaw Volume 2, 132.

57. Worthen, *Early Banking in Arkansas*, 51, 5–58, 68, 86.

58. *Arkansas Gazette*, November 8, 1836.

59. *Arkansas Gazette*, December 12, 1838; Worthen, *Early Banking in Arkansas*, 25–37.

60. Worthen, *Early Banking in Arkansas*, 97–98; *Arkansas Gazette*, November 21, 1837.

61. Crawford to Collins, October 25, 1838, Chickasaw Volume 2, 7–8.

62. *Arkansas Gazette*, July 18, 1838.

63. *Arkansas Gazette*, June 13, 1838.

64. *Arkansas Gazette*, July 10 and November 8, 1839, July 15 and July 22, 1840, and July 7, 1841.

65. Brown to Harris, January 9, 1837 (Frame 368) and September 23, 1837 (B314); Collins to Harris, July 27, 1837 (C339), and April 24, 1838 (C659); Collins to Crawford, December 20, 1838 (C940), M234-R924.

For Collins' relation with Glasgow & Harrison, see Collins to Harris, September 25, 1837 (C443), January 26, 1838 (C536), March 15, 1838 (C609), April 14, 1838 (C659), September 18, 1838 (C829), October 8, 1838 (C681), M234-R924.

66. *Arkansas Advocate*, July 1, 1841.

67. Hitchcock, *A Traveler*, 230; *Arkansas Gazette*, May 9, 1838.

68. Hitchcock, *A Traveler*, 230.

69. 27th Congress, 2nd Session, *House Report 453*, 1–3.

70. Hitchcock, *A Traveler*, 229.

71. *Ibid.*, 230–31; Charles B. Penrose to Spencer, April 9, 1842 (S3137), M234-R924.

72. 27th Congress, 2nd Session, *House Report 453*, 3; *Arkansas Gazette*, May 20, 1842, and June 21, 1843; John C. Rives, *The Congressional Globe* Volume XXIV, Part III (Washington, D.C.: 1852), 1830.

73. *Arkansas Gazette*, February 24, 1841, and May 5, 1841, and October 20, 1841.

74. *Arkansas Gazette*, November 7 and December 12, 1838, November 18, 1840, November 17, 1841, and July 6, 1842.

75. Kenny A. Franks, "Missionaries in the West: An Expedition of the Protestant Episcopal Church in 1844," *Historical Magazine of the Protestant Episcopal Church* 44 (1975), 326–27.

Attrition of the "Incompetent" and Orphan Funds

DURING HIS VISIT TO THE CHICKASAW NATION in 1841, Ethan Allen Hitchcock heard allegations of fraud regarding the "incompetent" and orphan funds. He became convinced there was truth in the allegations. One of the leading figures in the allegations was Daniel Saffarans, the trader from Tennessee who had speculated in Chickasaw lands before removal and followed the Chickasaws to the Indian Territory. Although he was open to making money anywhere it could be found, Saffarans turned his attention to the possibilities of making money in the credit economy of the Chickasaw District, particularly the "incompetent" and orphan funds held by the U. S. government, and the rations and commutation funds due late-arriving Chickasaws during the 1830s. Unlike the general Chickasaw fund, raided by Glasgow & Harrison and others, Saffarans took the lion's share of funds due individual Chickasaws.

(237)

The "incompetent" class of Chickasaws had been so labeled by the Chickasaw Commission, established by the Treaty of 1834. Their job was to decide which Chickasaws were incapable of conducting their own business or handling their money. Many of them were indebted to Mississippi merchants and others when they moved to the West, and both they and their creditors understood that all would be paid in the West.[1] The Treasury Department invested their funds in stocks in the banks of various states, established an account for each Chickasaw in the amount of the person's land sale, and planned to pay the interest derived from the account in the form of an annuity in the West. On the eve of removal, some of the Chickasaw leaders had asked that 20% of the monies due the "incompetent" Chickasaws be paid them to meet removal expenses, but Commissioner of Indian Affairs Carey

A. Harris determined that all of the funds should remain in U. S. government hands until the "chiefs in council," the exact wording of the 1834 supplemental treaty, decided that it was advisable to pay. Harris strictly interpreted the phrase "in council" to mean all of the chiefs and argued that the invested money was drawing 5% interest and that the "incompetents" would receive subsistence for twelve months after they arrived in the West, where they would have more need of their funds than before removal.[2] This was good in theory, perhaps, but the reality proved to be that poor quality and supply of subsistence during the next two years was probably not what Harris had in mind. The Chickasaws, desperate for cash and expecting payment of their money, found it necessary to turn to creditors.

By mid-1838, individual Chickasaws were asking Western Superintendent William Armstrong for the money due them. He realized that it was only a matter of time until the Chickasaw leaders called for payment of not only the interest but the principal as well and suggested paying out $100,000 and keeping the rest invested. He also predicted that he would ultimately "have the trading community to contend with, that always have power in Indian country, and especially when combined, as will be the case in this instance."[3] Given Armstrong's apparent involvement in the rations fraud that was going on at the time, his relationship to the traders might, at the least, be considered dubious. What combination of traders he had in mind in 1838 is uncertain, but one emerged during the ensuing months. Harris sent Armstrong a roster of the "incompetents" and the amounts due each, paid out the interest that had accumulated on the "incompetent" reserves, but decided to guard as much of the investment as possible. He directed Armstrong to stress the importance of protecting the principal, and if traders created difficulty, he was to revoke their licenses and eject them from the territory.[4] Thus Armstrong had not only specific information about the "incompetent" fund that the traders would eventually find useful but also authority to oversee their activities, of which he approved, despite his protests otherwise.

As Armstrong had predicted, the Chickasaw leadership began to press for payment of the funds. "The Chickasaws came over with considerable money," Armstrong said, "but little of which is left among them." In September 1838, the Chickasaw leaders debated the question, ultimately asking for half of the fund, over $300,000, but because only two commissioners were present, Armstrong did not pass their petition on to Washington.[5] When T. Hartley Crawford replaced Commissioner Harris in October, he stood firm against payment of the principal, arguing that the interest was sufficient for the "incompetents."[6] Crawford remained true to his pledge until the traders, with political assistance, later prevailed upon the secretary of war.

Although Crawford's argument made fiscal sense regarding the long-range wellbeing of the Chickasaws, the dire economic conditions of the Chickasaws in the West made a compelling argument. It was their money, after all. On February 14, 1839, the Chickasaw commissioners and other leaders in council at Boggy again petitioned for payment, apparently beginning to feel pressure from the Chickasaws. The commissioners said "that their first object in declaring Chickasaws incompetent was to save their money for them until they arrived west of the Mississippi, when we promised and expected they would be paid." Those with money had been generous in loaning funds, they said, but now many of those were suffering as well.[7] According to Armstrong, "The Indians are much dissatisfied at the commissioners who decided them incompetent. The commissioners feel uneasy."[8] But Crawford held the line. The Chickasaws were still due an additional seven months' rations, which should suffice until the interest on the fund could be paid the following year, he argued, and he told the Chickasaw commissioners and leaders it would be a mistake to withdraw the principal.[9]

Then politicians entered the debate. Senator T. H. Williams of Mississippi began pushing to clear the titles to "incompetent" Chickasaw lands for which purchase agreements met the treaty provisions. Crawford channeled the deeds that were in good order to the president.[10] With the increased clearing of "incompetent" Chickasaw deeds, Ishtehotopa and the Chickasaw leaders continued to petition Crawford for both the "incompetent" interest and principal. Crawford resisted. No, he said, the interest was much more to their advantage. The "incompetent" fund had earned almost $52,000 by July 1, 1839, over half of which had been paid, and the remainder was forthcoming.

Crawford questioned why people lately considered "incompetents" by the commissioners could now be suddenly "competent."[11]

The Chickasaw commissioners seemed determined to try every avenue to have the incompetent fund paid out. Armstrong reported it difficult to reconcile the Chickasaws to investment when they were needy. The "incompetents" were developing strong resentment against the commissioners, who, with Agent Benjamin Reynolds, had promised to pay them in the West. "Such is the dissatisfaction," Armstrong wrote, "that the commissioners who declared the Indians incompetent feel very uneasy." In September 1839 the Chickasaws wanted to send a delegation to Washington to discuss the "incompetent" and orphan fund investments, as well as the creation of a fort on their frontier to protect them from "refugee Cherokees, Kickapoos, Caddoes, Delawares, Shawnees, and Comanches."[12] Crawford held firm once more, arguing that he was preparing a payment of interest accrued on the "incompetent" fund and that the invested stocks could be sold only below par, resulting in a great loss. The treaty did not indicate that the Chickasaws would be paid in the West but that the money would remain in trust. The Chickasaws could send a delegation to Washington if they wished, but he would tell them face to face precisely what he had already said.[13]

Crawford's responses apparently had the desired effect. By early 1840 the Chickasaw leaders had reversed themselves. Now they concluded that payment of the interest alone and protection of the investment were in their best interest. However, they wanted payment of both the orphans' interest and that of the "incompetents." They also began to press the government for details regarding their land sales. By the eleventh article of the Treaty of 1834, they were supposed to receive a report six months after the land sales began and thereafter at six-month intervals. Was there not any part of the land sales that had been completed? They had never received a report. Now they wanted some figures on sales, expenses, and stocks, as well as the names of the heads of families, the amount of land each individual had received, who purchased it, and the amount paid. They were clearly suspicious: "If we had a full statement of all the lands that have been disposed of at public auction, or otherwise disposed of, the day and date of such

(240)

transactions, and the different prices, and all the above required information, it would enable us to find out some of the frauds that have
taken place."[14]

Why the leadership suddenly switched positions is uncertain. Their
repeated requests for the "incompetent" funds had been steadily rejected, and Crawford had been willing to entertain a request only from
the seven commissioners who had made the Treaty of 1834. That was
problematic because one commissioner had died, leaving only three
in the West, while the remaining three were still in Mississippi, "yet
detained in the indispensable duties of their office." In response, the
western leaders had nominated another to replace the deceased member, giving them a majority, and it was these four who had chosen to
accept payment of only the interest, perhaps because they could "do no
better."[15]

Their decision caused a counter movement in Mississippi. With
headquarters in Holly Springs, the Mississippi group reacted immediately upon learning about the western leaders' decision. One effort
came from Benjamin Love, who had remained at Holly Springs after
removal. Love had been one of the Chickasaw commissioners who had
gone to Washington in 1834 and negotiated the sale of the Chickasaw
lands in preparation for removal. After the sale was announced, Love
later said, "Our country was filled with white adventurers, who were
both disposed and encouraged to mingle freely with us. The habits
of our people were suddenly changed, their ability as individuals increased, and their necessary wants urgent, in this new state of affairs."
During the next three years, land sales and preparations for removal
occupied everyone's thought, he said. Merchants supplied credit to the
"incompetent" Chickasaws to see them through the interim. Chickasaws, like Love, also supplied credit. Love was in what he called "easy
circumstances, owned many likely negroes, a very large and valuable
stock, a productive plantation, with a valuable property in his treaty
reserve, without indebtedness to any body." Speculation would have
been easy, he said, and he had tempting offers, but he took his duty as
a commissioner seriously, concerning himself with seeing the Chickasaws through the interim and the removal. To assist those without
means, he secured their cash loans and debts for horses, provisions,

(241)

and clothing. He did so without fear because he believed the money would be forthcoming to the incompetents upon removal. He was a man of influence, considered a "preferred creditor at all times." However, "the more clamorous and uncompromising" whites left him no choice but to pay the debts to keep his people out of jail. Thus by 1840 he had "sold much of his property while it would sell—negroes and lands—to relieve himself from such liabilities, and provide the necessary support for his family." Much had been sold by execution, and suits had begun for much more. At the current prices in Mississippi, he doubted if the remaining property would pay his debts. If he had gone west and taken his property when the Chickasaws emigrated, he might have been safe from such loss.[16]

Love claimed that his yielding to the appeals of his fellow Chickasaws for financial assistance was a direct result of his dual role of acting for the government and for his people. The pressure had been so great that he had thought about resigning, but the appeals of Agent Benjamin Reynolds and the threat of the other commissioners to follow his example had caused him to stay. He had advanced an estimated $30,000 in livestock and goods with the full expectation of payment upon the Chickasaws' arrival in the West. The "competent" Chickasaws had paid up. What remained was entirely "incompetent" debt, ranging from $50 to $2,000 per person. His efforts had kept the Chickasaws from "loitering in the country and retarding their removal," and had helped to curb the "inducement to the shrewd to prey upon the improvident." Love was clearly alarmed that the decision of the western Chickasaw leaders had accepted the War Department's position that only the interest should be paid the incompetents. He was being "sacrificed to the bad faith of those who had left him here to meet the storm, while they are securely to reap the fruit of his sacrifices." Love alleged that some "sinister influence" from traders in the West might be afoot.[17]

In May 1840, Love filed an appeal for payment of his claim, supported by testimony from William Carroll, formerly in charge of Chickasaw land sales but also a speculator; U. S. Representative Jacob Thompson; James Davis of Holly Springs, former general counsel for the Chickasaws, who was now being accused by creditors of the Chickasaws of practicing fraud upon them for having helped persuade them to wait for collection until after removal; and David Hubbard, a land speculator from Tennessee. Hubbard said of Love, "He was wealthy and unembarrassed, and by becoming their security, and taking their debts upon himself, as I am informed and believe, he has become embarrassed, and I learn his property will be sacrificed to pay the debts of those incompetent persons." Hubbard and Davis were both land speculators who had a vested interest in collecting as many Chickasaw debts as possible. Davis was a member of the Pontotoc and Holly Springs Land Company, which in 1836 had purchased seventy-seven and one-quarter sections of Chickasaw land from the New York and Mississippi Land Company, a group of eastern capitalists. Hubbard had arranged the sale. As the economy soured in the years following 1837, sales lagged. Most members of the Pontotoc and Holly Springs Land Company went bankrupt. In 1842, the company returned more than half of the land to the New York company. That same year Davis took his slaves to Texas to escape his creditors and fell into disrepute.[18]

Love's claim opened the door to others and further attrition of the Chickasaw funds. His concern about the "sinister influence" of traders in the West may have been simply an attempt at political leverage, but it had reference to the decision of the western commissioners and leaders not to pay out the principal in order to protect the Chickasaw investment. He would have had to look no farther than Holly Springs to find evidence of "sinister influence"—if he had chosen to call it that— on the part of traders whose main goal was to get at the Chickasaw money.

A campaign was headed there by Felix Lewis, working through Representative Jacob Thompson, who worked in their behalf in Washington. Lewis listed a number of firms and individuals and estates that were owed money by the "incompetent" Chickasaws. The idea of incompetence, Lewis argued, was to protect the "incompetents" so that they could provide for themselves during removal and sustain themselves afterward. Merchants clearly believed that if they extended credit, payment would be forthcoming. During the period following the end of the rations in the West, traders continued to supply goods on credit, fully expecting to be paid. The recent reversal of the Chickasaw leaders in their opinion about payment astonished Lewis as an "act of

(243)

perfidy" that was a result of "some influence."[19] All of the persons Lewis listed may have had claims, but so did he, and he had strong reasons
for wanting the "incompetents" paid. He and his business partner,
Daniel Saffarans, had trading houses in the Chickasaw Nation west.
Together, they would ultimately take the lion's share of the Chickasaw
"incompetent" fund. Lewis and Saffarans, like other land speculators,
had been stricken a heavy blow by the soft land sales after 1837. Added
to the sagging economy was statehood for Arkansas and independence
of Texas, both of which attracted farmers who could find land more
cheaply there than in Mississippi.

Love's appeal persuaded Secretary Joel Poinsett to ask the Chickasaws to meet in council again and examine the validity of Love's claims
against the fund, and if the claims were valid, to ask for payment of
the fund once more. Then Commissioner Crawford was authorized to
pay Love's claim. Crawford alerted Jacob Thompson in the House and
Thomas Hart Benton in the Senate of the plan, which would require
payment of part of the principal.[20] While there may have been "some
influence" to protect the principal, there was some Chickasaw criticism
of the commissioners' decision to give up their demands for payment
of the principal. According to Agent Upshaw, the decision had caused
"great dissatisfaction" among the Chickasaws, which he feared would
lead to "considerable difficulty." The cause was the miserable condition
of many of the "incompetents," whom, he said, "have no stock, either
of hogs or cattle, and are destitute of clothing and provisions."[21] Crawford instructed Armstrong to have the Chickasaws request stock sales
under Article 4 of the treaty. Power to determine if the debts were valid
was vested in Armstrong. He was to use his own judgment to get at the
truth and to obtain forceful evidence. The government would pay Love
from the interest due the individual debtors, but other creditors must
sign an agreement to take Chickasaw invested stock at par for debts
owed them.[22]

The commissioners complied with Poinsett's request. Assembled in
council near Fort Towson that summer, they acknowledged the debts
and the right of creditors to collect Love's claim and others as well. They
rescinded the request for interest only, requested payment of sufficient
principal to settle the debts, and asked Armstrong to determine the evi-

(244)

dence of their indebtedness. In early October, Armstrong ordered investigation of the validity of claims in the presence of Chickasaw leaders at Doaksville and Boggy Depot, the two largest trading centers.[23]

Between November 20 and December 29, Upshaw and the Chickasaw leaders investigated hundreds of claims. They reported 109 held
by Benjamin Love for over $18,000; 105 held by Daniel Saffarans and
Felix Lewis for more than $22,000; 371 held by John Penn and Felix
Lewis for over $32,000; 132 claims held by Daniel Saffarans & Compa-
ny for $20,000; and 43 individual claims by Saffarans, James Colbert,
Thomas Colbert, Charles Colbert, Isaac Alberson, and Slone Love for
$68,000. When the Chickasaw commissioners endorsed these claims,
they washed their hands of the affair. Any future debts traders might
obtain against the Chickasaws would have to be collected without the
commissioners' help. Also, they asked that all of the "incompetents" be
paid what was due them, plus interest, in 1841. Armstrong strongly supported the commissioners, who felt responsible for the debts by having
encouraged the delay in payment until after removal. Armstrong also
defended the traders in Indian Territory, portraying them as life savers
who made it possible for the "incompetents" to survive on the Blue and
Boggy, long distances from the trading centers in the West.[24]

The War Department faced a dilemma. Secretary John Bell accepted Armstrong's total of more than $166,000 in claims, but stock
belonging to the indebted Chickasaws was just nearly $143,000. Even
with the interest due on the invested funds, the debts would absorb
their stock and interest, and they would still be in debt. Love's claim
had been reduced when he had received the interest due his debtors
in 1840. Rather than let the debts continue, the creditors were willing to take the "incompetent" stock at par, even though it would not
bring that much on the market. Thus the War Department decided to
transfer certificates of stock, state bonds, and interest of the "incompetent" Chickasaws, primarily to the firm of Saffarans and Lewis, who
by March of 1841, had bought up others' claims, and were owed more
than $160,000.[25]

This settlement with Saffarans and Lewis was generally condemned by Chickasaws and created suspicion among them. The "incompetents" themselves hardly understood what had happened to

their money. Greenwood, one of the old pre-removal chiefs, for example, "harped" on the "incompetent" fund and its being deposited in banks. The Chickasaws, he said, could not understand why they could not get at it or how their money could be gone. There were also general charges that the sale of the "incompetent" claims was "corrupt." Supposedly the Chickasaw commissioners had gathered at Boggy Depot, where Saffarans and Lewis had their store and were "there treated with every luxury the country affords free of charge, supplied with whiskey, etc.; and thus induced to recommend the payment of that fund to Saffaran [*sic*] and Lewis." Greenwood, for example, believed that there had been collusion between Agent A. M. M. Upshaw and the merchants, that Chickasaw Commissioner Slone Love was in league with them, and that Isaac Alberson, the chief representing the Chickasaw District in the Choctaw National Council, might also be implicated. In reality, Love and Alberson had both privately criticized Upshaw severely and wanted him removed, but Greenwood believed that they had finally realized how the people felt about the agent and were only trying to "protect themselves." Love and Alberson apparently did not want to appear instrumental in the removal of Upshaw, although complaints about Upshaw could be heard throughout the nation. If Upshaw, Love, and Alberson were in league, it was easy to understand why the latter two might want to separate themselves from him. Although Alberson "talked very obscurely" and "talked in a circle," he went on record with Hitchcock, asking him to inform the president of his concerns about Upshaw.[26]

(246)

Criticism of the sale of the "incompetent" stocks came from other quarters. Pitman Colbert called the merchants "speculators" who had "shamefully" cheated the "incompetents." There was "not a white man in the country sufficiently friendly with the Chickasaws to tell the truth or say a word for them." One of the younger Colberts also bitterly complained, calling the purchase a "perfect robbery, that they have charged $150 and as high as $200 for a horse not worth over $30." Johnson McKinney was also highly critical of the Chickasaw leaders and the agents for selling the claims. He considered it scandalous and called the merchants "swindlers" who, like the agents, were guilty of "robbery." Some claims had been sold to merchants at the Choctaw Agency, one of whom was the firm of Berthelet, Heald & Co., who had a store there and at Fort Towson and Boggy Depot. R. M. Jones, a Choctaw partner of the firm, attempted to persuade McKinney to collect debts that Chickasaws owed Choctaws by funneling trade to Jones, who would take the claims. McKinney refused, saying that the Chickasaws would sooner or later have money and could pay. McKinney alleged that the merchants charged double prices for their goods when they presented their bills for payment.[27] The merchants were undaunted by such rumors and accusations.

Successfully settling their claims against the "incompetent" Chickasaws through the transfer of stocks at par, Daniel Saffarans and Felix Lewis apparently concluded that they had struck on a good thing. They presented themselves as life savers of the Chickasaws; at their own risk they had extended credit, assuming that the "incompetent" funds would eventually be paid. They had acted with the sanction of the Chickasaw commissioners, who had reaffirmed their actions when they assisted in auditing the firm's records and authorizing payment. In the wake of the settlement, other "incompetents" who were due money went to them and asked them to finance livestock and other things they needed and take their share of the stock in payment. When Saffarans and Lewis sought the sanction of the War Department for such a course, the in-house reply was "no answer necessary."[28]

Whether Secretary Bell's response was tacit consent is uncertain, but Saffarans and Lewis pursued their course anyway. According to Armstrong, they brought an estimated $50,000 worth of goods into the Indian Territory, expressly to trade with the Chickasaws. By summer 1841 the "incompetent" Chickasaws who still had money due them had amassed huge debts. The chiefs and commissioners in council at Boggy Depot in July 1841 claimed to have examined the accounts accumulated after March 1 of that year and approved them. Their logic was that the Mississippi claims had been settled; those who amassed debts in the West should have theirs paid as well. Upshaw and Armstrong, in turn, approved the accounts for more than $84,000.[29]

Without question, Poinsett's decision in 1840 to trade stocks at par for individual debts opened a broad avenue to attrition of the Chickasaw "incompetent" fund. The settlement in the winter of 1840-41 had

(247)

liquidated the existing debts both east and west of the Mississippi. Now the goal of merchants was to create more debts, in effect to keep the cycle going. Saffarans returned to the Indian Territory in the spring of 1841 and personally looked after his business through the summer and fall. During that time, there was "constantly some one of the commissioners" in his Boggy Depot trading house where the "incompetents" came, sometimes 50 to 100 miles, to get articles they needed. Saffarans said, "It was then suggested by the commissioners, whether there could not be some way devised by which much labor and trouble could be saved to these poor old Indians, and proposed to me to give them a credit on our books, so that they could send and get such things as they might want." Thus he developed a due bill system. He gave each person a due bill in the amount of the individual's claim. It worked to the Chickasaws' benefit, Saffarans claimed. In some instances he gave due bills to Indians to whom the "incompetents" owed money, thus settling many debts. "The incompetent Indian would bring up his creditors, and get me to give them due bills for what was owing them and have charged to his account. In some cases where they did not want to take the whole debt at the time the transfer was made, the creditor would take my due bill for the balance, and looked to me for pay." [30] It was this system that apparently gave rise to complaints from the Choctaws and created difficulties for Saffarans.

(248) The merchants' practices came under fire from the Choctaws. In October 1841, Peter Perkins Pitchlynn of the Choctaw Nation complained to the secretary of war about the actions of not just Saffarans and Lewis, but other traders as well. "The Chickasaws are my people," he said. "I am allied to them by blood and by many personal and warm friends, whom I have been attached to from the days of my boyhood." He called the traders unscrupulous. "We have suffered much from speculators; but if your licensed traders are permitted to defraud and swindle us in this manner, and they are not arrested, and that shortly, then we shall be a peeled people indeed." [31]

Pitchlynn based his complaint on the allegations of Joseph Dukes, A. Robinson, Robertus Wilson, and Thomas J. Pitchlynn. Dukes claimed that Saffarans & Lewis charged 300% to 400% on goods they sold and held against the "incompetents'" claims for money due them. Dukes alleged that the Chickasaw commissioners had allowed this state of affairs to occur. Saffarans and Company had a "full sweep" of the "incompetent" fund, and "their next aim will be the orphans, and, perhaps even grasp at the general annuity." Dukes wanted the Choctaw legislature at its next session to eject all white traders from the Choctaw Nation. Even Choctaws like Robert Jones, he alleged, was in collusion with the "speculators."[32] Robinson called Saffarans and Company "Chickasaw speculators," who raised prices by 100%. Like Dukes, he endorsed the movement to put them out of the nation.[33] Wilson reported that after Saffarans and Company obtained a settlement of their claims in the spring, "they made a rush, and have the balance bought up." They had not yet got the Chickasaw leaders to approve the sale of the state bonds but had convinced them the bonds were worth only half their value and traded the Chickasaws the other half in high-priced goods. "It is said that they keep whiskey; and James Colbert, half drunk, to interpret for them. Old Isaac Alberson told me that they had commenced buying the orphan claim of money. So the doors are open to the Chickasaw money, and they will pull out the whole amount, general funds and all, if not put a stop to."[34] Finally, Thomas J. Pitchlynn reported in late September that Saffarans & Lewis had left the nation, having obtained some $200,000 of the "incompetent" Chickasaw claims. "All the merchants in Doaksville are purchasing them," he said. "I think they are a day after the feast. O, how it galls me to think what poor fools the Chickasaws are to allow such conduct to go on, and not to inform the Government of it! I think every white man who is living in the nation without a Choctaw family ought to be ordered out of it forthwith. They are sucking, as it were, our very veins for the last drop."[35] These men may have been Choctaw Nation meddlers, as Saffarans later claimed, but they were dead right about their plans for the Chickasaw fund.

Saffarans had, indeed, left the Indian Territory for Washington, where he arrived to claim payment of debts based on his due bills only a short time after Peter Pitchlynn had been there complaining about his tactics. In collecting his claims, Saffarans rallied his Whig friends to intervene in his behalf, including Ephraim H. Foster of Nashville and Balie Peyton of his hometown, Gallatin, Tennessee.[36] Foster had

(249)

been elected to the Senate in 1837 but had resigned in 1839 because he refused to take instructions from the Democratic Tennessee State Legislature. Thus he held high currency among Whigs in 1841. Peyton was elected to Congress as a Jackson Democrat in 1833 and 1835. In 1840, however, he campaigned for Harrison, who appointed him as U. S. Attorney at New Orleans. Saffarans prevailed upon these men to work for payment of his claims with Albert M. Lea, acting secretary of war between John McLean and John C. Spencer, both of whom succeeded Bell.

In October, Saffarans presented a claim for more than $84,000 in "incompetent" Chickasaw stock, based on notes from individual Chickasaws, transferring their stocks to him. Commissioner of Indian Affairs Crawford balked, saying that questions had been raised about the price and quality of goods his firm had supplied. Saffarans claimed that he was in a bind. He had bills for orders for $50,000-$60,000 in goods in eastern cities, due in November and December. He asked Secretary John C. Spencer to transfer $60,000 in State of Maryland stocks, which Spencer promptly did. Spencer held up the balance of Saffarans & Lewis's claim because the charges Pitchlynn had made were grave. Although he claimed to have little doubt that the traders were honest, he ordered Armstrong to examine their books and those of other trading houses in the Choctaw Nation in the presence of the Chickasaw commissioners.[37]

(250)

Saffarans "confidentially" approached Lea to use any remaining influence he had with the secretary's office. He had no fear, he argued, that Armstrong's investigation would show any wrongdoing but was afraid that Armstrong might take too long. Inaction might embarrass him financially and hold up other business he had before the War Department. Saffarans claimed that he had not been told who made the charges against his company but he felt certain that it was not the Chickasaws; "for I am acquainted with all of the principal men in the nation," he said, "and they have all been eyewitnesses to more or less of our operations in their country." His chief clerk at Boggy Depot had informed him that two "white Choctaws," one of whom was Robertus Wilson, had tried to circulate a memorial to expel white traders from the Choctaw Nation, but the Chickasaws had refused to sign. It was a scheme laid to defeat Saffarans & Lewis, Saffarans claimed, "not because we don't do those we trade with as much justice as any other traders, but it is because we have more information and do more business than any other traders," apparently Saffarans' nicer way of saying they had a virtual monopoly. He laid the scheme at the feet of the Pitchlynn family, even though he claimed not to know who his accusers were, because Wilson was Peter Pitchlynn's brother-in-law. Pitchlynn, his brother Thomas, and their mother owed him $500 or $600, Saffarans claimed, and were angry because he had tried to collect it.[38]

Although his statements to Lea were allegedly "confidential," Lea felt it "due" himself to pass them on to Secretary John C. Spencer because Lea had overseen the earlier partial payment of Saffarans' claims. Also, he confirmed the Pitchlynn family's hostility because Peter Pitchlynn had recently asked not only Lea but the president to remove all white traders from the Indian Territory.[39]

Armstrong and the Chickasaw commissioners went to Boggy Depot, where they examined the books of not only Saffarans & Lewis but Berthelet, Heald & Co., who also had a store there. The latter had also been in the business of trading goods for Chickasaw stock in the "incompetent" fund. Armstrong called partners Berthelet, Heald, and Jones "gentlemen of the first standing. General Jones is a Choctaw. I have known him since he removed to this nation in 1832, and I have always found him honest and correct. The other two are gentlemen of high character." He had even higher praise for Saffarans & Lewis. And he made sure that no enterprising company might see the investigation of buying up incompetent stock as a moment of weakness and attempt to move in on the licensed traders of the nation. "The merchants of the nation have all participated, with one exception, in the trade. I consider them men of good character and standing; none other need apply to me for a license."[40] Besides the two he investigated, Armstrong had in mind the firms of Doak & Tim and D. & S. Folsom.

Armstrong's report gave Saffarans & Lewis glowing praise. His inspection of the company had been attended by not only the Chickasaw commissioners but "generally some three to five hundred Indians." He reported that the goods and livestock, which the traders had supplied the Chickasaws, were of sound quality and fairly priced, given the dis-

(257)

tance they had to be hauled, and that the firm had literally saved the lives of the incompetents. Because the government had not paid the Chickasaws the money due them upon arrival in the West, the traders had let them buy on credit the goods they needed to survive and the livestock necessary to establish herds. The traders had even allowed them to buy in larger quantities than they needed, providing a surplus to trade for debts they owed Choctaws and other Chickasaws. This economy had been better, Armstrong argued, than what would have resulted from payment, for there were signs of economic recovery and well being everywhere. If they had received money, he said, the "incompetents" would have spent it and would now be destitute. Finally, Armstrong blasted the Pitchlynn family as Choctaw interferers who were deeply resented by the Chickasaws and who lived too far from the scene to know what they were talking about.[41]

Armstrong vouched for the goods and for the fact that they met the Chickasaws' needs. Saffarans & Lewis stocked dry goods such as Mackinaw blankets, domestic calicoes, mixed satinets, Merrimack blue prints, dark fancy prints, plate prints, fancy chintz, cotton stripe, bleached domestics, ticking, brown shirting, sheeting, scarlet and blue stroud, and English gingham; groceries such as sugar, coffee, flour, bacon, and corn; tools such as axes, hoes, chains, augers, and wagons; riding equipment such as spurs, saddles, and bridles; clothing such as Kip brogans, russet brogans, seal pegged and calf brogans for men, women's brogans, and shawls. The traders bought the goods in New York and other places in the East or in New Orleans and shipped them primarily by way of Van Buren, Arkansas, and then overland to the main trading places in the Choctaw Nation proper and the Chickasaw District. Most of these items were marked up an average of 100% from the purchase price, which Armstrong apparently did not consider exorbitant. Saffarans & Lewis had also supplied over one thousand cattle, seven or eight hundred hogs, and a number of horses and work oxen.[42]

The Chickasaw commissioners also defended both the traders and themselves, claiming the prices charged the Chickasaws were not as high as alleged. "Our people are not so ignorant as to give such prices for goods; they understand generally how to trade. In most cases, with Saffarans & Lewis, one or more of the commissioners have generally been present, and almost invariably one or two of their clerks, and our own educated young Chickasaws, in whom we confide." They clearly did not like Peter Pitchlynn, and, like Armstrong, blasted the Pitchlynn family as Choctaw meddlers. The commissioners felt that they were on the line. It was they who had declared the people "incompetent," under the assumption, they claimed, their action would protect the people's money by keeping it from the Chickasaws until they arrived in the West. Because the money had been invested and was unavailable, the people had been forced into debt. "We are unwilling," the commissioners wrote, "for censure to be thrown upon us when we feel conscious we have done our duty; and hope that the Government will not sanction interference by such designing men as Messrs. Pitchlynn and others. It would be time to listen to these complaints when our own people, who are alone interested, complain."[43]

Despite what the commissioners said, Chickasaws *had* complained about the traders' tactics. Ethan Allen Hitchcock had heard a number of complaints about the merchants upon his arrival in the Chickasaw District in late 1841. Without question, his visit coincided with a growing contention among the Chickasaws regarding leadership. Criticism of the commissioners and of Upshaw was mounting. But even some of the commissioners and their supporters had serious concerns about the sale of the "incompetent" funds. At Doaksville, Hitchcock found the Chickasaws in that area reluctant to talk in the presence of Upshaw. Slone Love told him that Captain Greenwood wanted to see him, and on the road, Hitchcock was urged by Henry Colbert and his mother to visit the old chief. At Greenwood's, on March 1, 1842, a number gathered to complain bitterly against the agent and charged that the sale of the "incompetent" claims had been "corrupt." Although the traders argued that they had "relieved" the wants of the Chickasaws, the outside observer could legitimately question whether the traders had not created the wants that they had then lucratively "relieved." "If they traded without express authority, would it not be fair to pay the money to the original claimant and leave him to settle with the traders. If the latter have traded fairly the honesty of the Indian will pay him, the chance is equal," Hitchcock observed.[44]

His observations led him to the conclusion that purchase of the

(253)

"incompetent" and orphan funds should stop or be regulated. "The Government assumed guardianship over both and both are at the mercy of speculators," he wrote, "and fare worse under Government protection than those deemed competent to manage their own affairs." However, it might be too late to reform the system. "Traders have large claims on the Indians and from the nature of the case, provide for bad debts by a large advance on their goods." He added, "An attempt to restrict the trade would be likely to produce indirectness in it, resulting in heavier charges by the traders to cover the increased chances of bad debts." One possible solution, he concluded, was that the government could issue a clear rule that traders could not trade in Indian country except at their own risk. If they traded on credit, they could not enter the Indian nation to collect debts. "As a rule, if he trades honestly the Indians will pay. If they refuse payment it is *prima facie* evidence of extortion and fraud on the part of the trader."[45] Before he left the Indian Territory, Hitchcock concluded that Armstrong was a main player in the fraud surrounding delivery of subsistence rations to the Chickasaws and other tribes. Unfortunately, Armstrong was in charge of overseeing trade in the Indian Territory and approved of the traders' tactics.

Armstrong well knew that *inflation* and *speculation* were the key words that described the economy of the Indian Territory. He also knew how the merchants had managed to gain control of the "incompetent" claims. Here is how it worked. Saffarans and Lewis or another trading house bought a Chickasaw's claim for money due him from sale of his land in Mississippi. For every ten dollars due the Chickasaw, the merchant put an "X" on the back of the agreement. The Chickasaws could take payment only in goods. If a claim was worth $200, the claimant could have $200 worth of goods. If he took part of the payment, the merchant erased the appropriate number of "X's" from the back of the agreement. Denominations less than ten, "change" in effect, were given in the form of due bills that could be redeemed in goods only at the merchant's store. The agreement between the Chickasaws and the trader remained on deposit with the trader until the amount was used up. One person who owed another could take the person to the trader to pay the debt in goods by having the trader subtract from the amount on deposit. When Hitchcock encountered this system in 1842, the due bills were called "Brandon money." He did not know what the term meant until a Chickasaw handed him some due bills, little slips of paper containing handwritten notes. He gave an example: "Four dollars in goods. IIII charged S & Lewis. A. P. Sheldon." The Roman numerals stood for each dollar like the "X" stood for ten. These pieces of paper circulated like paper money.[46]

This system enriched the traders and cheated the Chickasaws. The traders made payment only in goods that had been marked up sometimes 100% from their cost to the trader. When a due bill came in for payment, the trader automatically reduced the face value by 50%. Thus on the four-dollar due bill that Hitchcock copied, Saffarans and Lewis would have paid two dollars in goods that had been marked up perhaps 100%. Hitchcock stopped short of calling this fraud on the Chickasaws; it was at least, he said, a cheat on the government, which would pay the trader the full amount of the claim.[47]

It is uncertain whether this system was tied to the Brandon Bank in Mississippi or the Chickasaws simply took the name of the bank to describe discounted or worthless paper money. Either way, the name was apt. Established at Brandon, Mississippi, in 1838, the bank was a failure from the start. It was funded primarily by paper money it held on Planters Bank in Mississippi. Although Mississippi banks supported it at first, Memphis banks discounted it by 25 percent. People who held Brandon money in the fall of 1838 found that the money was trading at 35% below par. The banks in towns along the Mississippi, which were the most solvent banks of the time, would have nothing to do with Brandon money, even those in Natchez and Vicksburg.[48]

Testimonials by Armstrong and the commissioners in behalf of the merchants and their "Brandon money" system reached Washington well in advance of Hitchcock and the evidence he had garnered. In February 1842, the War Department paid the remainder of Saffarans' claim from the previous fall and those of Doak & Tim and D. & S. Folsom. In March, it paid additional claims by Saffarans. That same month, Berthelet, Heald & Co. submitted their claims for $80,000, and the department advanced them $50,000.[49] Then Hitchcock reached Washington on the heels of congressional investigation of fraud in Indian removal.

(255)

Although Hitchcock's findings about the role of Armstrong and other government officials in rations fraud were unpopular with Spencer, what he learned from Hitchcock about the traders' due bill system had a telling effect. With the department's ongoing attempt during the spring and summer of 1842 to contain the scandal regarding fraud in Indian affairs in the Southwest, Spencer had a vested interest in avoiding the exposure of another. Saffarans was in Washington at the time Spencer learned of the due bill system. He expressed his objection to it to Saffarans, who immediately went to the Indian Territory and issued orders calling in all due bills in circulation and instructing his agents to issue no more.[50]

Saffarans developed a plan to consolidate the claims of all the traders, a process he had started earlier that year. In early April, Josiah S. Doak had sent Saffarans the last paperwork on the incompetent claims he held. Apparently tired of the business, Doak & Tim had chosen to bow out: "Those is the last we expect to have any thing to do with, as I am desirous to have the matter closed as soon as possible."[51] With Spencer's disapproval of his due bill system, Saffarans, too, had decided it was time to get out of the "incompetent" business. On July 1, 1842, Saffarans & Lewis, Doak & Tim, Berthelet, Heald & Co., and D. & S. Folsom issued a joint notice from Doaksville, calling in all due bills for "incompetent" claims, saying it was the wish of the secretary of war that the bills be paid. Knowing Saffarans' success in the settlement of claims, the other firms asked him to examine their books. Saffarans apparently prevailed on William Armstrong, at whose request Chickasaw Agent Upshaw and military officers from Fort Towson and Fort Washita examined the traders' accounts as Armstrong had done earlier. They, too, gave the traders a vote of approval as did the Chickasaw commissioners, and on October 27, 1842, Saffarans submitted the claims of all the traders for payment, which was forthcoming within days.[52]

It may never be certain how much of the Chickasaw "incompetent" fund went to Saffarans and Lewis, but it was a large amount for the 1840s. The following summary gives an idea. In March 1841 the War Department transferred New York, Indiana, Maryland, and Kentucky bonds to the traders. More than $22,000 went to Saffarans and Lewis, over $32,000 went to Penn & Lewis, and more than $20,000 to Daniel Saffarans & Company. In October of that year, Saffarans received $58,000 in Maryland bonds, and in February 1842, $30,000 in Kentucky bonds. In March 1842, Saffarans received more than $19,000 in Maryland and Kentucky bonds, and in November Saffarans & Lewis received over $14,000. In 1843 and 1845, Saffarans received more than $2,000. Thus in four years, Saffarans and his associates received almost $200,000 of the "incompetent" Chickasaw fund, nearly half of the amount received by all merchants in the Indian Territory.[53]

Although he capitulated on the due bill issue, Saffarans nevertheless defended it. He blamed its creation on the Chickasaw commissioners. Though it was a system that had worked to the benefit of the "incompetent" Chickasaws, he claimed, he pledged to bring the system to an end within ninety days, not only in his firm but in all the others as well. Spencer responded, "I am satisfied by the within explanation, believing Colonel Saffarans from the representations of members of Congress from Tennessee and of the Hon. Balie Peyton, to be an honest man."[54] In reality, Saffarans had little to lose. The "incompetent" fund had little left in it. Besides, he had already turned his attention toward other Chickasaw funds.

Saffarans had told Albert Lea in late 1841 that he had "much business" before the War Department, unconnected to the "incompetent" claims. Part of it was the Chickasaw orphan fund claims, money held in trust from the sale of orphans' land, which he had acquired in the same way he had acquired the "incompetent" claims. He had tried to push some of them during a trip to Washington in the spring of 1841, consulting with John Bell and T. Hartley Crawford, but he did not have sufficient proof to pursue them at the time. When the department ordered the examination of his books that fall regarding the "incompetent" claims, he hesitated in pushing the orphan claims.[55] With the "incompetent" claims settled, however, he could pursue the orphan money in earnest.

The Chickasaw commissioners had believed that the orphans, like the "incompetent" Chickasaws, needed protection until they reached an age or circumstance that would allow them to handle their own affairs. They, like others, moved west with the expectation of receiving payments due them in the new country. Chickasaw orphans had be-

gun to apply for payment of their funds soon after removal. The first
to petition for his funds was Cyrus Harris, an orphan at removal, but
in 1839 a man married with a family and considered "one of the most
intelligent and respectable young Chickasaws belonging to the tribe."
His claim was supported by Armstrong and the Chickasaw commissioners. The only response the Chickasaws received was that when the
claim was considered, the government would let them know.[56] Crawford was, in fact, guarding the orphan fund as he had done the "incompetent" fund. His stated policy was to pay only the interest received on
the $146,000 of orphans' invested money in Arkansas State stocks.
He planned to pay those who had married or come of age their share
of the interest, provided a majority of the commissioners named in the
fourth article of the Treaty of 1834 would agree to it. He would not pay
out the adult or married orphans' shares of the principal because the
stocks could not be sold at par as a result of lingering national economic difficulties. Months passed, and instead of paying the interest
to the orphans, Crawford invested it in Pennsylvania State stocks. In
1841, however, he finally ordered a payment of the interest to those who
had reached legal age or were married.[57]

After nearly two years had passed with no action taken on the Harris petition, the Chickasaw commissioners and chiefs renewed their request for the orphan fund. In some ways their argument was the same
as that regarding the "incompetent" Chickasaws: it was their money,
and they needed it. "It certainly is reasonable to suppose," they said,
"that people must be clothed and fed." But with the orphans, there
were other issues. They sent the government a roster of those who had
come of age, were married, and had land in Mississippi that had not
sold because of the economic conditions of recent years. "A great many
of them," said the leaders, "have some education, and bid fair to be
of service to their nation. It is our wish . . . that they be permitted to
sell their lands as other competent Chickasaws did. It is our wish that
our people should all be put on an equality." Their displeasure with the
state of affairs was evident: "We petition for nothing in which our treaty does not bear us out; but it appears that we are always the last that
are attended to. When the time came (Agreeably to our treaty) to move
from Mississippi, we moved without the Government having to send

her army to drive us off, like the Cherokees. We made our treaty, and we intended to stand to and abide by it. We have always been the friend of our great father the President of the United States, and we always will be; and we ask nothing more than a compliance of our treaty."[58]

Before the end of 1843, Saffarans and his partner Felix Lewis depleted the Chickasaw orphan fund. By the time Secretary Spencer directed Saffarans and the other merchants to cease issuing due bills, Saffarans had already gotten a number of orphans in debt to him in the amount of their claim. Spencer's directive regarding the competents did not stop him from giving credit to orphans in the amounts of their claims. He also acted as attorney of record for those whose lands remained unsold east of the Mississippi. When the War Department decided to settle the "incompetent" claims by trading Saffarans-invested stock at par, it opened the door for similar action regarding the orphans. Thus in 1842 and 1843, Saffarans and his partner acquired almost $179,000 of Arkansas and Pennsylvania stock and interest. Also, by the end of 1841, Saffarans had begun to buy yet unsold orphans' lands in Mississippi. Of the orphans land sold after 1839, Saffarans and Lewis bought ninety-nine quarter sections and Saffarans bought sixty-nine, or the equivalent of eighty-four orphan claims.[59]

But that was not all. Saffarans was also gleaning his share of the general Chickasaw fund. Besides the orphan claims that he had pending when the War Department examined his books in 1841, he also had "considerable business to do" for his "friends in Mississippi, and some of the most influential in North Mississippi, and also of the right stripe."[60] Saffarans no doubt referred to the merchants holding Chickasaw debts, but he also meant Chickasaws who had remained in Mississippi but later decided to join their people in the West.

Late removals had been a constant phenomenon since the main removals had ended. In 1839, Commissioner Crawford sent Upshaw to Mississippi to see former Agent Benjamin Reynolds about Chickasaw money he was still holding and directed him, while he was there, to try to persuade those remaining in Mississippi to remove. He was to emphasize that the removal was closed, and that if they did not go west with him, they would be left to their own resources should they decide to remove later. Those who removed themselves, however, argued that

(259)

they should be indemnified at a rate equal to that given in 1838 to the Colberts. While the War Department had not encouraged that mode of removal, Crawford believed it "reasonable" that they be paid. Thus he ordered Armstrong to make rolls of those who removed by their own means but also those who had joined organized removal parties en route.[61]

Not only did those who removed themselves have little luck in collecting their reimbursement, but those who asked for assistance in moving were also denied. Benjamin Love, Charles Eastman, and others were put off because there was no money in the Chickasaw fund to be expended. The only assistance the Department would offer was subsistence once they reached the West.[62]

In September 1842, backed by four of the Chickasaw commissioners, Saffarans sought an agreement with the War Department to remove all remaining Chickasaws who wished to go west for $30 per person and 25 cents a day for each horse. He was to be paid out of the interest on the general Chickasaw fund upon their delivery at Fort Smith. The idea was that Saffarans & Lewis would advance the money to the Chickasaws and collect from the Chickasaw fund through the War Department. They were to earn 6% on the money owed until they were paid. Some accepted Saffarans as their agent. One party of 188 in the fall of 1842, for example, netted him $9,000. But many distrusted him and his motives and were suspicious of his claims to be an emigration agent because the Chickasaws had been adamant all along that they did not want removal agents acting for them. They also believed he was trying to collect for Chickasaws who removed on their own at earlier times.[63]

Months before he made a formal agreement with the War Department, Saffarans had been acting as agent for Chickasaws who wished to remove. In early 1843, he sought to expand his efforts. He received reassurance that claims would be paid to any who could show evidence of self-removal. During the next four years, Saffarans, through his attorney Joseph Bryan, filed dozens of claims to collect the thirty dollars due each person for whom he had financed removal.[64]

Saffarans found other ways to get at the Chickasaw fund. He bought up the claims of those who held old debts against the United States for various reasons. He had the power of attorney, for example, for William McGilivray, Immahholatubby, and Ubbetunheyah to collect for the hire of wagons and teams during the general removal. He held a like claim for Captain Greenwood, deceased. Upshaw supported Saffarans' claim, saying some of Greenwood's surviving children were minors, some of whom had come of age since the old chief's death some six years after removal. Saffarans also acquired the claim for the services by J. M. Skelton as issuing commissary for the Chickasaws.[65] Apparently, whenever Saffarans found opportunity to acquire Chickasaw funds, he took it.

If he ran into difficulty in collecting his claims, Saffarans called on men like Armstrong and Upshaw. Upshaw used the influence of his office whenever he was asked, always urging the War Department to pay up. His arguments were patent: when the late Chickasaws arrived, they were destitute of cash and would have suffered had it not been for "private aid," which allowed them to start anew in the western country. In exchange, Saffarans bought out by either power of attorney or direct order the Chickasaws' claims against the government. Benjamin Love had done likewise, and although he had sent his claim for payment, all of it had not been paid, so he sold his claim to Saffarans. Saffarans had not taken advantage, Upshaw argued. All of the claimants were either "white men or intelligent half breeds and capable of protecting their own interests in any business transactions whatever."[66]

(261)

In February 1845 the Senate launched an investigation of the transfer of bonds or other money held in trust for the Chickasaw and Choctaw "incompetents" or orphans. The body wanted to know who received the money and sought a review of the decisions of the secretaries of war, beginning with Joel Poinsett, regarding the funds. The Choctaw orphan fund remained intact, and in his report Commissioner Crawford insisted that the decisions regarding the Chickasaw funds had been made by the secretary of war, who had investigated each claim and had guarded against fraud.[67] By that time, Saffarans had drained the Chickasaw fund to the extent possible. Certainly the easy money had ceased to flow, and he was ready to move on to other ventures.

It is difficult to say how much of the Chickasaw money passed into the hands of Daniel Saffarans and his partner Felix Lewis as a result of their purchase of "incompetent," orphan, or self-removal claims. It was a huge amount, a veritable fortune for its day. In some ways it had been easy to deplete the Chickasaw fund, for certain factors had worked in Saffarans' favor: risk, inflation, and Chickasaw single-mindedness in using their own money. Saffarans settled with his fortune in Memphis, where he became a well-known figure. Lewis faded from the scene. Despite the financial cost to them, the Chickasaws had reached one of their main goals: to get all of their people to the West. That goal was a necessary step in reestablishing themselves as an independent nation once more, separate from the Choctaws.

NOTES

1. T. Hartley Crawford to William Armstrong, June 2, 1840, Chickasaw Vol. 2, 78–80, in National Archives Record Group 75, Records of the Office of Indian Affairs, Records of the Commissary General of Subsistence, Chickasaw Removal Records.

2. C. A. Harris to Benjamin Reynolds, April 30, 1837, Chickasaw Vol. 1, 149–50.

3. Armstrong to Harris, June 19, 1838, 28th Congress, 2nd Session, *Senate Report 160*, 6.

4. Harris to Armstrong, August 8, 1838, Chickasaw Volume 1, 273–74; *Senate Report 160*, 6–7.

5. Armstrong to Harris, September 28 and October 12, 1838, *Senate Report 160*, 7–8.

6. Crawford to Armstrong, November 17, 1838, and Joel R. Poinsett to D. Thompson, February 11, 1839, Chickasaw Vol. 2, 10–11, 30–31; *Senate Report 160*, 8.

7. Ish-to-ho-to-pa, et al., to Martin Van Buren, February 14, 1839, *Senate Report 160*, 8–9.

8. Armstrong to Crawford, February 22, 1839, *Senate Report 160*, 8.

9. Crawford to Armstrong, March 29, 1839, *Senate Report 160*, 10.

10. Crawford to Thomas H. Williams, March 2 and 8, April 16 and 23, 1839; Crawford to James H. Henry, March 16, 1839; Crawford to Solomon Clark, et al., June 4, 1839; Chickasaw Volume 2, 35, 37–39, 52, 55–59.

11. Crawford to Armstrong, September 9, 1839, Chickasaw Volume 2, 69–70.

12. Extract of a letter from Armstrong, August 17, 1839; Armstrong to Crawford, September 24, 1839, and Ish-te-ho-to-pa, et al. to President, September 3, 1839, *Senate Report 160*, 10–12.

13. Crawford to Armstrong, November 9, 1839, *Senate Report 160*, 13. Crawford to Armstrong, June 2, 1840, Chickasaw Vol. 2, 80. The interest payment Crawford had promised occurred in July 1840. See Crawford to Armstrong, July 18, 1840, Chickasaw Volume 2, 95.

14. Armstrong to Crawford, May 20, 1840; Ish-to-ho-to-pa, et al. to Upshaw, April 11, 1840, *Senate Report 160*, 14–15.

15. Benjamin Love to Secretary of War, May 25, 1840, *Senate Report 160*, 8.

16. Love to Poinsett, May 15, 1840, *Senate Report 160*, 15–17.

17. Love to Secretary of War, May 25, 1840, *Senate Report 160*, 16–18.

18. Love to Poinsett, May 21, 1840, James Davis to David Hubbard, December 31, 1839, and Hubbard to Poinsett, May 27, 1840, *Senate Report 160*, 15–16, 19, 20; Mary Young, *Redskins, Ruffleshirts and Rednecks: Indian Allotments in Alabama and Mississippi, 1830–1860* (Norman: University of Oklahoma Press, 1961), 142–43.

19. Felix Lewis to Jacob Thompson, May 4, 1840, and Thompson to Crawford, May 23, 1840, *Senate Report 160*, 21–24.

20. Poinsett to Crawford, May 28, 1840, *Senate Report 160*, 21; Crawford to Thomas H. Benton, June 1, 1840, Chickasaw Vol. 2, 85–87, and *Senate Report 160*, 24–25.

21. A. M. M. Upshaw to Crawford, August 23, 1840, *Senate Report 160*, 25.

22. Crawford to Armstrong, June 2, 1840, Chickasaw Vol. 2, 78–80.

23. Ish-to-ho-to-pa, et al. to President, August 12, 1840; Armstrong to Upshaw, October 6, 1840, *Senate Report 160*, 25–26, 28.

24. Upshaw to Armstrong, December 29, 1840, enclosed in Armstrong to Crawford, January 5, 1841, *Senate Report 160*, 27, 28–29.

25. Crawford to John Bell, March 22 and April 12, 1841; Crawford to Armstrong, March 25, 1841, Chickasaw Volume 2, pp. 138–40, 147–48.

26. Ethan Allen Hitchcock, *A Traveler in Indian Territory: The Journal of Ethan Allen Hitchcock, late Major-General in the United States Army*, ed. Grant Foreman (Cedar Rapids, IA: The Torch Press, 1930), 197–99.

27. *Ibid.*, 200–01.

28. Daniel Saffarans and Felix Lewis to John Bell, March 1841, *Senate Report 160*, 35.

29. Ish-te-ho-to-pa, et al. to President, July 15, 1841, Upshaw to Crawford, August 20, 1841, and Armstrong to Crawford, August 26, 1841, *Senate Report 160*, 36–38.

30. Saffarans to John C. Spencer, November 7, 1842, *Senate Report 160*, 60.

31. P. P. Pitchlynn to Secretary of War, October 25, 1841, *Senate Report 160*, 38.

32. Joseph Dukes to Pitchlynn, September 4, 1841, *Senate Report 160*, 39.

33. A. Robinson to Pitchlynn, September 27, 1841, *Senate Report 160*, 40.

(263)

34. R. Wilson to Pitchlynn, September 17, 1841, *Senate Report 160*, 40.

35. Thomas J. Pitchlynn to Peter P. Pitchlynn, September 21, 1841, *Senate Report 160*, 41.

36. Ephraim H. Foster to Albert M. Lea, September 30, 1841, and Balie Peyton to Lea, October 7, 1841, *Senate Report 160*, 45.

37. Saffarans to Spencer, October 29, 1841, with endorsement; Spencer to D. Kurtz, October 30, 1841; Kurtz to Armstrong, and Saffarans & Lewis to Crawford, November 13, 1841, *Senate Report 160*, 42–43, 50; Crawford to Armstrong, November 5, 1841, Chickasaw Volume 2, 155–56.

38. Saffarans to Lea, November 19, 1841, *Senate Report 160*, 43–44.

39. Lea to Spencer, November 26, 1841, *Senate Report 160*, 44–45.

40. Armstrong to Crawford, December 1, 1841, and January 9, 1842, *Senate Report 160*, 45, 51.

41. Armstrong to Crawford, January 9, 1842, *Senate Report 160*, 45–47.

42. *Ibid.*, and Statements P15, T2, T3, T4, and T5, *Senate Report 160*, 45–46, 48–49, 53, 55, 56–58.

43. Ish-to-ho-to-pa, Isaac Alberson, James Wolf, and Slone Love to Armstrong, January 4, 1842, *Senate Report 160*, 47–48.

44. Hitchcock, *Traveler*, 196–97, 215.

45. *Ibid.*, 186, 187, 202.

46. *Ibid.*, 249–50.

47. *Ibid.*

48. *Memphis Enquirer*, September 1, 1838, and October 6, 1838.

49. Statement V1; Berthelet, Heald & Co., to Crawford, March 24, 1842; Spencer, Statement R3, *Senate Report 160*, 51, 62–63. For abstract of indebtedness of Chickasaws to various companies, see National Archives Record Group 75, Records of the Bureau of Indian Affairs, Entry 254, Abstracts of Disposition of Lands, Volume 2, 157 ff. See also, Entry 929, Records Relating to Indian Trust Funds, Ledger for Trust Funds of Chickasaw Incompetents and Minors, 1837–43.

50. Saffarans to Spencer, November 7, 1842, *Senate Report 160*, 60.

51. Josiah S. Doak to Saffarans, April 9, 1842, *Senate Report 160*, 59.

52. Notice, July 1, 1842; Saffarans to Crawford, October 27, 1842; Statements T2, T3, T4, T5, and V1, *Senate Report 160*, 52–58, 59, 63–64.

53. Document V1, *Senate Report 160*, 62–63.

54. Saffarans to Spencer, November 7, 1842, and Spencer's endorsement, November 8, 1842, *Senate Report 160*, 61.

55. Saffarans to A. M. Lea, November 19, 1841, *Senate Report 160*, 43.

56. Armstrong to Crawford, March 27, 1839; Ish-to-ho-to-pa, et al. to

Armstrong, January 28, 1839; D. Kurtz to Armstrong, May 4, 1839, *Senate Report 160*, 65; Crawford to Armstrong, May 4, 1839, Chickasaw Volume 2, 52–53.

57. Crawford to Armstrong, November 9, 1839; Crawford to J. M. Porter, October 3, 1843, *Senate Report 160*, 13, 68; Crawford to Armstrong, July 16, 1840, Chickasaw Volume 2, 91–94.

58. Armstrong to Crawford, March 10, 1841, and Ish-te-ho-to-pa, et al., Memorial, November 25, 1840, *Senate Report 160*, 66–67.

59. Crawford to Spencer, December 24, 1841, Saffarans to Crawford, October 2, 1843, and Crawford to Porter, October 3, 1843, *Senate Report 160*, 67–72.

60. Saffarans to Lea, November 19, 1841, *Senate Report 160*, 43.

61. Crawford to Upshaw, March 7, 1839, and Crawford to Armstrong, March 19, 1839, Chickasaw Volume 2, 36–37, 40–41.

62. Crawford to Benjamin Love, July 24, 1840, August 20, 1842, and September 30, 1841, Chickasaw Volume 2, 97, 149–50.

63. Ish-te-ho-to-pa, et al., to J. C. Spencer, August 10, 1842, Record Book of the Chickasaw Nation, June 2, 1837–August 1855 (Oklahoma Historical Society Microfilm CKN 30), 20–21; Crawford to Saffarans, October 1 and November 1, 1842, Crawford to Armstrong, October 1, 1842, and Crawford to J. M. Porter, June 26, 1843, Chickasaw Volume 2, 232–34, 255, 305; Second Auditor to William Medill, July 17, 1848, and C. F. Eastman to Jacob Thompson, January 16, 1844, enclosed in Thompson to Crawford, January 19, 1844 (Chickasaw Emigration A233 and T1147), National Archives Microcopy M234, Letters Received by the Office of Indian Affairs, Roll 144. This source is hereafter cited as M234-R144.

64. Armstrong to Crawford, April 9, 1843, and Saffarans to Crawford, February 14, 1843 (Chickasaw Emigration A1430 and S3334), M234-R144; Crawford to Saffarans, February 25, 1843, Chickasaw Volume 2, 283. Too numerous to cite, correspondence relating to Saffarans' various claims can be found in the "B" documents of M234-R144 for the years 1844–48.

65. Joseph Bryan to Crawford, February 5, May 25, 1844, and October 3, 1844 (Chickasaw Emigration B1933, B2027, B2227), and Bryan to William Medill, August 14, 1846, October 31, 1845, and November 30, 1846 (Chickasaw Emigration B2734, B2577, B2792), M234-R144.

66. Upshaw to Crawford, September 16, 1844 (Chickasaw Emigration U168), M234-R144.

67. William Wilkins to W. P. Mangum, March 1, 1845, and Crawford to Wilkins, February 26, 1845, *Senate Report 160*, 2–3.

RECLAIMING THE
CHICKASAW NATION

WHEN ETHAN ALLEN HITCHCOCK visited the Chickasaws in 1842, he found that economic recovery following removal was slow. By most accounts, recovery did not begin in earnest until the early 1850s because of the Chickasaw's scattered settlement pattern, the credit economy, fear of the western tribes, Choctaw domination, and delays in organizing government.[1] Perhaps the greatest cause was the need for the Chickasaw people to escape from Choctaw dominance and to reestablish themselves as a separate nation. Economic recovery could not, and did not, occur until the Chickasaw people consolidated their numbers in the Chickasaw District and established an autonomous government. In the debate over what type of government they would have, Chickasaw leaders and their followers nearly split the Chickasaw people into two factions. However, both sides—traditionalists and constitutionalists—had a common goal: freedom from Choctaw domination. The process of establishing their government, which brought an end to their removal era, lasted for nearly two decades after removal, and it demonstrated their fierce nationalism, which allowed them to rise above threats of factionalism that often rent the population of other removed tribes.

Hitchcock found the Chickasaws smarting under Choctaw domination. Members of both nations denied the assumption on the part of U. S. officials that the Choctaws and Chickasaws were essentially the same people. That assumption had driven U. S. attempts for a number of years to get the Choctaws to take the Chickasaws in after removal and for the Chickasaws to agree to submit to Choctaw control. The old Chickasaw leaders, however, argued that their people had no traditional stories about separation from the Choctaws, concluding that

(267)

the Chickasaws and Choctaws were not traditionally one people. The Choctaws as well told Hitchcock that their customs differed altogether from those of the Chickasaws, an idea Hitchcock found strange because of the similarity of languages. The Chickasaws argued that although the languages were the same in structure, they varied widely in vocabulary and the Choctaws had dialects that the Chickasaws had difficulty understanding. They felt "humiliated under the Choctaw agreement," Hitchcock said. "They feel as if they have purchased themselves into degradation."[2]

The old chiefs such as Greenwood, who had seen Chickasaw government go through a number of drastic changes, were particularly outspoken in their dislike for the Choctaws. He claimed that the Choctaws were dishonest and inhospitable, using the example of the Chickasaw delegation's trip to the West to find a suitable land for settlement. The Choctaws, he told Hitchcock, "trailed off" the Chickasaws' horses "and made them pay for their recovery, and they would hardly give a traveler a meal of victuals." Nor did Greenwood like the Choctaws' Christian preaching and camp meetings: "Jumping, singing, hallowing, crying. Don't like it," Greenwood told Hitchcock.[3]

Political differences also upset the Chickasaws. Directly following the Treaty of Doaksville in 1837, the Choctaws had changed their constitution to accommodate the Chickasaws. The Chickasaw District became one of four political districts along with Mosholatubbee, Pushmataha, and Apuckshunnubbee. Each district was empowered to elect a chief every four years. Members of the General Council were elected each year, the number from each district based on population. The Chickasaws, however, did not elect a chief or members of Council until 1841.[4] In 1842, the four district chiefs of the Choctaw Nation were John McKinney, Isaac Folsom, Jim Fletcher, and Isaac Alberson, who represented the Chickasaw District.[5] Alberson was formerly one of the four district chiefs of the Chickasaw Nation east of the Mississippi River and had served since 1834 as one of the seven Chickasaw commissioners. In addition to the elected officials who dealt with the Choctaws in council, fifteen to twenty captains served as "advisors to the chief." The Chickasaw agent dealt with the chief in all national issues, except land, a matter still controlled by the commissioners.[6]

Chickasaw feeling toward the Choctaws was not hostility, Hitchcock argued, just partiality to "their old customs, laws, and usages."[7] Certainly Greenwood's dislike for the present condition was a longing for the old Chickasaw style of government, a feeling he shared with other old leaders. Hitchcock described him as about sixty and "destitute" of white culture. McGilbrey (i.e., McGilivray) was even older, and, like Greenwood, disliked whites, their ways, or imitation of them.[8]

Feelings against the Choctaws were not a penchant of just the old men. There was a general fear that the Chickasaws would lose their identity by becoming a part of the Choctaw Nation. There was widespread dislike for Choctaw laws and resentment that the Chickasaws were overruled in the Choctaw council.[9] They were clearly underrepresented. Upon removal, the Chickasaws had settled throughout the Choctaw Nation and were slow to settle in the Chickasaw District. The Chickasaw District, therefore, had fewer Council members, and Chickasaws living in the Choctaw districts had little power.[10]

On a basic level, Chickasaw men resented the marriage of Chickasaw women to Choctaw men, who were lured to the women because of widespread stories of Chickasaw wealth. Intermarriage between members of the nations created difficulties. Because the Chickasaws were matrilineal, children belonged to the mother, and their blood was traced through her. If a Chickasaw man married a Choctaw, he would retain his right to the Chickasaw national fund during his life, but at his death, his children would have no right. A Choctaw man, however, marrying a Chickasaw, could enjoy the benefits of her right during his life and at his death, the children would retain their rights.[11]

At stake, clearly to many Chickasaws, was Chickasaw identity. Hitchcock summed up Greenwood's position as follows: "Greenwood says the Chickasaws have always had a *king* and other chiefs, perpetual. When they came to this western country their people scattered among the different districts and have done nothing about their government and some of their chiefs have died. As for the Choctaw laws they seem like the white man's laws and the Chickasaws have never been accustomed to them and don't like them."[12] Without question, the old chief understood that governmental independence was the key to his people's identity and that removal had disrupted it and threatened the

(269)

very root of Chickasaw society. His statement that they had always had a king and other chiefs signifies his preference of governmental form. Although he was no doubt thinking of the government of his youth, those days were gone forever. The traditional government had undergone steady change during the previous forty years. Yet it was the vestiges of traditional governmental forms that had seen the Chickasaws through the trauma of the earlier stages of removal, and these vestiges would be fundamental in taking them through the final stage: reconstruction of the Chickasaw Nation.

Ishtehotopa's tenure as minko would bring an end to a governmental system that was perhaps as old as the Chickasaw people themselves. He would be the last in a long line of hereditary minkos. Traditionally, Chickasaw society had been governed by clans, from which were selected leaders of the towns and of the nation as a whole. Each clan had a council of elders and a minko, whom the clan selected. At the national or tribal level, the ranking leader was the minko, chosen from one of the high ranking clans. The minko was assisted by the tishu minko, or medicine leader, who served as speaker of the national council. The council was made up of clan chiefs, whose task it was to deliberate issues confronting the people.[13]

These structures had undergone significant changes, however, by the time Ishtehotopa became minko in 1820. Ishtehotopa became minko following the untimely death of Chehopistee, who had served only a short time after the death of his, as well as Ishtehotopa's, maternal uncle Chinnubbee.[14] Traditionally, and like the minko to some degree hereditary, the tishu minko was selected from the beloved family. Before Ishtehotopa's leadership, the chiefs, as these leaders were commonly called, were better known than the minkos.[15] The chief served as speaker of the national council.[16] By the late eighteenth century, the role of chief took on greater significance, the nation depending on him to deal with the Americans and other international powers. By the time of the Treaty of Hopewell, European powers had shifted, causing major shifts in Chickasaw lines of authority in government. Expulsion of the British, with whom the Chickasaws had aligned themselves, left the field to the Spanish and the Americans. Eventually aligning with the Americans, the Chickasaws found it necessary to step aside from hereditary lines of chiefs and looked to the sons of James Colbert as "chiefs": William, George, and Levi.[17] Levi replaced George in 1813. At the same time, however, Tishomingo became the hereditary head chief, replacing Mingo Mataha, who had served at the same time as William and George Colbert.[18] Levi Colbert, who was considered "principal chief and spokesman of the nation,"[19] maintained his position as such until he died in 1834.

Much has been said about the self-serving influence of the Colbert brothers in Chickasaw affairs.[20] Malcolm McGee said that the Chickasaw nation was not displeased with the land cessions made to Levi Colbert in the Treaty of 1816. The treaty commissioners thought Colbert greatly helped and that his management of the nation showed better statesmanship than any chief before or after him except George Colbert.[21] Josiah W. Walton, secretary to Levi, said that he was "shrewd and influential and that his word or advice was law among his people and they loved him. Other chiefs, captains, and even the Chickasaw kings, in the latter period, appeared to be 'Boy kings,' who looked up to him."[22] In addition, it was a Chickasaw practice to vest political power in certain families through matrilineal descent. It may have been that the Colbert brothers were connected, through their mother, to one of the beloved families of the eighteenth century.

Whatever the reality of Levi Colbert's leadership, throughout his period of service, the Chickasaws remained devoted to the old forms of leadership. The traditional hereditary chieftaincy resided in Tishomingo, who signed the treaty of 1816. Malcolm McGee made a fine distinction: Colbert was "chief," and Tishomingo was "head chief."[23] In 1833, John Eaton, one of Jackson's treaty negotiators, considered Tishomingo chief with Colbert.[24] Colbert died the following year. No one was appointed to replace him. Although Tishomingo appears to have been recognized officially as head chief in the years directly preceding removal, Emmubbee seems to have held the more traditional position as advisor to minko Ishtehotopa. He was referred to by Upshaw, the superintendent of Chickasaw removal, as "counceller to the King."[25] Unfortunately, Emmubbee was murdered on the eve of removal in 1837. No one seems to have replaced him as one with a close relationship to the minko. Tishomingo removed about 1839. What happened to him after removal has been debated.[26] However, consensus seems to be that he was the last of the hereditary chiefs who rose to his position in the traditional manner.

Chickasaw deviation from the old hereditary government by investing power in the Colbert brothers was not the only innovation in their government during the two decades preceding removal. The nation had been divided into four districts in 1818. In addition to the chiefs who sat in council, each district had a chief. Districts chiefs remained the same from 1818 to 1831: Samuel Sealy in the southwest, William McGilivray in the northwest, Tishomingo in the northeast, and Apassantubby in the southeast. Appasantubby died in 1831 and was replaced by Isaac Alberson.[27] The district chiefs served until removal. However, after 1830 and 1832, respectively, neither they nor the traditional leadership could function as a government without facing prosecution in the states of Mississippi and Alabama. Whether Tishomingo was exercising his authority as traditional head chief or chief of his district when he seized the traders' goods in 1831, the effect was the same. It was a test case for both the state of Mississippi and the Chickasaw government. For the next three years, the Chickasaws operated without a government, at least one visible to the non-Chickasaws living among them. Those years coincide, significantly, with perhaps the lowest point of Chickasaw morale before removal.

Then in 1834, the Chickasaw leaders took a step that in effect created a governing body that could function openly for the Chickasaw people. In the Treaty of 1834, supplemental to the Treaty of Pontotoc, the Chickasaw negotiators created the Chickasaw Commission. The treaty commissioners were Ishtehotopa, Levi Colbert, George Colbert, Martin Colbert, Isaac Alberson, Henry Love, and Benjamin Love. Whether they knew it or not, the Chickasaws had struck on a brilliant strategy by giving these men a bureaucratic name, quite acceptable to the Americans. By avoiding terms like "chief" and "council," forbidden by Mississippi law, they had created a political structure that would replace the recently emerged district chief structure and form a governing body that would represent the Chickasaw people and see them through the hard years of removal and Choctaw domination that lay ahead.

The U. S. government was a willing partner in these developments, even though officials at the time may not have realized the significance of what they were doing. While only a few years earlier Andrew Jackson had denied that there was a way the Chickasaws could salvage their government under state law, his agents in 1834 helped do just that. John Eaton, concerned that neither Levi Colbert nor Tishomingo was present in 1832, refused to negotiate with a group who went to Washington in an attempt to remake the treaty of 1832. In addition, the Chickasaws needed seven delegates to do business, he said, and refused to negotiate because only four were present.[28]

Through all the changes in their government, the Chickasaws retained a respect, even a reverence perhaps, for the old hereditary leadership. In the treaty of 1801, for example, minko Chinnubbee, head chief Immattauhaw (Emattaha), and former head chief Chummubee signed before George Colbert. In the treaty of 1805, Chinnubbee and Immattauhaw signed before Colbert. In the treaty of 1816, Chinnubbee and Tishomingo as well as four other chiefs, three of whom became district chiefs, signed before Levi Colbert. In the treaty of 1832, Ishtehotopa and Tishomingo signed before Levi Colbert.[29]

The treaty of 1832 makes clear the homage paid the old chiefs and the hereditary government. The Chickasaw negotiators wanted to show their gratitude "to their old chiefs, for their long and faithful services, in attending to the business of the nation" by taking care of them in their old age. They gave a pension for life to "their old and beloved chief Tish-o-mingo, who is grown old, and is poor and not able to live, in that comfort, which his valuable life and great merit deserve." They also created a pension for their "old and beloved Queen," Puc-caun-la [or Pakaunli], who was "very old and poor."[30] The language here tells it all. By "old and beloved" chief and queen, the Chickasaws meant traditional, and by "grown old," and "very old and poor," they meant aged.

By 1842, when Hitchcock visited the Indian Territory, the remaining influence of the minko and the old chiefs was nearing its end. Choctaw historian Muriel Wright has written that at the time of removal Ishtehotopa "was merely the nominal head of the Chickasaws, the real control in the hands of the sub-chiefs and certain prominent mixed blood members of the Nation."[31] Perhaps so, but the reverence

(273)

for the "old" chiefs no doubt contributed to the effective role of the Chickasaw Commission as the de facto government of the Chickasaw people from 1834 to 1841, when Isaac Alberson was elected to represent the Chickasaw District in the Choctaw National Council. By 1842, only three of the original Commissioners were still living; Ishtehotopa, Isaac Alberson, and Benjamin Love. James Colbert had replaced Levi Colbert, who died in 1834, and James Gamble had replaced Charles Colbert, who was elected in 1840 and died in 1842. James Colbert (a second by that name), had replaced Martin Colbert, who died in 1840; James died in 1842 and was replaced by Joseph Colbert. Slone Love replaced Henry Love, who resigned in November of 1840.[32]

Previous to Hitchcock's visit, there had been some dissatisfaction with the commissioners over their handling of the "incompetent" fund. Because the Chickasaws were unsuccessful in gaining access to their funds, those who had been listed as "incompetent" began to resent the commissioners who had labeled them so. As early as 1839, the commissioners felt it necessary to defend their actions by asserting their intent to protect the people's assets. Hitchcock suspected that the merchants and contractors had bought them off. He wrote that the commissioners "collected at Guy's at the Depot where Saffran [sic] and Lewis have the store, and there treated with every luxury the country affords free of charge, supplied with whiskey, etc., and thus induced to recommend the payment of that fund to Saffaran [sic] and Lewis."[33]

(274)

In 1844, payment of the first annuity since removal drew lines between groups contending for authority over the Chickasaw funds. Contention first arose over where the money would be paid. Armstrong directed Upshaw to hold the payment in the Chickasaw District. The Chickasaws hired two clerks to pay out the $60,000—a considerable sum—to heads of families. In wake of the payment, contention arose. The payment lasted two or three weeks, yet some Chickasaws failed to enroll for payment and later claimed that Upshaw and the commissioners who oversaw the payment took their money. Others complained that the payment did not last long enough.[34]

As time for the annuity payment approached in the summer of 1845, contention over where the payment would take place and to whom it would be paid surfaced again. The commissioners, who had been a unified de facto government during removal and after removal, were now divided. A majority of them argued that they were the proper Chickasaw authorities and that the government should pay the annuity in the Chickasaw District. Ishtehotopa, backed by Pitman Colbert, both of whom lived at Fort Towson seventy or eighty miles from the Chickasaw District, argued that the government should pay the annuity to the commissioners, not heads of families, at whatever point they might determine outside the District. William Armstrong alleged that this plan was backed by white men, and he believed that to follow it would be unfair. On the other hand, he believed that the credibility of the commissioners was under fire following the annuity payment of 1844. In addition, the Treaty of 1834 had given the commissioners authority over land matters, but said nothing about funds.[35]

Armstrong, who had been present at the Treaty of Doaksville in 1837, argued that both Choctaws and Chickasaws had insisted on a separation of their financial affairs. The reason the Chickasaw District was set aside was to ensure Chickasaw control over their funds. There were specific objections to doing Chickasaw business inside the Choctaw nation because the Choctaw chief could not allow someone else to call a council. Both sides distinctly understood, Armstrong said, "that their monied affairs were to be managed and payments were to be made in their own district." Thus he recommended that the payment should be made to District Chief Alberson as representative of the nation.[36]

(275)

On July 18, 1845, the Chickasaws came closer to a factional division than they had been since the late eighteenth century. At the request of the Colbert party, after a four-day council of the Chickasaw leadership at Boiling Springs near Fort Washita, the Chickasaw Commissioners—Ishtehotopa, Isaac Alberson, Benjamin Love, Slone Love, James Wolf (who had replaced James Colbert), Joseph Colbert, and James Gamble—resigned. They reasoned that their task had been primarily to oversee land matters. With those matters all but finished, they resigned to cut down national expenses and to attempt to unite the parties of Chickasaws. They also resigned with the understanding that no other commissioners would be appointed to replace them.[37]

After the commissioners resigned on the fourth day, the council adjourned, agreeing to reconvene in one hour. Alberson and his party returned and waited for several hours, but Pitman Colbert's party did not return.[38] Apparently in an attempt to wrest Chickasaw government from Alberson and other officials elected from the Chickasaw District, Colbert's party, whose support rested in Chickasaws who resided in the Choctaw districts, met and elected a slate of officials to rival Alberson's party.[39] The lines were clearly drawn but reflected complex political dynamics that were not so clear. Alberson's party favored a constitutionally elected government over the Chickasaw district as part of the Choctaw Nation under the Treaty of Doaksville of 1837 and the Choctaw constitution. Although they had old chiefs Chickasaw Nahnubbee, Newberry, and others among their ranks, they included a large number of American-educated Chickasaws such as Cyrus Harris, Gabriel Love, Joseph Perry, James Gamble, and others. Colbert's party, with whom Ishtehotopa sided, favored the traditional hereditary government led by the minko and chiefs, supported by Chickasaws who lived in the Choctaw districts but resented Choctaw political dominance.[40]

The Colbert "government" attempted to use the annuity payment of 1845 as political leverage. With Edmund Pickens their designated treasurer, they asked the government to turn the 1845 annuity funds over to him for distribution, claiming that it was the wish of a majority of the Chickasaws. Alberson's party alleged ulterior motives behind the move. They wanted a government agent to make the payment as in 1844 because they had no faith that Pickens could guarantee an honest disbursement. Because of the party rift among the Chickasaws, they doubted that any one of their members could disburse the funds to everyone's satisfaction. They were especially dubious of Pickens' ability, calling him "uneducated and utterly and notoriously incompetent." They also suspected that money was behind the move, believing that "the sole object of the proposed change is to enrich an Indian trading establishment," Pitman Colbert's, and otherwise raid the Chickasaw national treasury by paying high salaries to party loyals.[41]

According to the Alberson party, Pitman Colbert and his followers had manipulated facts to gain support for their attempted governmental takeover. Of the estimated 4,300 Chickasaws in the Chickasaw District, no more than 100 or 200 favored Colbert's annuity payment plan. Colbert had used the fact that a few families had been left off the

(276)

annuity rolls in 1844 to convince some Chickasaws that fraud had been committed by the government. Colbert also appealed to "that portion of the people who oppose innovation and prefer old Indian customs," Alberson's party argued, by putting Pickens nominally under the authority of Ishtehotopa, whom they called "a weak, credulous, ignorant but well meaning man, who was the Hereditary chief under the old exploited tribal government." Distrust of the Colbert family's potential rise to power once more is evident, and it is clear that the Alberson party wanted Chickasaw government to go in a new direction. "It is quite natural," they said, "that those who lost their last years annuity should be induced to desire a change and that those who are attached to ancient customs should be gratified by a proposition to restore them partially in the person of their former Chief. But can any one believe that the majority or even a respectable minority would with their eyes open consent to place their entire fund at the disposal of a trader? Yet the prime mover in this whole affair, the acknowledged leader of the party who pushes it, is Maj. Pitman Colbert an Indian trader at Doaksville. The King, Ish ta ho to pa and the Disbursing Chief, Mr. Pickens are indeed disconnected with any trading establishment, but the former is completely under the control of Maj. Colbert, and the latter is avowedly and officially to look for advice and assistance to Maj. Colberts son in law Mr. Sampson Folsom, himself an unsuccessful merchant."[42]

(277)

William Armstrong, who had anticipated such a political rift for some time, sided with the Alberson party, duly elected to represent the Chickasaw District. He urged the U. S. government to recognize only officials from the District and to reject the efforts of the Colbert Party. "Meanwhile," he said, "in advance of instructions, it is my intention to pay the Chickasaw annuity myself to the Chickasaw people enrolled in companies under Captains chosen by themselves, and looking to the Chief as the proper representative of their tribe."[43] And he did so. Although this settled the issue, "the feelings aroused at that time helped to serve as a basis for politics among the Chickasaws for many years," argue some historians.[44]

In 1846, Colbert's party once more attempted to persuade the government to turn over the interest on the Chickasaw fund to Edmund Pickens, the Colbert "government's" treasurer. Alberson and his followers protested what appeared to be an attempt at government patronage. They cited as proof the fact that just before the 1845 annuity payment began, Ishtehotopa asked that "$4,000 be set apart for his particular use." They said, "It is well understood that the greater part of this sum was intended for a Texas lawyer who had acted as Maj. Colbert's council in this matter, and who is expected to aid him in pressing it at Washington." Why pay a lawyer, they asked, to argue for a fair distribution of funds when the government did it without charge? The Alberson party argued that the removal treaty of 1834 laid the groundwork for payment of the annuity, not to particular Chickasaws but on an individual basis by government officials.[45]

Coincidental with the annuity controversy in 1845, political friction began to increase between the Chickasaws and Choctaws. That year, the Choctaw General Council passed a law refusing payment of salaries out of the Choctaw national funds to any councilors elected from the Chickasaw District. Bitter feelings also arose that year over Chickasaw dissatisfaction with the eastern boundary line of the Chickasaw District. In 1846, a movement arose among some Chickasaws to obtain a separate district to be ruled by their own government. Their actions simply added to growing Chickasaw dissatisfaction with Choctaw domination, but it would take a decade for the Chickasaws to achieve a separation. According to Choctaw historians Wright and Hudson, "The Chickasaws were placed in an anomalous position in that they not only participated in the government of the Choctaw Nation but also kept up their former tribal organization as well. It was but natural that they would have a deeper interest in the latter especially since that organization, in which only Chickasaw officials took part, had full charge of their financial affairs."[46]

During the preceding decade, the Chickasaws had moved slowly, but deliberately, toward constitutional government. They had not politically organized the Chickasaw District until July of 1841, when they elected Isaac Alberson district chief, Slone Love district speaker, James Gamble district secretary, and eight representatives to the Choctaw General Council: Elahpombia, Chickasaw Nahnubbee, Ishkiltaha, Enaloa, William Barnet, James McGlothlin (McLaughlin), John Gaines, and Shippawa. However, Alberson and five of the eight representatives failed to attend the Choctaw Council on October 1 that year. The following year the Chickasaws reelected Alberson and Love unanimously and elected a new slate of council representatives, whose attendance in council was much greater.[47]

In 1843, the Choctaw Nation changed its constitution to give more balanced representation to the districts. Some Choctaw districts were dissatisfied with the structure of the General Council. Because of population, Apuckshunubbee District had dominated it. The Council changed the constitution to provide for a senate and a house of representatives. Each district had the same number of senators and one house member for every 1,000 of the population. Despite the changes, Chickasaws remained underrepresented because, as late as 1851, only an estimated two-thirds of the people had settled in the Chickasaw District.[48]

The averted political schism in 1845 consolidated the authority of the elected officials and moved the Chickasaws along the constitutional road. These officials began to unify the people by reaching out to the remaining officials of the old form of government. Slone Love as treasurer was directed to pay the captains for their services. Perhaps in an attempt to mollify Ishtehotopa and the old chiefs, the government provided for a pension of $100 a year for life to Ishtehotopa, William McGilivray, and Thomas Sheko "for their services rendered the Chickasaw People."[49] By 1846, the district legislative branch was more sophisticated in the wake of the Choctaw law reorganizing the government, and the district had an organized judicial system. James McLaughlin was chief, Isaac Alberson Jr., speaker, and James Gamble secretary. Senators were Benjamin Love, Enaloa, and Edmund Pickens, and representatives were Robert Love and Gabriel Love. Henry Love was supreme court judge, and William Love and Johnson Frazier were inferior judges. Captain of the light horse police was Ahfahmah.[50]

That same year, the district officials began to take other steps to consolidate their political authority. They sought to purge from the annuity rolls any persons ineligible to participate. All were eligible who had received allotments in Mississippi or Alabama, provided they had moved west and were still citizens of the nation. Exceptions were the "heirs of Molly & Betsy Meeks who were discarded by the general consent of the Chickasaws." White and Choctaw women who were married to Chickasaws at the time of the Treaty of 1834 and had remained married were eligible as were their offspring, but all who had married into the Chickasaw tribe after the treaty were not. The next year, they determined that the annuity of any person who died after registering for the annuity and before payment should be used to satisfy any claims against that person. In an attempt to overcome criticism that had attended earlier annuity payments, those who were overlooked in the payment could appeal for payment from the general Chickasaw fund. The officials took other steps to consolidate their authority. In January they began to discuss establishment of a manual labor school and set salaries for district officials, including a new office called "school trustee,"[51] although they had no school system at the time.

The council at Boiling Springs in July 1847 also certified the captains who would oversee the annuity for that year. Each captain was responsible for the payment of a certain number of families, registering the people under his authority for payment. The list of captains reflects the state of Chickasaw government on its way from traditional to constitutional governing systems. Of the 24 captains on the list, who represented 4,341 Chickasaws, six were elected by vote, 15 were appointed by the chief, two were self-made, and one, Ishtehotopa, was hereditary. His name appears at the end of the list of captains, followed by the title "Hereditary King." As late as January 1847, his mark as "King" had appeared first on documents, followed by other signatures and marks. By January 1848, his name appears last on the list of Captains without title, his residence listed as Kiamitia.[52] After that, his name disappears from the Chickasaw records altogether.

The officials continued to try to diffuse the ongoing political contention over the annuity payment by stabilizing the process. In early 1848 at Brushy Council House, the council directed that children born after registration and before the date of the payment should receive an annuity. They requested the agent to pay the annuity at Boggy Depot "until such time when the situation of our people may be changed." They said, "It is a subject which has caused much contention and the Depot at this time is central for all and will it is seriously hoped do away with all ill feeling."[53]

The council in early 1848 also dealt with remaining issues related to removal. A committee, established to consider strategies regarding "several important subjects relative to the Tribe," recommended that the "competent funds better known as Col. B. Reynolds receipts" be located and the matter taken to Congress to assist the Chickasaws in getting their money, which Reynolds had held for them when they left Mississippi and had not returned to them.[54] Also, on March 17, Chief James McLaughlin and leading men asked the government to pay the equivalent of nineteen months' subsistence rations in money to Chickasaws newly arrived from the old nation, saying "each Chickasaw has the right to receive the same subsistence as another." They added, "Those who remained so long behind are principally families who had lost their husbands shortly after we emigrated, had large families and were unwillingly detained. It would therefore look very bad, if they were not to receive so good treatment as those more fortunate."[55] The commissioner of Indian affairs had reduced the ration period for late comers to seven months, and the Chickasaws had earlier asked that the twelve-month period be restored.[56]

Beginning in 1848, the Chickasaws also began to send delegations to Washington on a regular basis. Chief James McLaughlin, Pitman Colbert, Isaac Alberson, Edmund Pickens, Shippawa, James Gamble, Davis James, and John McGilvery made up the first delegation, whose agenda included investigation of the details of the Chickasaw fund, adjudication of all unsettled claims, education, unsold land in Mississippi, and, most significant, a new home for the Chickasaw people "to the realizing of securing to themselves some bright hope of a better day ahead of them then [sic] they are now experimenting [sic] under the Yoke" of the Choctaws. The following November, acting Chief Isaac Alberson Jr. signed the appointment of James Davis, Jackson Frazier, Maxwell Frazier, and Gabriel L. Love to serve as the second delegation in 1849.[57] The makeup of these delegations suggests that the controversy of three years earlier was at rest, for they consisted of members of both sides. And during the next few years, their delegations' agendas changed little, particularly on the issue of financial matters and separation from the Choctaws.

By the early 1850s, majority sentiment among the Chickasaws was

(281)

for separation. The major obstacle facing them was the difference between their interpretation of the Treaty of Doaksville of 1837 and the Choctaws' understanding of the agreement. To the Chickasaws, the Choctaws had agreed to sell a part of their land to the Chickasaws. The Choctaws argued that they had not.

The reasons for separation expressed in Washington by the fourth delegation in 1851 makes plain the Chickasaw position on the matter. First, Winchester Colbert, Sampson Folsom, and Jackson Frazier argued that because the Chickasaws were only one quarter the size of the Choctaw population, the Choctaw council made all the laws, and as a small minority, the Chickasaws felt that their voice was neither "felt nor heard." The Chickasaws "unanimously opposed" some Choctaw laws. Second, members of both tribes had rights everywhere, but the Choctaws treated those Chickasaws living in the Choctaw districts as intruders, an accusation that was "frequently thrown up to them as a reproach" that they had no rights in Choctaw country. The result was "many private difficulties" that sometimes ended in death. Third, the boundary between the Chickasaw District and the Choctaw districts had not been settled to Chickasaw satisfaction. It remained a cause of "excitement," which had recently "approached near rupture." Fourth, the Choctaws paid officers of the nation except Chickasaws. The Chickasaws had paid a large sum of money to live in the Choctaw Nation and did not think that they should also have to support the Choctaw government. They would not submit much longer. Finally, these points of contention had estranged the Chickasaws and Choctaws. "The Chickasaws are dissatisfied with their present political condition," the delegation wrote. "Nothing but a separation from the Choctaws will ever satisfy them."[58]

The Chickasaw delegates worked diligently. On June 22, 1852, the Chickasaws signed a treaty that went a long way toward winding up the business of removal. Negotiated by Edmund Pickens, Benjamin S. Love, and Sampson Folsom, the treaty provided for the sale of the remaining Chickasaw lands in the east, a settlement of their claims arising from removal, and establishment of rules for management of the Chickasaw fund. Then on November 4, 1854, they and the Choctaws came to an agreement that settled the long-standing dispute over the eastern boundary of the Chickasaw District.[59]

Only one major goal had to be reached for the removal process to be complete: establishment of a separate country for the Chickasaws. In 1855 they sent delegates Folsom and Pickens back to Washington to accomplish that goal. The Choctaw General Council appointed Peter P. Pitchlynn, Israel Folsom, Dickson W. Lewis, and Samuel Garland as delegates with authority to secure "final and satisfactory settlement of all unadjusted Choctaw matters." Commissioner of Indian Affairs George W. Manypenny pushed hard to reach an agreement because he wanted the Choctaws and Chickasaws to relinquish any claim to lands west of the hundredth meridian, and he wanted a lease on their commonly held land between the ninety-eighth and hundredth meridians as a territory on which to resettle other removed tribes. The Choctaws wanted to settle what was called their Net Proceeds claim. The Chickasaws were single minded: They wanted a country where they could govern themselves.[60] Because all three parties had an agenda, the time was right for action.

The Chickasaws got what they wanted in an agreement reached on June 22, 1855. They were granted the lands between the recently established eastern boundary of the Chickasaw District and the ninety-eighth meridian. The Choctaws and Chickasaws received $800,000 for relinquishment of their title to lands west of the one hundredth meridian and lease of the district between the ninety-eighth and one hundredth meridians. The Choctaws received three-fourths and the Chickasaws one-fourth. The agreement guaranteed the right of any Chickasaw or Choctaw citizen to settle in either nation with full rights of citizenship, but they could participate in the national fund of only their chosen nation. For their separate lands, the Chickasaws agreed to pay the Choctaws $150,000 out of their national fund. Although the Chickasaws were dissatisfied with terms regarding the survey of their nation's boundaries, the U. S. Senate ratified the treaty on February 21, 1856.[61]

The Chickasaws lost no time in establishing their own government. They met in convention at Good Spring (Tishomingo City) on August 1, 1856, where the officials of the Chickasaw District closed their affairs. They provided for depositing the $200,000 due them under the

treaty with agent Douglas Cooper until a national government could
be formed. Then the convention members reorganized into a constitutional convention with Joel Kemp as chairman. They charged a committee with drafting a constitution. They reassembled in Tishomingo
City on August 30 and ratified the document.[62] Modeled after the U. S.
Constitution, it contained a bill of rights, guaranteeing the individual's
civil liberties. Free males nineteen or older could vote. The constitution
established executive, legislative, and judicial branches of the government. The two-house legislature consisted of a senate and house of
representatives. The judiciary consisted of supreme, circuit, and county
courts. For legislative and judicial purposes, the Chickasaw Nation was
divided into Panola, Pickens, Tishomingo, and Pontotoc counties.[63]
With the constitution ratified, the first election took place. Cyrus Harris was elected from a field of three candidates by a small majority as
first governor of the new Chickasaw Nation. He was succeeded two
years later by Dougherty (Winchester) Colbert, whom Harris defeated
in 1860.[64]

Thus the Chickasaws had concluded the final step in the removal
process—reclaiming their nation. The election of Harris closed the
removal era. It was a remarkable feat for a people who had lived without a functioning government of their own for two and a half decades.
The constitutional framework established in 1856 made for a smooth
transition in government that boded well for the new nation, and the
Chickasaw people began to lay the groundwork for the present, modern Chickasaw Nation.

NOTES

1. Arrell Gibson, *The Chickasaws* (Norman: University of Oklahoma Press,
1971), 216–25.

2. Ethan Allen Hitchcock, *A Traveler in Indian Territory: The Journal of Ethan
Allen Hitchcock*, ed. Grant Foreman (Cedar Rapids, IA: The Torch Press,
1930), 200, 218, 173; Hitchcock to J. C. Spencer, April 29, 1842 (H1029),
National Archives Microfilm Publications, Microcopy M234, Letters
Received by the Office of Indian Affairs, Roll 138. Microcopy M234 is
hereafter cited as M234, followed by the roll number.

3. Hitchcock, *A Traveler*, 200.

4. Muriel Wright and Peter J. Hudson, "Brief Outline of the Choctaw and Chickasaw Nations in the Indian Territory 1820 to 1860," *Chronicles of Oklahoma* 7 (December 1929), 400.

5. Hitchcock, *A Traveler*, 219–20.

6. William Armstrong to T. H. Crawford, June 10, 1845, *http://www.chickasawhistory.com/CHICl__45.htm*, retrieved July 17, 2004.

7. Hitchcock, *A Traveler*, 199–200.

8. *Ibid.*

9. *Ibid.*, 172, 183.

10. Wright and Hudson, "Brief Outline," 400–01.

11. Hitchcock, *A Traveler*, 172, 183.

12. *Ibid.*, 199.

13. Gibson, *The Chickasaws*, 21–22.

14. Before Chehopistee, his maternal uncle Chinnubbee had been minko from the early 1790s until 1819. Before Chinnubbee was Hair Lipped King, who died about 1791. Malcolm McGee, "Chickasaw History According to Malcom [*sic*] McGee," *http://www.chickasawhistory.com/mcgee.htm*, retrieved January 1, 2004; Treaty of 1832. McGee, born in 1760, had gone to the Chickasaw Nation in 1768. By 1800 he was serving as an interpreter for the Nation. He lived with the Chickasaws until removal, remaining in Mississippi for a few years before joining them in the West, where he died on November 5, 1848. See editor's note, McGee, "Chickasaw History."

15. Tobeutubby, or White Man Killer (called Pimataha or Paya Mataha by the Americans), had been active in the 1750s and 1760s. He was head chief with Red King, his uncle. He was followed by Wolf's Friend, then Chummubee or Mingatuska (minko tushka, red warrior), a nephew of old Tobeutubby and one of the Chickasaw representatives that went with Piomingo to the Treaty of Hopewell in 1786. Chummubee was followed by Mingo Mataha, who, with Chinnubbee, signed the Treaty of 1801 as Immuttauhaw and the Treaty of 1805 as E'mattaha. McGee, "Chickasaw History"; Richard Peters, ed., *Public Statutes at Large of the United States of America* (Boston: Charles C. Little and James Brown, 1846), 7: 66, 90.

16. Gibson, *The Chickasaws*, 21–22.

17. William Colbert rose steadily in power in the late 1790s and by 1797 had solidified his influence when he defeated an attempt by Wolf's Friend and Piomingo to place the Chickasaw Nation in the Spanish camp. George Colbert replaced his brother William. James R. Atkinson, *Splendid Land, Splendid People: The Chickasaw Indians to Removal* (Tuscaloosa: University of Alabama Press, 2004), 177–79, 198.

18. While William seemed to have risen to power by virtue of his personal charisma and achievements, George was appointed by minko Chinnubbee to act as principal chief because of his ability to speak English. He served for twelve years, his name appearing on the Treaties of 1816 and 1818. He resigned in 1813 to go with his brother William to fight the Creeks. McGee, "Chickasaw History"; Atkinson, *Splendid Land*, 201.

19. Atkinson, *Splendid Land*, 207.

20. See, e. g., Gibson, *The Chickasaws*, particularly Chapter 7.

21. McGee, "Chickasaw History."

22. Andrew Grant Gregory, "The Chickasaw Indian Colbert Family: An American Dynasty Era 1729–1907," *Journal of Monroe County History* 5 (1980), 41.

23. McGee, "Chickasaw History."

24. Monte Ross Lewis, *Chickasaw Removal: Betrayal of the Beloved Warriors, 1794–1844* (Ann Arbor, MI: University Microfilms International, 1985), 101–05.

25. Upshaw to Harris, June 2, 1837 (Chickasaw Emigration U10), M234-R143.

26. At the time of removal, Tishomingo made his home at Bethany in present-day Lee County, Mississippi (Sections 13 and 24, Township 7, Range 5 East). He was robbed of $1,000 shortly after the sale of his land. Benjamin Ellis, an upstanding citizen of Ellistown, was indicted for the crime.

    Historian Cushman says Tishomingo died in 1839, a year before Ishtehotopa. Ishtehotopa lived at least until 1848, probably longer. Cushman is incorrect about the minko, and he may be wrong about Tishomingo. Choctaw historian Muriel H. Wright says that he supposedly died and was buried at about 102 years of age near Little Rock about 1838 while on the removal trail. However, other evidence suggests that he completed the journey to the West. A story in the *Memphis Commercial Appeal* on November 1, 1894, tells what allegedly happened upon his arrival in the West. The storyteller claims to have attended a party that migrated overland to Fort Coffee, arriving in March 1839. He told how they found ruined rations stored at the frontier depots. Added to this situation was an outbreak of smallpox just as the party crossed the Arkansas River at Dardanelle, Arkansas. They carried the disease to those already encamped at Fort Coffee and the result was a fatality "about the worst that has been seen." One of the first fatalities was Tishomingo, encamped with his family about two miles from the fort. According to the storyteller, the old chief's daughter came to him, claiming the family was too poor to bury him with proper ritual. He pleaded with Captain John Stuart, who he said was commandant at the fort. Soldiers gave Tishomingo a military funeral attended by those

Chickasaws who "were able to climb out of bed."

Who the storyteller was is uncertain. He says that he was "generally chosen to act as interpreter." The self-description fits John Mizell. Whoever he was, there are a number of problematic points in his narrative. For example, the smallpox epidemic of 1838 did not decimate the Chickasaws as he suggested. Most had been inoculated. Also, although Tishomingo had been robbed before he left for the West, it is not likely that he was destitute upon arrival. And, certainly, the Chickasaws would not have relied on the federal troops to bury such an important figure in their society.

This is the same story told by Charles Johnson, who wrote under the name "Boggy," in the *New York Times* in July 1894. The story however, is about Captain Jim Brown, a well known Chickasaw leader who had fought in the Red Stick War.

Adding to the mystery of Tishomingo's last days is the eulogy for someone by that name written by Choctaw Peter Pitchlynn in 1841. It has been argued that the man referred to was a Choctaw called Tishomingo, but Malcolm McGee, who told his story of the Chickasaws in 1841, stated that Tishomingo died that year. Evidence in Pitchlynn's writing suggests that the deceased might have been, in fact, the old chief. Pitchlynn referred to him as a Choctaw because the Chickasaws were at the time citizens of the Choctaw Nation, a large number of whom had settled near Eagletown. Pitchlynn's description of his military service fits Tishomingo, and Pitchlynn twice refers to the "brace," which some historians have silently changed to "brave," apparently assuming it was a typographical error. Literally, with the death of Tishomingo, the last of the old braces (pairs, i. e., minko and chief) was gone. With Tishomingo's death, only Ishtehotopa remained. Homage to, and recognition of, him as minko lasted nearly until his death, apparently in the late 1840s. With his demise ended an era in Chickasaw government. See H. B. Cushman, *History of the Choctaw, Chickasaw and Natchez Indians*, ed. Angie Debo (Norman: University of Oklahoma Press, 1999), 403–04; Muriel H. Wright, *A Guide to the Indian Tribes of Oklahoma* (Norman: University of Oklahoma Press, 1951), 87; Richey Henderson, *Pontotoc County Men of Note* (Pontotoc: Pontotoc Progress Print, 1940), 5–10; Boggy of Arkansaw, "Capt. Jim Brown, U.S.A., Chickasaw Indian," *New York Times* July 31, 1894; "On the Cover: War Chief Is Honored," *Chickasaw Times* 7 (April/May/June 1978), 2, 7–8; McGee, "Chickasaw History."

27. McGee, "Chickasaw History."

28. Lewis, *Chickasaw Removal*, 101–05.

29. Treaties of 1801, 1805, 1816, 1832.

(287)

30. Peters, ed., *Public Statutes at Large*, 7: 386.

31. Wright and Hudson, "Brief Outline," p. 397.

32. Lewis, *Chickasaw Removal*, 107; Upshaw to Crawford, July 2, 1842 (U117), M234-R138; Ish-te-ho-to-pa, et al., to J. W. Porter, February 8, 1844 (B1972), M234-R139.

33. Armstrong to Crawford, February 22, 1839 (A551), M234-R137; Hitchcock, *A Traveler*, 164–65, 168–69.

34. Armstrong to Crawford, June 10, 1845 (A1836), M234-R139.

35. *Ibid.*

36. *Ibid.*

37. A. M. M. Upshaw to Armstrong, July 20, 1845 (A1862), M234-R139.

38. E. Steen, et al. to Armstrong, undated, enclosed in Armstrong to Crawford, July 27, 1845 (A1862), M234-R139.

39. Albertson [*sic*], et al. to Crawford, July 22, 1845, enclosed in *Ibid.*

40. Alberson, et al. to William L. Marcy, undated, 1845, enclosed in *Ibid.*

41. *Ibid.*

42. *Ibid.* Historians Wright and Hudson argue that Colbert represented the majority of Chickasaws, which the Alberson party disputed. However, insufficient evidence exists to support either claim. See Wright and Hudson, "Brief Outline," 402.

43. Armstrong to Crawford, July 27, 1845 (A1862), M234-R139.

44. Wright and Hudson, "Brief Outline," 402.

45. Alberson, et al. to William L. Marcy, undated, enclosed in Armstrong to Crawford, July 27, 1845 (A1862), M234-R139.

46. Wright and Hudson, "Brief Outline," 403, 406.

47. Record Book of the Chickasaw Nation (Oklahoma Historical Society Microfilms, Roll CKN-30), June 2, 1837–August 1855, 7, 20.

48. Wright and Hudson, "Brief Outline," 400–01.

49. List of Captains of 15th September 1845, Record Book (CKN-30), 27.

50. List of District Officers in July 1846, *Ibid.*, 28.

51. Post Oak Grove Chickasaw District, October 31, 1846; Laws Passed the Council of July 1847; and Post Oak Grove, January 1, 1847, *Ibid.*, 29, 35, 37, 39.

52. Post Oak Grove, January 1, 1847, and A List of Captains at the Annuity of January and February 1848, *Ibid.*, 35, 47.

53. Brushy Council House, February 17, 1848, *Ibid.*, 46a.

54. Post Oak Grove, January 28, 1848, *Ibid.*, 44.

55. James McLaughlin, et al. to A. A. M. Upshaw, March 10, 1848, Chickasaw Letters—1848.

56. Chickasaw Chiefs and Captains to Upshaw, May 3, 1847, Chickasaw Letters—1847, *http://www.chickasawhistory.com/CHICl__47.htm*, retrieved December 31, 2006.

57. Boiling Springs, March 17, 1848, Record Book, June 2, 1837—August 1855, p. 59; Resolutions of the Chickasaw Council, 19 March 1848, Upshaw to William Medill, April 28, 1848, and Isaac Alberson Jr. to Upshaw, November 4, 1848, *http://www.chickasawhistory.com/CHICl__48.htm*, retrieved December 31, 2006. For the consistency in Chickasaw arguments, see, for example, the fourth delegation's proceedings in 1851 in 4th Delegation's Proceedings, April 26, 1851, April 29, 1851, May 1, 2, 3, 7, and 10, 1851, Record Book, June 2, 1837—August 1855, unpaged.

58. 4th Delegation's Proceedings, April 26, 1851, Record Book, June 2, 1837—August 1855, unpaged.

59. Wright and Hudson, "Brief Outline," 404—05, 407.

60. *Ibid.*, p. 408.

61. *Ibid.*, 408—09, 410.

62. Gibson, *The Chickasaws*, 255—56.

63. *Ibid.*, 256—57; Wright and Hudson, "Brief Outline," 410—11.

64. "Governor Cyrus Harris," *Chickasaw Times* 7 (July—September 1978), 10, reprinted from *Chronicles of Oklahoma*.

CONCLUSION

I N THE SUMMER OF 1856, the Reverend Mr. Thomas C. Stuart visited the Chickasaws. His objective was to see how his former mission acquaintances and students were faring. His visit was pleasing but sad. Some of the converted still lived, but others had passed away. Some that he had implored through his sermons to seek salvation were still listed among the sinners. The Chickasaws had passed through a hard trial: "For several years after they emigrated they were very much dissatisfied. Sickness prevailed among them and many of their old people died." Now, however, he found them "contented and happy." Everywhere he looked, he saw evidences of "advances made in civilization." He was struck by the change in dress since he had last been among them. "They have almost universally laid aside the Indian costume," he wrote, "and assumed, at least in part, the white man's dress. Among the largest number collected on the occasion, I saw but two clad in the old Indian style. These are called subbees, in a way of derision, just as a certain class amongst us are called 'old fogies.'" The Chickasaws lived in good log houses with stone chimneys, and they had "abolished the office of chiefs and councils for a government of the people, and . . . organized a regular state government, with a written constitution after the model of our sovereign states."[1]

Stuart attended the first meeting of the new government when the first governor was elected and inaugurated. His former student Cyrus Harris was one of three candidates standing for the office. No one had received a constitutional majority, so the decision fell to the legislature. Of the thirty votes cast by the twelve senators and eighteen representatives, Harris received seventeen. Besides Harris, six of the senators had attended Stuart's Monroe mission. The speaker of the House had attended the Martyn school, and House member Archibald Alexander had gone to the Caney Creek school. Despite the number of

American-educated members present, all of the proceedings of the first legislature were conducted in the Chickasaw language.[2]

Among the senators was Stuart's former student James Gamble, who was also the translator. Stuart had visited the grave of Gamble's mother, one of his early Monroe converts, whose Chickasaw name meant "There is none such," baptized Catharine, and known as Aunt Kitty. Her son, "James Gamble—named and supported, I think, by a society of ladies in Rocky River congregation," had begun his American-style education at the Monroe Mission and completed it at Mesopotamia, Alabama. Stuart was proud to say, "He is now decidedly a great man of his nation—is a senator in their legislature—is national interpreter and translator, and is their commissioner to Washington City to transact their business with the Federal Government."[3]

Stuart's visit to the West brought back memories of his first meeting with the Chickasaw chiefs and council in 1820. In remembering his visit to Tishomingo City, the seat of Chickasaw government in 1856, he wrote to his old-time friend David Humphries with whom he traveled in 1820, "This was the name of a venerable old chief who was present at our council in 1820, and signed our articles of agreement. His office was that of chief speaker, and his name signifies 'king's servant.' It was well for the Chickasaws to cherish and perpetuate his memory by giving his name to the capital of their new government."[4] At that 1820 council, as well, Ishtehotopa had been installed as minko. Although the Chickasaws could not have fathomed it at the time, he would be the last hereditary "king."

What changes had come to the Chickasaws in the thirty-six years that elapsed between Stuart's first and last visit to the Chickasaws! They had seen their leadership debilitated by Mississippi and Alabama laws and by the pressure of encroaching American population. They had been forced to sell their ancient tribal homeland and see it invaded by non-Chickasaws. They had suffered the trauma of removal to a new land and its environment. They watched as their national and individual trust funds dwindled as a result of fraud and a debt economy. They had tolerated Choctaw political domination with smoldering resentment. But through it all, they remained a unified people and reestablished their nation in the West.

Victimized as they were, they refused to remain victims. They suffered, but through the suffering demonstrated a strong self-assurance, a determination to control their own destiny, and a sense of nationhood that had ensured their survival for centuries before removal and that has sustained them for more than one and three quarters of a century since. Removal was more than a physical trek from Mississippi and Alabama to Indian Territory. It was a significant part of the journey of the Chickasaw people toward becoming what the Chickasaw Nation is today.

NOTES

1. E. T. Winston, *"Father" Stuart and the Monroe Mission* (Meridian, MS: Press of Tell Farmer, 1927.), 78–79, 80.

2. *Ibid.*, 79.

3. *Ibid.*, 77.

4. *Ibid.*, 81.

BIBLIOGRAPHY

UNPUBLISHED PRIMARY SOURCES

Croffut, William A. William A. Croffut Papers. Library of Congress.

National Archives Record Group 75. Records of the Bureau of Indian Affairs.

Letters Received by the Office of Indian Affairs, 1824–81. Microcopy M234.

Records Relating to Indian Trust Funds, Ledger for Trust Funds of Chickasaw Incompetents and Minors, 1837–43.

Records of the Commissary General of Subsistence. Chickasaw Removal Records. Special film labeled 1847 Chickasaw Census Roll.

Records of the Commissary General of Subsistence. Chickasaw Removal Records, Entry 253, Chickasaw Volumes 1, 2, and 3.

Records of the Commissary General of Subsistence. Chickasaw Removal Records, Abstracts of Disposition of Lands, Volume 2.

National Archives Record Group 217. Records of the U. S. Department of the Treasury. Accounting Officers of the Department of the Treasury, Entry 524, Chickasaw Payments, 1833–66.

Pontotoc County, Mississippi, Records. Wills, Books 1 and 2; Deeds, Book 3.

Records of the Chickasaw Nation. Record Book of the Chickasaw Nation, June 2, 1837–August 1855. Oklahoma Historical Society Microfilm CKN30.

Wilson, John. "Old Monroe Presbyterian Church and Cemetery, 1821–23." Algoma, MS: n. d. Typescript in Pontotoc County Library, Pontotoc, Mississippi.

(295)

PUBLISHED PRIMARY SOURCES

Fisher v. Allen (1832)," http://www.chickasawhistory.com/Fisher__htm.

American *State Papers*. Military Affairs. Vol. 1, 1831.

"Chickasaw Letters—1839," http://www.chickasawhistory.com/CHICl__39.htm.

"Chickasaw Letters—1845," http://www.chickasawhistory.com/CHICl__45.htm.

"Chickasaw Letters—1847." http://www.chickasawhistory.com/CHICl__47.htm.

"Chickasaw Letters—1848." http://www.chickasawhistory.com/CHICl__48.htm.

Cushman, H. B. *History of the Choctaw, Chickasaw and Natchez Indians*. Ed. Angie Debo. Norman: University of Oklahoma Press, 1999.

Frank, Kenny A. "Missionaries in the West: An Expedition of the Protestant Episcopal Church in 1844." *Historical Magazine of the Protestant Episcopal Church* 44 (September 1975), 318–33.

Gerstacker, Friedrich. *Wild Sports in the Far West.* Boston: Crosby Nichols and Company, 1859.

Hitchcock, Ethan Allen. *Fifty Years in Camp and Field: Diary of Major-General Ethan Allen Hitchcock, U.S.A.* Ed. W. A. Croffut. New York: G. P. Putnam's Sons, 1909.

_____.*A Traveler in Indian Territory: The Journal of Ethan Allen Hitchcock.* Ed. Grant Forman. Cedar Rapids, IA: Torch Press, 1930.

"Infant Pontotoc celebrated Fourth in patriotic fashion in 1838." *Journal of Pontotoc County Historical Society* 1 (Summer 1999), 70–71.

Jackson, Andrew. *Correspondence of Andrew Jackson.* Ed. John Spencer Bassett. 7 Vols. Washington, D. C.: Carnegie Institution, 1926–1935. Reprint ed. New York: Kraus Reprint Co., 1969.

Johnson, Neil R. *The Chickasaw Rancher.* Rev. ed. Ed. C. Neil Kingsley. Boulder: University of Colorado Press, 2001.

"Mississippi Chickasaw Land Sales—1836." *http://www.chickasawhistory. com/land__p__1.htm*

McGee, Malcolm. "Chickasaw History According to Malcom [*sic*] McGee," *http://www.chickasawhistory.com/mcgee.htm.*

Parsons, John E., ed. "Letters on the Chickasaw Removal of 1837." *New York Historical Society Quarterly,* 37 (1953), 272–83.

Peters, Richard, ed. *Public Statutes at Large of the United States of America.* Vol. 7. Boston: Charles C. Little and James Brown, 1846.

Swanton, John R. *Chickasaw Society and Religion* [Forty-second Annual Report of the U. S. Bureau of American Ethnology]. Lincoln: University of Nebraska Press, 2006.

U. S. Congressional Serial Set:
    23rd Congress, 2nd Session. *House Document 83.*
    27th Congress, 2nd Session. *House Report 453.*
    27th Congress, 2nd Session, *House Report 454.*
    27th Congress, 2nd Session. *House Report 604.*
    27th Congress, 3rd Session. *House Document 65.*
    27th Congress, 3rd Session. *House Report 271.*
    28th Congress, 2nd Session. *Senate Report 160.*

Wilshire, Betty C.*Marshall County, Mississippi, Probate and Will Records.* Carrolton, MS: Pioneer Publishing Co., 1996.

Bibliography

NEWSPAPERS

Arkansas Advocate

Arkansas Gazette

Army and Navy Chronicle

Chickasaw Times

Memphis Enquirer

Missionary Herald

Van Buren Press

SECONDARY SOURCES

Armstrong, Kerry M. "Was It James or John Allen?" *http://www. chickasawhistory.com/allen.htm.*

Atkinson, James R. *Splendid Land, Splendid People: The Chickasaw Indians to Removal.* Tuscaloosa: University of Alabama Press, 2004.

Braden, Guy B. "The Colberts and the Chickasaw Nation." *Tennessee Historical Quarterly* 17 (March 1958) and (December 1958), 222–48 and 318–35, respectively.

Elliott, Jonathan. *The American Diplomatic Code, Embracing a Collection of Treaties and Conventions between the United States, and Foreign Powers, from 1778 to 1834, with an Abstract of Important Judicial Decisions, on Points Connected with Our Foreign Relations.* Washington: Jonathan Elliott, Junior, 1834.

English, Jo Claire. *Pages from the Past: Historical Notes on Clarendon, Monroe County, and Early Arkansas.* Clarendon, AR: J. C. English, 1976.

"The Family of General James Winchester, Part Two." *http://www.rootsweb. ancestry. com/~tnsummer/winch2.htm.*

Foreman, Grant. *Indian Removal: Emigration of the Five Civilized Tribes of Indians.* Norman: University of Oklahoma Press, 1972.

Gibson, Arrell. *The Chickasaws.* Norman: University of Oklahoma Press, 1971.

Gregory, Andrew Grant. "The Chickasaw Indian Colbert Family: An American Dynasty Era 1729–1907." *The Journal of Monroe County History* 5 (1980), 38–42.

Harlow, Jerry Anderson. "Cotton Gin Port." In Monroe County Book Committee, *A History of Monroe County, Mississippi.* Dallas: Curtis Media Corp., 1988.

Henderson, Richey. *Pontotoc County Men of Note.* Pontotoc, MS: Pontotoc Progress Print, 1940.

Lewis, Monte Ross. "Chickasaw Removal: Betrayal of the Beloved Warriors, 1794–1844." PhD Dissertation. North Texas State University, 1982.

Little, Carolyn Yancey. "Samson Gray and the Bayou Meto Settlement, 1820–1836," *Pulaski County Historical Review* 39 (Spring 1984), 2–16.

Littlefield, Daniel F. Jr. "African Slavery Among the Chickasaws: Some Problems in Historiography." Third Mid-America Conference on History. Springfield, Missouri. September 19, 1981.

Litton, Gaston, ed. "The Negotiations Leading to the Chickasaw-Choctaw Agreement, January 17, 1837," *Chronicles of Oklahoma* 17 (December 1939), 417–27.

Longnecker, Julia Ward. "A Road Divided: From Memphis to Little Rock through the Great Mississippi Swamp," *Arkansas Historical Quarterly* 44 (Autumn 1985), 203–19.

McAlexander, Herbert H. *A Southern Tapestry: Marshall County Mississippi, 1835–2000*. Virginia Beach, VA: The Denning Company, Publisher, 2000.

"Mary Black." *http://anpa.ualr.edu/trail__of__tears/indian removal__project/people/Black__Mary.htm.*

Pierson, J. Diane. "Lewis Cass and the Politics of Disease: The Indian Vaccination Act of 1832," *Wicazo Sa Review* 18 (Fall 2003), 9–35.

Silver, James W. "Land Speculation Profits in the Chickasaw Session." *Journal of Southern History* 10 (February 1944), 84–92.

Summers, Cecil Lamar. "The Trial of Chief Tishomingo, the Last Great War Chief of the Chickasaw Indians," *The Journal of Monroe County History* 3 (1977), 28–38.

Winston, E. T. *"Father Stuart" and the Monroe Mission*. Meridian, MS: The Press of Tell Farmer, 1927.

Worthen, W. B. *Early Banking in Arkansas*. Little Rock, AR: Democrat Printing Co., 1906.

Wright, Muriel, and Peter J. Hudson. "Brief Outline of the Choctaw and Chickasaw Nations in the Indian Territory, 1830 to 1860." *Chronicles of Oklahoma* 7 (December 1929), 388–18.

Wright, Muriel. *The Indian Tribes of Oklahoma*. Norman: University of Oklahoma Press, 1951.

——————, "Notes on Events Leading to the Chickasaw Treaties of Franklin and Pontotoc, 1830 and 1831." *Chronicles of Oklahoma* 34 (Winter 1956–1957): 465–83.

Young, Mary Elizabeth. *Redskins, Ruffleshirts and Rednecks: Indian Allotments in Alabama and Mississippi, 1830–1860*. Norman: University of Oklahoma Press, 1961.

(305)